Race for
SUSTAINABILITY
Energy, Economy, Environment and Ethics

T0323513

Race for
SUSTAINABILITY
Energy, Economy, Environment and Ethics

Ken Hickson

Sustain Ability Showcase Asia, Singapore

 **World Scientific**

NEW JERSEY · LONDON · SINGAPORE · BEIJING · SHANGHAI · HONG KONG · TAIPEI · CHENNAI

Published by

World Scientific Publishing Co. Pte. Ltd.

5 Toh Tuck Link, Singapore 596224

USA office: 27 Warren Street, Suite 401-402, Hackensack, NJ 07601

UK office: 57 Shelton Street, Covent Garden, London WC2H 9HE

Library of Congress Cataloging-in-Publication Data
Hickson, Ken.
 Race for sustainability : energy, economy, environment and ethics / by Ken Hickson (Sustain
Ability Showcase Asia, Singapore).
  pages cm
 Includes bibliographical references and index.
 ISBN 978-9814571357 (softcover : alk. paper)
 1. Sustainable development. 2. Energy development--Environmental aspects.
3. Renewable energy sources. 4. Sustainability. I. Title.
 HC79.E5H53 2014
 338.9'27--dc23

                                            2013034652

British Library Cataloguing-in-Publication Data
A catalogue record for this book is available from the British Library.

In-house Editor: Lee Xin Ying
In-house Designer: Lionel Seow

Typeset by Stallion Press
Email: enquiries@stallionpress.com

Printed in Singapore

Contents

Introducing the Race for Sustainability

There's a sense of urgency about all this. It's a race against time. It's a race the world is in danger of losing.

We're on about the urgent need to fix the world's unhealthy dependency on fossil fuels, which contribute most of the deadly greenhouse gas emissions damaging the atmosphere and bringing about unheard of changes to our climate.

The science is in. Without exception, the world's international agencies — the United Nations, the World Health Organisation, the World Bank, the International Energy Agency, among others — recognise the gravity of the global problem and call for more to be done to deal with its ramifications.

As long as we continue to dig up and burn fossil fuels; as long as we continue to destroy and burn rainforests; as long as we continue to make, drive, consume, waste products and resources, we stay on the path to destruction.

Dramatic, yes. Painful, yes. But how else will we understand how real is the global problem if we do not hear it the way it is.

But this is not all doom and gloom. In this book — as well as in my previous encyclopaedic effort "The ABC of Carbon" — I go out of my way to write about the issues and the opportunities.

This book is made up mostly of what I have talked about and written about over the last year or so.

You will also meet some great men and women who are profiled because they have something significant to say. I've met them and talked to them so I know they are well and truly off the starting blocks in this race.

This book has been written and produced in Singapore and much of its attention has been on events happening in Asia. But its focus and reach is truly global.

There are many governments who are doing more than we give them credit for. Singapore is among the most committed.

Likewise, most of the leading corporations around the world are taking serious, deliberate and meaningful steps on the sustainability journey.

We report the wise words of the International Energy Agency (IEA) and the UN Framework Convention on Climate Change (UNFCCC). We hear from Sir Richard Branson and the Carbon War Room. One of the world's most remarkable visionaries, Amory Lovins of the Rocky Mountain Institute, makes a welcome appearance.

Leaders and visionaries, yes, but also men and women who are prepared to take a stand and to continue to contribute positively through their own organisations or in society at large.

We deal with energy efficiency a lot because we realise it is so important and can make such a difference. Waste management and air pollution both figure prominently.

We look at moves to a cleaner energy future in Asia. We see what's happening as buildings turn green inside and out.

We see how the events industry is becoming sustainable in a big way. If the London Olympics can set the highest sustainability mark — and produce a new global gold standard — any event of any size or scale can do it.

That very much means that events like the Formula 1 Grand Prix in Singapore — a night race and arguably the most energy-inefficient event in the world — can also be measured and managed in a sustainable fashion.

This motor racing event — talking and writing about it — prompted this book's title. But the scope and scale of it all goes beyond that topic to cover all things of concern in the sustainability landscape.

We're said it before — and we won't hesitate to repeat it — that sustainability is made up of four E's: Energy, Economy, Environment and Ethics. This goes beyond the "triple bottom line" of John Elkingham — people, planet and profit — with the three pillars being economic, social and ecological.

We don't think that achieves the sustainable balance that we need for our world, our countries, our companies, or our communities. Energy must be part of the equation. It is a critical pillar. So is Ethics. Not to devalue the importance of "people", but to us an ethical approach to all we do is essential.

Whether we talk about corporate social responsibility or the even bigger picture of sustainability, we must place equal importance on energy, economy, ethics and the environment.

We hope the book's contents will reach to people in all walks of life and business. We do want people to wake up to what's happening in their own street, town, city and country. And to come to realise that we can make some changes for the better.

It does come down to human behaviour and human choices.

We can have the best technology in the world — and we are surely at that point where we are very well equipped with what's needed. We can have the most expensive machinery and the biggest and best buildings. But if we continue to use resources irresponsibly — if we continue to waste food, water and energy, like we have been doing too date — we are not even in the race.

Because it all comes down to you. People matter and people have power. With all the options and the choices available. A power for good or a power abused.

For too long, we have said it is someone else's problem: Governments. Industry. Oil companies. Forest owners.

Well, the news is out. Just as the science is in. It is your problem and it is my problem.

This book attempts to raise issues and present opportunities. It gives you — the reader — access to a wealth of current and useful information and an introduction to people and organisations who are making a difference.

Read well. Act soon.

Ken Hickson
August 2013

What People Are Saying in This Book

Sir Richard Branson, chairman of the Virgin group, who founded the Carbon War Room:
"War is not a nice thing, but a carbon war is the right thing because it's a call to arms… it is a war worth fighting."

Christiana Figueres, executive secretary of the UNFCC:
"The world faces a big gap between commitments to reduce greenhouse gas emissions and the reductions that scientists say will be needed to minimise catastrophic effects."

Dr. Fatih Birol, chief economist of the International Energy Agency:
"It is an economic sin that only one third of all economically viable energy efficiency potential is being realised. In terms of international energy policy implementation, this is an epic failure."

Dr. Vivian Balakrishnan, Singapore's Minister for the Environment and Water Resources:
"Energy efficiency is, at this point of time, the only game in town. Given that every joule, every kilowatt hour, is drawn from imported energy, we have to conserve and be as efficient as possible."

Lord Paul Drayson, former UK Minister, on motor sport:
"This is the way in which the world needs to move. History begins in 2014 with the first FIA electric race. It will give young people an insight into a future that is fun and cool but which does not damage the environment."

Amory Lovins, Rocky Mountain Institute, who wrote *Reinventing Fire*:
"Old buildings can be better than new. There is the temptation to tear down and start afresh, but smart retrofitting can mean up to 75% savings on energy use."

Dr. Nasir Hassan, regional adviser on environmental health for the WHO:
"Outdoor air pollution is identified as the cause of 800,000 deaths a year, while nearly 50% of pneumonia deaths among children under five are due to particulate matter inhaled from indoor air pollution."

David Fogarty, on Double Helix DNA sleuthing:
"The logging increases global warming with heightened carbon emissions, and landslides through loss of watersheds. It causes loss of livelihoods in forest communities and dents global timber prices."

Doug Woodring, founder of Ocean Recovery Alliance:
"Already, over 10% of fish tested in oceans contain pollutants from plastic in their tissue. The growing plastic waste stream is a resource worth capturing and channelling into products that enhance life, rather than degrade it."

Kwek Leng Joo, Managing Director of CDL:
"Natural calamities. Climate change. Economic crisis. Business failures. Governance letdowns. Food shortages. Resource scarcity. Ethical lapses. Social breakdowns. Many companies in Singapore and around the world continue to operate in a seemingly indifferent manner, either ignoring or oblivious to the impact and risks these environmental, social and governance issues have on their business."

Why Sustainability Matters

Section 1

1 F1 at Odds with Singapore's Race for Sustainability

This is a "hot button" story which refuses to go away. It started in September 2012 and it demonstrated that writers/journalists have an advocating role to play by not only reporting, but drawing attention to issues and opportunities. I made the discovery a year ago that in the same month Singapore was hosting its National Energy Efficiency Conference, an international Corporate Social Responsibility summit, launching a five month long climate change awareness campaign called "Our Green Home" and the Singapore Environment Council's "G1" event, there was also, arguably, the biggest polluting event on the planet — a night time Formula 1 motor race. This article updates my early revelations but starts with the heading and the letter which appeared in the Sunday Times on 27 September 2012...

Photo adapted from David (2009), WikiMedia Commons (public domain) by Lionel Seow: www.commons.wikimedia.org/wiki/File:RafflesAvenue.JPG.

S ingapore's decision to commit to another five years of the Formula 1 (F1) race needs to be tinged with some trepidation ("Five more years for S'pore race", *The Sunday Times*, 23 September 2012).

The F1 race here is arguably the most "energy inefficient" event in the world, largely because it is held at night and requires a massive amount of extra lighting. Along with an overdose of fuel burn from the cars, the air is polluted and Singapore's greenhouse gas emissions in the atmosphere increases. All the additional air-conditioned hospitality buildings and accompanying electric-charged entertainment must also be taken into account.

And this was all happening in the same week that Singapore hosted its National Energy Efficiency Conference, and the same month the National Climate Change Secretariat launched a five-month-long series of exhibitions and roadshows highlighting climate change's impact on Singapore.

Using less energy is a primary message delivered to all.

With this in mind, it would be advisable for the organisers of the Singapore Grand Prix to build energy efficiency into the next series of events, conduct a complete energy audit, measure its environmental impact and take all these into account when evaluating its total economic benefit to Singapore.

Interestingly, the race also coincided with the news that Singapore had won an international award for its i Light Marina Bay — Asia's first and only sustainable light art festival — which attracted over 500,000 visitors to Marina Bay in March ("i Light Marina Bay Wins Award", *The Sunday Times*, 23 September, 2012). It was measured and managed for sustainability like the London Olympics, which set a new global "gold" standard for events — ISO 20121 (Event Sustainability Management System).

Maybe Singapore should secure another new motor racing event — Formula E — which was unveiled recently as a global championship involving only electric cars.

That would put Singapore truly in the race for sustainability.

Kenneth Hickson.

Yes, I have to admit. That was me. One and the same person. I wrote that letter and the *Sunday Times* published it.

More recently (in June 2013), I was interviewed on the same subject by Nobuko Kashiwagi for the United Kingdom based UBrain TV (a web-based service) — see www.ubraintv.com — and I was asked about how to make events more sustainable, as this was something our company Sustain Ability Showcase Asia (SASA), was in the business of doing.

I explained that our company had offered to be involved in the F1 event in Singapore as we believed it could be run in a more sustainable fashion.

Of course, we couldn't — or wouldn't — stop the cars and the entertainment. But as it is a night-time event, it requires massive use of lighting and I believe there is the opportunity to introduce some significant energy saving measures. Manage the lighting better. There is also the opportunity to manage water, the hospitality, air conditioning, waste, etc. All this will add up to reducing the environmental impact of the event.

I made the point that events in themselves are inherently unsustainable, involving lots of people and energy, but there are guidelines and an international sustainability standard to follow. It is ISO 20121, called the Olympic gold standard because it was developed and used to provide a standard of sustainability for the London Olympics in 2012.

If the London Olympics can be sustainable, so can the F1 or any event in the world for that matter.

The story continues. And as recently as late June 2013, came the announcement from Federation Internationale de l'Automobile, or FIA, that for the next ten years the aim was to help turn motor racing events around the world towards sustainability. At the same time a commitment to introduce a new class Formula E, for electric cars.

Implications for the global sport of motor racing and all host countries of F1 events. Implications for Singapore.

But let's track the race for sustainability story back to September 2012. I think I raised a few eyebrows, when my newsletter came out with the headlines and the commentary (even before the letter appeared in the Straits Times), as follows:

Race for Sustainability?

This month is special for Singapore (September 2012). It presents its National Energy Efficiency Conference with overseas and local experts and delegates; hosts an international CSR summit and launches a five month long climate change awareness campaign called "Our Green Home" at a Singapore Environment Council "G1" event. But to top all that, Singapore hosts arguably the biggest polluting event on the planet — a night time F1 motor race. Besides being energy inefficient — all those lights as well as powerful fuel guzzling cars — it would be the most unsustainable event ever. In the same month, the Singapore Zoo welcomed two pandas from China to an appropriately air-conditioned cool cage. We know that air conditioning uses about 70% of Singapore's stationary energy. All too much to take in? Enough to make your editor take to riding a Singapore-built bamboo-framed bike! Definitely the most sustainable and energy efficient form of transport in the world.

————◦————

In the next issue of my newsletter — issue 175 dated 16–30 September — I couldn't resist another niggling commentary. Drawing attention to the wealth of excellent material from experts at the National Energy Efficiency Conference and the decision to proceed with another five years of F1 racing:

Abuse of Power?

We are talking about the misuse of energy here, not political power or human rights. We are concerned with the waste of a finite resource. Of the pollution caused by fossil fuels to the atmosphere and the air we breathe. A lot of talk — and some action — is going on to get countries, cities and companies to clean up their energy act. Energy efficiency is usually identified as the easiest way to go. Stop the waste of energy. And save money on your power bills at the same time. So this week's National Energy Efficiency Conference is drawing on some of the best brains and some of the best examples from business around the world. There are also a lot of good ideas and applications on clean energy and even cleaner transportation in this issue. And while Singapore suffers in silence with the massive energy use (waste?) associated with its F1 night time races — look at all the lights and cars! — there's an announcement from the international motorsport body that a new electric vehicle race is scheduled for the future. A move in the right direction, which might make more of us think about the real energy cost and environmental impact of unsustainable car racing events against the economic benefits.

In the same issue, we reported on a move by FIA to introduce Formula E — a racing series for electric vehicles.

Getting on Track with Electric Vehicles to Share and Race

Electric vehicles represent a balance between the need for mobility and the impact of private transport on the environment, with its high energy efficiency and low overall emissions. And now, finally, the FIA has woken up to the opportunity presented by cleaner burning transport with the introduction of Formula E — a racing series for electric vehicles, to begin in 2014.

We repeated the article from Theo Leggett for BBC News (28 August 2012):

Formula E Electric Car Racing Series Is Launched by FIA

In the world of motor racing the internal combustion engine is king.

Circuits around the world regularly echo to the earsplitting howl of racing V10s and V12s at full throttle. But perhaps, not for much longer.

Motorsport's governing body, the Federation Internationale de l'Automobile, or FIA, has announced plans for a brand new motor racing series, designed exclusively for electric cars.

The new championship, known as Formula E, is due to begin in 2014.

Manufacturers are being invited to design and build their own cars, which will race on city-centre circuits around the world.

It will be run by Formula E Holdings, a consortium of investors led by the Spanish billionaire Enrique Banuelos, who made his fortune in real estate and agribusiness.

The FIA says it represents "a vision for the future of the motor industry over the coming decades".

Four-wheeled bicycles

The thinking behind the series is simple: electric cars have an image problem, and the series' backers think motor racing can help to resolve it.

Until recently, battery cars were simply impractical. They were slow, heavy and expensive and had very limited range between charges.

That situation is now changing, with the launch of models such as the Nissan Leaf and Ford Focus Electric, which have reasonable performance and batteries which can cope with longer journeys.

But sales remain very sluggish. In the US, nearly 13 million cars were sold last year, but fewer than 20,000 were electric.

Cars such as the electric Nissan Leaf can cope with longer journeys.

"Electric cars haven't been cool up until now," says motor industry analyst Jay Nagley, who runs the cleangreencars.co.uk website.

"Until the Nissan Leaf came along they were basically four wheeled bicycles, with a battery pack and a terrible safety record. So there is a need to change the image."

But can motorsport help to make electric cars sexy? One man who thinks so is British businessman, part time racing driver and former government minister Lord (Paul) Drayson.

His company, Drayson Racing Technologies, has spent the past two years developing an electric racing car, and he is acting as scientific adviser to the new championship.

"This gives us the perfect way to showcase the performance of electric cars," he says.

Formula E investors are led by Spanish billionaire Enrique Banuelos.

"People think they're slow. We will show that it's possible to do 200 mph, or 0–60 in three seconds. Our ultimate goal is to create a sporting spectacle which is both sustainable and exciting."

He believes the series will not only promote electric cars, but help to develop them as well — making road cars better.

"A lot of R&D still needs to take place, and motorsport has always been a tremendous driver of R&D," he says.

"Many of the things we take for granted on our road cars started out on a racing car. Even the humble rear view mirror was first fitted to a race car in the US in the 1920s."

Fast but silent

Yet the idea of electric motorsport has plenty of critics. They claim that electric cars lack something which motorsport fans yearn for — noise, and plenty of it.

But according to Lord Drayson, they're missing the point.

"What we're trying to do is create a new racing experience. It will be a different type of car, racing through the city streets, before new audiences, in places where we haven't raced before."

He believes that while older fans may lament the lack of a howling exhaust note, young people simply won't notice.

Even the most sophisticated electric racing cars have some limitations.

Chris Aylett, the chief executive of the Motorsport Industry Association agrees.

"It will be a very trendy, very modern, futuristic form of racing," he says.

"We're not talking about appealing to the grey market with these cars. We're looking at the 15 year old today who will be tomorrow's car buyer."

This isn't the first time that motorsport has attempted to embrace environmentally friendly technologies.

This year's Le Mans 24 hours was won by a diesel-electric hybrid, while F1 cars have been using energy recovery systems for the past two years. Technically, that makes them hybrids too.

But the new series is certainly a radical venture. And in order to get around some of the limitations which affect even the most sophisticated electric cars, it has had to embrace some very radical ideas.

The batteries in the new cars are expected to run down relatively quickly. So when a driver comes into the pits, he won't just change his tyres.

He'll change the whole car — swapping it for a new, and fully charged machine.

Serious Thinking about Sustainability

We did some research ourselves which also uncovered that FIA had been doing some serious thinking about sustainability for a while. How to green the sport and reduce its impact on the environment.

FIA has been working on a sustainability policy for some time. It is encouraging countries and venues for motor racing events to be more sustainable. An extract from its 2009 proposed policy:

Carbon Neutrality

It is proposed that the total activity of putting on a motorsport championship or series should be carbon neutral. In line with the polluter pays principle, the FIA should offset its own regulatory presence, and encourage others to offset their own emissions by making offsetting a condition of involvement to a championship or series. The FIA will not regulate carbon assessment or offsetting methods, but simply require demonstration that both have been undertaken. In order to further assist race organisers, the FIA will make available a non-exhaustive list of recommended auditors and offset providers. Such action in offsetting will gain respect of environmentalists if it is part of a wider long-term strategy for emissions reductions.

Technology Promotion

Energy recovery technologies should be promoted through motorsport. The best method of integrating the various levels of hybridisation, ensuring equivalency, and promoting their qualities, is in an efficiency-based formula as described in point one. Although many automobile manufacturers are developing hybrids, there is a strong opinion that they do not represent a cost effective means of reducing fuel consumption and CO_2 emissions, but are increasingly demanded by the market place. Energy Recovery Systems technology, however, is fundamental to the future of the automobile, including these hybrids. Motorsport can make a useful contribution to development and marketing. Technology such as fly wheels reducing dependence on batteries and concentrating on the internal combustion engine load shift proves to be the most promising way forward.

Best Practice

Best environmentally sustainable practice in the holding of motorsport events, both circuit-based and rallies, and including energy use, carbon offsetting, noise control, waste disposal, water protection, spectator traffic management, and physical damage to the local environment, should be established in consultation with Autorite Sportive National (ASNs, the national sporting organisation in each country authorised to stage FIA approved motor racing events) and circuit operators. Existing best practices should be pooled and commonly established, and best practice guidelines should be published.

———<○>———

As recently as 26 June 2013, the FIA reported:

Creating an Environment for Change

Introducing a proposed action plan for sustainability, the FIA yesterday put the focus on environmental awareness in motorsport.

Yesterday's plenary session on sustainable motorsport saw Deputy President for Sport Graham Stoker present a new Action for Environment campaign which the Federation will today present to the World Motor Sport Council.

Following an opening introduction from Nick Nuttal of the United Nations Environmental Programme (UNEP) in which he explained how motorsport, through technological innovation, is ideally placed to deal with a resource-constrained future, Stoker outlined the new campaign.

"We had a very constructive working group with input from some pretty high-powered experts and ASNs and we tried to create a workable framework that we are now taking forward and which we are calling Action for Environment," he said.

"The goal is that within a decade we will be a best practice exemplar in terms of environmental sustainability," he added. "The action plan is divided into two parts — Measure and Improve and the second, Innovate and Promote. On the first, we will provide you with the necessary tools so you can demonstrate at ASN level and at a FIA level that you can operate in a sustainable way."

"On the other side, we will use the unique position we have in motorsport and in mobility to try to innovate and to spread new technology for the benefit of society," he added. "We will back that up with a proper action plan, with publicity, statistics, information — all the things you need when talking to other stakeholders, be they companies, local authorities or with central government."

"This initiative is going before the World Council tomorrow (Friday) for approval and we will then seek to implement it. I commend this to you strongly, as I believe, indeed I think we all believe, that along with safety this is the other major issue we have to deal with."

In outlining the measurement tools available as part of the plan, Deputy President Stoker referred to the FIA Institute's recently launched environmental accreditation scheme which was explained by FIA Institute Deputy President Garry Connelly.

"The FIA Institute last year announced a new programme, which is a complete framework for environmental accreditation for all stakeholders — events, circuits, team owners, everyone involved in motorsport. McLaren is the first company to achieve excellence and the Institute itself had its audit last week and we hope to be accredited."

"We would encourage you to do it," he added. "Why? Well, as President Todt said in his opening address here, if we don't do things ourselves, others will do them for us and they may regulate us in a manner we may not appreciate. We have to be proactive. From the smallest to the largest ASN, this is achievable now for you and I encourage you to get involved."

Commenting on his company's need for sustainability credentials, McLaren Managing Director Jonathan Neale said that while the team is this year celebrating its 50th anniversary, in that time over 100 F1 teams have failed.

"It's really important from an economic and from an innovation perspective that we stay ahead in the process of making our sport sustainable in the widest economic sense."

"From about 2007 onwards we started to take a much more proactive approach to this on the basis that out investors, shareholders and sponsors, the people who want to use this wonderful sport as a marketing platform, wanted to see from us that we were being proactive and that this was externally accredited."

"We were one of the first 500 UK companies to get a carbon trust certificate, and we were re-awarded that in 2012. Over four years, we reduced our carbon footprint by 20%. We did that for very good economic reasons — simply, waste costs."

Peter Gregory from FIM also spoke about the motorcycle sport federation's long involvement in sustainability stretching back to 1993. He outlined how the organisation has appointed an environmental steward and holds 12 sustainability seminars each year.

Lord Drayson, who this week set a new speed record in an electric car, also spoke about the merits of the new Formula E Championship saying that the series was the right way forward for motorsport.

"This is the way in which the world needs to move," he said. "History begins in 2014 with the first FIA electric race. It's an opportunity for us to engage with urban teens who are very interested in technology. It will give young people an insight into a future that is fun and cool but which does not damage the environment."

Last Words?

Besides writing about the issue, I have gone out of my way to draw the attention of the Ministry of Environment and Water Resources (MEWR), the National Environment Agency (NEA), the Singapore Tourism Board (STB) — which is itself actively encouraging organisers and hosts to work towards sustainable event measurement and management — and the Singapore GP organisation.

SASA has a team of people in Singapore capable of measuring and managing sustainability and energy aspects of events — as was done for the i Light Marina Bay festival (see the case study in Section 6, Chapter 22).

Not only did the lighting festival keep its carbon footprint "incredibly low", a concurrent energy saving campaign involving 47 properties over the three week period managed to collectively save 210,000 kWh of energy electrically, by being persuaded by the SASA team, acting on behalf of the Urban Redevelopment Authority (URA).

NEA was surprised we managed to get so many buildings to voluntarily reduce their energy use in this way.

One person who has worked with SASA — including undertaking energy metering for i Light Marina Bay — is an energy efficiency expert based in Singapore, Adrian Bukmanis, of Energenz. He did a walk-around the F1 (in September 2012) and had this to say:

"There is definitely room for improvement (e.g. all the hospitality suites are cooled with 'one tick' split units). Given that Singapore has signed up for another five years, I would suggest that they should be setting a yearly target for improvement (in energy efficiency) and engaging a solid group of professionals to help with that. I would like to be involved to make the event as 'lean and green' as possible."

SASA has offered to undertake a "sustainability assessment" of the 2013 F1 event. To meter — wherever possible — and measure the energy use of the event.

We need to come up with a benchmark. To measure the environmental impact of the event — through energy use alone — and see where things can be improved. A full sustainability assessment would also look at all other aspects of the event, including waste, water, access and transport.

It came to light during exploratory discussions that the extra lighting for the event, covering the whole distance of the track, remains on for 24 hours a day over the three-day period of the event. While we heard this from a very reliable source, it cannot be verified, but it seems surprising that an event run at night should need to leave all those powerful lights on during the day and night.

It doesn't take an Einstein to work out where there could be an immediate and significant saving of energy in the running of F1 in Singapore.

One can hope that Singapore recognises the opportunity to be a leader in sustainability — for F1 and all other events — and gets on top of, or maybe even ahead of, the international policy introduction for sustainability in motor racing events. McLaren is setting an example. So is Lord Drayson. And Formula E will be a good start in 2014.

The Race for Sustainability is on. Singapore needs to make sure it gets off to a flying start from the starting grid in 2013, or do we have to wait another year?

Sources

- www.sph.com
- www.abccarbon.com
- www.fia.com
- www.draysonracingfe.com
- www.mclaren.com
- www.bbc.co.uk
- www.singapore-f1-grand-prix.com

2 Impactful Advocacy: Sense and Sustainability

For a good overview of sustainability — both the issues and the opportunities — I can do no better than refer to an article I was invited to contribute for the 2012 annual issue Social Space, produced by the Lien Centre for Social Innovation and published in the section on Impactful Advocacy. I also set out the all important four E's of sustainability — Energy, Economy, Environment and Ethics. This is the nearest thing to an academic paper I have produced in the last couple of years, complete with reference notes. Here is an updated version...

Sense and
Sustainability

Like the proverbial chicken and egg, climate change and sustainability are inextricably linked: it is impossible to decide which comes first, but urgent solutions are needed. Here's a timely lesson on the four E's of Sustainability — energy, economy, environment and ethics.

Climate change is generally accepted by over 90% of the world's scientists as being human-induced. Like road accidents or nuclear disasters, it is definitely not an act of God as we still label various "natural" disasters like earthquakes, tsunamis and floods.

Remarkably — and scientifically — we are seeing evidence today that points the finger to climate change as setting off major geological events. Rising sea levels, dramatically reduced arctic ice and melting glaciers — and perhaps even the extraction of oil, gas and minerals out of the earth — can set off a geological chain reaction leading to earthquakes and tsunamis.

If that is stretching our faith in climate scientists — and bringing out a storm of protests from the climate deniers and sceptics — let's just settle for all the other evidence we have that our climate is changing and bringing about with it an undeniable increase in extreme weather events, rising sea levels, higher average temperatures, more out-of-control bush fires and the prospect of climate refugees displaced by any of these events.

We have to accept that there's a nexus here. Climate and its consequential impact can no longer be separated from all the other essential resources we need: water, food and energy.

So here's where sustainability comes in.

Man has long exploited the planet's natural resources, but the exploitation, especially in the burning of fossil fuels, really started in earnest with coal and the Industrial Revolution (between 1750 and 1850 in Europe). But our natural resources are finite. The usage at current levels cannot go on. It is not sustainable, especially when there is a preponderance of evidence linking the effects of our energy consumption with climate change.

Arguably, the first person to really put two and two together was Swedish chemist Svante Arrhenius. In a paper he presented in 1895, he came up with the theory of the importance of carbon dioxide (CO_2) content in the atmosphere for the climate, which he labelled "the greenhouse effect".[1]

First, he determined how much cooling might result from halving the earth's CO_2 content during a long period without volcanic activity. Then he turned the equation around to demonstrate what would happen if industrial emissions grew enough to double the amount of CO_2 in the atmosphere. He predicted a warming of about 5°C, which at the time he believed might take another 2,000 years to happen.

The Nobel Prize winner for chemistry could not possibly have predicted the rate of industrialisation — or the hell-bent extraction and burning of fossil fuels — which has taken climate change and temperature rise to the brink in 200, not 2,000 years.

So with all this evidence before us — of both human-induced climate change and the renewed emphasis on sustainability — we need to be clear what we mean by sustainability.

There may be as many definitions of sustainability and sustainable development as there are groups trying to define it, says one consultancy in the US, Sustainable Measures.[2]

All the definitions have to do with:

— Living within the limits;
— Understanding the interconnections among economy, society, and environment; and
— Equitable distribution of resources and opportunities.

There is a view that sustainability is about more than three critical components — people, profit and planet. The "triple bottom line" was coined by the leading light in the world of sustainability — John Elkington.[3]

Some quotable quotes on sustainability:

"Sustainability is the next transformational business megatrend..."
— David Lubin, Sustainability Network and
Daniel Esty, Yale University.[4]

"Sustainability is the biggest issue facing business in the 21st century..."
— Bill Ford, chairman of Ford Motor Company.[5]

"Fortune 1000 Executives are aware of their own company's green efforts, but join the general public in ongoing skepticism of corporate America's commitment to sustainability."
— Gibbs & Soell Sense & Sustainability Survey 2011.[6]

"Sustainable development is...meeting the needs of the present without compromising the ability of future generations to meet their own needs..."
— The UN-commissioned Brundtland Report in 1987.[7]

"93% of 766 CEOs surveyed believe that sustainability will be 'important' or 'very important' to the future success of their company..."
— Accenture and the UN Global Compact.[8]

But in my language, sustainability is achieved through four, not three, components. There has to be a balance of four E's: energy, economy, environment and ethics.

Why Energy?

It is not sustainable for a company or a country to be totally reliant on the burning of fossil fuels to provide the energy it needs.

Burning fossil fuels is damaging the planet through pollution and excess greenhouse gases. We are rapidly depleting the earth's resources, and there must be a more sustainable way to produce and use energy.

Switching to cleaner, greener and renewable energy, like wind, solar, geothermal, hydro, tidal, wave and biofuels is a must if we are to be sustainable into the future.

Energy efficiency is also an answer to make a country and company sustainable.

Business is often showing the way.

In 2007 Google launched a Renewable Energy Cheaper than Coal (RE < C) initiative as an effort to drive down the cost of renewable energy. Its Clean Energy 2030 Plan is a proposal on how to shift the global economy from one that depends on fossil fuels to one that is based on clean energy.[9]

GE's Ecomagination project puts billions into clean energy investments around the world. In October last year, it announced an expansion of its footprint in India to connect with one of the country's fastest growing clean energy developers. The GE unit will invest US$50 million — its first renewable energy investment in India — to support the development of 500MW of wind projects. It is a small part of GE's US$6 billion portfolio of renewable energy investments worldwide.[10]

Why Environment?

We need to sustain life on earth. Human life depends on nature. We need biodiversity. Plants absorb CO_2. Clean water and productive land for food are reliant on a healthy environment.

There is an obvious nexus between environment and energy, water and food. We cannot emphasise enough the strong connection between sustainability and climate change, where human activity and industrialisation have directly contributed to damaging the atmosphere with excessive greenhouse gases from burning fossil fuels.

Nature is the unseen dimension of the nexus (of energy, water and food), says the International Union for Conservation of Nature. "With its functions integral to the three securities and their inter-dependence, nature is part of the infrastructure needed to manage the nexus and its resilience. Nature helps mediate the nexus links...without healthy ecosystems in well-functioning watersheds, the infrastructure built for irrigation, hydropower or municipal water supply does not function sustainably, and is unlikely to achieve the economic returns necessary to justify investments."[11]

It is simply not sustainable to continue to use up the earth's resources — oil, coal, gas — as they are not replaceable or renewable. That's not sustainable for the environment or for the economy and the planet as a whole.

Interface, which is the worldwide leader in design, production and sales of environmentally responsible modular carpets, has issued a call to action for other companies, large and small, to set bold goals in the pursuit of sustainability.[12]

Interface's "Mission Zero" is a commitment to eliminate negative environmental impact by 2020; the company pledged to obtain third-party validated environmental product declarations on all InterfaceFLOR carpet tiles globally by 2012.

This started at the top — by founder Ray Anderson — who set the highest possible standards for life-cycle analysis, for supply chain management, as well as production and distribution. Sadly, Anderson died in 2011, acclaimed as a global leader in sustainable business practices.

Why Economy?

Look at the economies that are out of shape and unsustainable: Greece, Italy and Spain. There's a need to have a balanced budget. To economise. Money might make the world go around, but when it gets out of hand — through overspending or mismanagement, even greed — things come crashing down.

We need to remind ourselves about sustainable development. It means meeting the needs of the present without compromising the ability of future generations to meet their own needs.

We need to go on an economy drive. We can no longer pursue profit at all costs. Or growth at all costs. Economic factors — for business, for communities, for countries — must be in balance with the other three.

Launched in 1999, the Dow Jones Sustainability Index (DJSI) tracks the financial performance of the leading sustainability-driven companies worldwide. Top of the list in different sectors are Adidas, BMW, Coca Cola, Intel, Philips, Samsung (Technology), Siemens, Swiss Re and Westpac, and Singaporean businesses, including CapitaLand, CDL and Keppel Land.[13]

Why Ethics?

Usually, we connect with ethics under a kindlier term — social or people factors — but it is ethics we are really need to be concerned about. Ethical behaviour, which is essential for business as it is for nations. That means transparency, compliance, corporate governance and corporate social responsibility.

Ethics impacts on labour policies and trade practices. It means running the business in a way that benefits all stakeholders, not just shareholders.[14]

Companies like Nike got into big trouble a few years back when it was revealed that their foreign manufacturing plants used child labour to make its running shoes and soccer balls. After initially denying it, Nike had to back-track under pressure from consumer groups and NGOs like Oxfam, who produced evidence from around the world.[15]

Being Clear about Sustainability

Simply put, sustainability is "a business approach that creates long-term shareholder value by embracing opportunities and managing risks deriving from economic, environmental and social developments", as defined by the DJSI and used as guidelines for its selected leading businesses.

Put another way, corporate sustainability leaders, according to DJSI, achieve long-term shareholder value by gearing their strategies and management towards harnessing the market's potential for sustainably produced products and services while at the same time successfully reducing and avoiding sustainability costs and risks.

It makes perfectly good commercial sense too. Sense and sustainability go together. Of course, there will be plenty who will scoff and suggest sustainability is just another costly exercise dreamt up by "greenies" masquerading as management consultants. But being responsible goes beyond being green. Ethical and environmental, as well as economy and energy, figure in the equation.

If companies are smart about the way they produce and distribute their products, they can actually save money — as well as energy, water, waste and other resources — and make more money for themselves and society. Walmart's supply chain management is a great example of this, now being taken notice of by many other businesses, including its competitors.[16]

Walmart states quite clearly what it stands for: "To be supplied 100% by renewable energy; to create zero waste; to sell products that sustain people and the environment." Not content to do all it can for itself, it has also led the business world by getting its supply chain on board the sustainability process.

That's real sustainability in action.

Along with sense and sustainability should be success and sustainability. It can work and it does work. We just have to wake up to the issues as well as the opportunities presented by climate change and sustainability.

Endnotes

1. Svante Arrhenius and the greenhouse effect is reported in my book, *The ABC of Carbon* (2009), Chapter A, and in many other places. The Nobel Prize winner's biography can be found here, www.nobelprize.org/nobel_prizes/chemistry/laureates/1903/arrhenius-bio.html.

2. For explanations and definitions of sustainability, www.sustainablemeasures.com/node/35.

3. The authors argued that this trend is comparable to mass production, manufacturing quality movement, IT revolution and globalisation. David Lubin and Daniel Esty, "The Sustainability Imperative", *Harvard Business Review*, May 2010.

4. Bill Ford was quoted here, social.ford.com/our-articles/technologies/green/documentary-series-aims-to-help-customers-make-a-greener-shift/.

5. A summary of the 2011 Gibbs & Soell Study, www.gibbs-soell.com/wp-content/uploads/2011/04/2011-Gibbs-Soell-Sense-Sustainability-Study_40511F.pdf.

6. The essentials from the 1987 Brundtland Report, www.un.org/documents/ga/res/42/ares42-187.htm.

7. "A New Era of Sustainability", UN Global Compact-Accenture CEO Study 2010, www.accenture.com/SiteCollectionDocuments/PDF/Accenture_A_New_Era_of_Sustainability_CE.

8. John Elkington's "triple bottom line" first appeared in his book, *Cannibals with Forks: The Triple Bottomline of 21st Century Business* (New Society Publishers, 1997). For more on him and his work go to, www.johnelkington.com/activities/books.asp.

9. An update on Google's work by the Breakthrough Institute, www.thebreakthrough.org/blog/2011/06/google_energy_innovation_can_h.shtml #moreO_Study.pdf.

10. GE is investing heavily through its Ecomagination project, www.ecomagination.com/.

11. "Putting Nature in the Nexus", International Union for Conservation of Nature, 2011 report, Bonn Conference, cmsdata.iucn.org/downloads/nexus_report.pdf.

12. The Interface sustainability progress report, www.interfaceglobal.com/Sustainability/Our-Progress.aspx.

13. This started at the top — by founder Ray Anderson — who set the highest possible standards for life-cycle analysis, for supply chain management, as well as production and distribution. Sadly, Anderson died in 2011, acclaimed as a global leader in sustainable business practices.

14. The Dow Jones Sustainability Index, www.sustainabilityindex.com/07_htmle/indexes/djsiworld_keyfacts.html.

15. In an article on ethics, "Ethical Issues in Practising Public Relations in Asia", *Journal of Communication Management*, 2004, 8(4), 345–353, www.emerald-insight.com/journals.htm?issn=1363-254X, I pointed out areas of importance for professionals and business people operating in different countries. These included cultural practices, as well as personal, professional, political, religious, racial, trade, business, legal, financial, environmental and social aspects.
16. An update on the Nike case study, business-ethics.com/2010/01/24/ 2154-nike-corporate-responsibility-at-a-tipping-point/.
17. According to Walmart's corporate data, "We provided our more than 100,000 global suppliers with a brief survey to evaluate their own sustainability. The survey, taken by our top-tier suppliers by 1 October 2009, represents a key step towards enhancing transparency in our supply chain. We are continuing to roll out this assessment in our international markets.", walmartstores.com/pressroom/news/9706.aspx?rss=All_Press_Releases.

Sources

- www.sustain-ability-showcase.com
- www.lcsi.smu.edu.sg

3

12 Steps to Sustainability in Business

A number of times over the last three years, I have been asked to give talks about sustainability and also provide some practical advice as to what companies, organisations, community groups and schools can do about it. So I came up with some practical steps — 12 of them — which I think help put it all in context and enable people in any organisation to start on the sustainability journey. While this is designed more specifically for a business, the steps can very easily be adopted by or adapted to any organisation, large or small…

1. **Commit to the sustainability journey** — this must come from the top. You must decide on principles and plans. Set targets and appoint teams.

2. **Get good advice** — there are good consultants around to advise and assist. The Singapore Compact for Corporate Social Responsibility and the Singapore Business Federation can point you in the right direction.

3. **Get certified** — start with a Green Biz Check or an Eco Office certification. You can aim for an ISO standard — ISO 14001 for Environment Management Systems or ISO 50001 for Energy Management Systems. Go for gold on the Global Reporting Initiative, the UN Compact or the Dow Jones Sustainability Index.

4. **Engage an energy auditor** — call on one of the 17 Energy Services Companies accredited by the National Environment Agency (NEA) or get your consultant to advise you.

5. **Become energy efficient** — look into all the ways you could become more energy efficient as an organisation. Look at your utility bills and install effective meters to measure your energy. Look to introduce an enterprise sustainability platform into your business.

6. **Find the bottom line benefits** — it won't take long to discover that becoming sustainable can save and make money for the business. You can get really sophisticated and explore the marginal abatement cost curve developed by McKinsey.

"12 Steps" mixed media by Dave Hickson.

7. **Commit to water and waste management** — there's money to be made by saving water, reducing waste and recycling too. The Public Utilities Board and the NEA can help you here.

8. **Set high ethical standards** — be transparent, practise good corporate governance and be ethical in all your business dealings whether at home or abroad. Take all these areas into account for ethical behaviour: cultural, personal, professional, political, religious, racial, trade, business, legal, financial, environmental and social.

9. **Corporate Social Responsibility** — also called Corporate Sustainability and Responsibility by Dr. Wayne Visser, it helps an organisation bring together all the necessary and good business practices.

10. **Embark on sustainability reporting** — guidelines have been produced by the Singapore Exchange (SGX) to help listed companies produce reports on sustainability in the same way as they would for financial reporting.

11. **Communicate effectively with all stakeholders** — it is essential to communicate within and outside the organisation to demonstrate that you mean business and to showcase your goals and achievements.

12. **Commit to conservation and community projects** — becoming a good corporate citizen is part and parcel of your sustainability journey.

Sources

- www.abccarbon.com
- www.nea.gov.sg
- www.csrsingapore.org/c
- www.sbf.org.sg
- www.greenbizcheck.com
- www.sustain-ability-showcase.com
- www.energynz.com
- www.waynevisser.com
- www.sgx.com

4

Profile — Christiana Figueres: Global Emissions Reduction Efforts

*Along with a select few journalists, I was not only able to hear UNFCCC Executive Secretary Ms. Christiana Figueres speak at an event in Singapore organised by the S. Rajaratnam School of International Studies (RSIS), but also had the chance to engage in an interview directly with her. I reported our encounter in my newsletter, **abc carbon express**. Joining me in the intimate interview situation with Ms. Figueres was Jenny Marusiak of Eco-Business.com. Her report is here too, to make up this profile of an important lady on a global mission...*

Impressed by the commitment by 33 countries and 18 regions to start emissions trading schemes and heartened that more major companies are investing in renewable energy and working towards a low-carbon future, United Nations Framework Convention on Climate Change (UNFCCC) Executive Secretary Christiana Figueres is hopeful that a "multilateral solution" to climate change impacts will come about sooner than later.

In October 2012, UNFCCC Executive Secretary Christiana Figueres was in Singapore. She was forthright and made an unemotional plea for recognition of the importance of a "multilateral solution" to climate change.

She also acknowledged positive moves by many countries and regions to introduce emission trading schemes — to put a price on carbon — in addition to those already in place in Europe, Australia and NZ.

She noted that in 2013, 33 countries will have committed to, or have in place, emission trading schemes, along with 18 sub-regional/regional schemes, including the state of California, which will regulate 20% of global emissions.

She was quoted earlier saying Asia is now "the new centre of the universe" for emission reduction efforts. At the Carbon Forum North America event in Washington D.C., she said the region currently leads the push towards cutting emissions through cap-and-trade and other market-based mechanisms, seen to be growing in the coming years.

In Singapore, she was quick to highlight the definite increase in investments, in Asia and elsewhere, in renewable energy production and other emission reduction programmes. She was pleased to see countries and companies taking action, particularly on energy efficiency measures — "because it makes perfect business sense" — and this will also reduce fossil fuel emissions.

When questioned on the current carbon price — through the European Emission Trading Scheme (ETS) — and its impact on genuine investments in renewable energy and other emission reduction projects, she recognised the price was low probably due to low demand (or lack of willing buyers) and a supply surplus of carbon credits, via the "successful" introduction of so many clean development mechanism (CDM) projects.

The UNFCC conference in Doha (November 2012) saw the much hoped for "second commitment" to the Kyoto Protocol and at the same time gave greater confidence that the CDM can deliver what it was intended to — meaningful mitigation measures/projects in developing economies and a suitable return by way of carbon credits for the investors.

In September 2012, the independent high-level panel set up to examine the Kyoto Protocol's CDM released its eagerly awaited recommendations by urging nations to intervene forcefully to address the crisis in the carbon market and substantially increase their expectations for cutting greenhouse gas emissions.

It pointed out that the "ability under the CDM to earn a saleable credit for each tonne of greenhouse gas emissions reduced" has spawned over 4,500 projects in 75 developing countries, from wind energy and efficient cook-stove projects to landfill gas and large industrial projects.

However, the CDM, the report continued, "credited with creating the first global environmental currency, is now under threat due to the current low prices paid for credits, the result of low demand and uncertainty over the timing and level of future demand, which is tied to countries' emission-reduction commitments."

According to the high-level panel, "if nations permit the CDM mechanism to disintegrate, the political consensus for truly global carbon markets may evaporate. Therefore, the panel calls on nations to increase their mitigation ambition by strengthening the pledges that have been made under the UNFCC and by adopting corresponding domestic policies and measures."

Ms. Figueres is hopeful for the continued success of the CDM and the Kyoto Protocol, but urges all parties to acknowledge three very important factors:

1. **Climate change is a global problem and transcends regional or national boundaries;**
2. **Countries can contribute to a low-carbon future in their own way;**
3. **We need to have a global accounting system in place to monitor emissions and the climate change mitigation and adaptation progress.**

While she makes no prediction in these volatile political and economic times, she maintains there is significant progress — even momentum — in the climate change negotiations for global commitments and expects the year-end meetings in Doha to produce a continuing forward movement.

———◆———

Joining me in the intimate interview situation with Ms. Figueres in Singapore on that October 2012 day, was Jenny Marusiak of Eco-Business.com, who collected a little more from the occasion:

Climate Negotiations: Minding the Gaps

UN climate chief Christiana Figueres told a Singapore audience that climate action was heading the right way, but lacks the urgency it requires.

Multilateral climate negotiations are "cumbersome but absolutely crucial" to responding to global warming, said the UN climate chief.

UNFCCC Executive Secretary Christiana Figueres said at a lecture hosted by RSIS that the world faced a big gap between commitments to reduce greenhouse gas emissions and the reductions that scientists say will be needed to minimise catastrophic effects.

"I have no doubt that the clean energy revolution is underway, and the tipping point (towards a low-carbon economy) is inevitable. But I am concerned about the timing and the speed," she added.

Current commitments from governments to reduce greenhouse gas emissions account for only 60% of the amount to keep global warming within the commonly accepted target window of 2°C.

To reach that target will take a combination of international government efforts and simultaneous action on national and regional levels from all sectors, said Ms. Figueres to the 200-strong group of policymakers, academics and other professionals at the Shangri-La Hotel.

The global climate negotiation process has helped spawn an "endless number of efforts on the ground pioneered by an increasing number of sectors and stakeholders", and has added climate change to the very short list of issues to which a truly universal response will be made, she added.

For example, she noted that in 2013, carbon prices in 33 countries and 18 sub-national regions will regulate 20% of global emissions.

She said governments were making progress on closing the three gaps identified at last year's talks in Durban, South Africa, which would help provide the policy certainty necessary to drive private sector action and investment.

The first gap is the time between the expiration of the only existing legally binding agreement on carbon emissions — the Kyoto Protocol — at the end of 2012, and a new global agreement slated for adoption in 2015 and implementation in 2020.

In an unusual step for the negotiations, she said, governments have managed to come up with a preliminary draft text for a second period of the Kyoto Protocol, the Doha Amendment to be used at upcoming talks in Doha.

Ms. Figueres told Eco-Business in an interview after the lecture that while countries commiting to the second period of the Kyoto Protocol initially will account for only 10–12% of global greenhouse emissions, the agreement would be an important reference point for work on the new global agreement through 2015.

"In and of itself, it is limited in what it can do with respect to the trajectory of global emissions. It is, however, very important in terms of its rules and maintaining the environmental integrity of the process," she said.

The second gap is the gap in financing developing countries to cope with climate change. In 2009, wealthy countries committed to provide "fast-start" funding of US$30 billion annually by 2012. The following year in Cancun, negotiators agreed to establish a $100 billion Green Climate Fund by 2020, and have since been struggling with how to implement the fund.

However, the climate fund committee is making progress. "We have much better traction to launch the Green Climate Fund and are working on resolving differing views and defining funding mechanisms," she noted.

Negotiations for the 2020 global agreement, known as the Durban Platform, aim to close the third gap — the lack of sufficiently ambitious emission reduction targets and the need for more countries to commit to making the required reductions.

In that too, governments are making progress with the input from governments, non-governmental organisations, businesses and other groups.

"We have some preliminary ideas…and first thoughts on how to deal with the very, very different national circumstances of countries in shaping an effective, fair and ambitious agreement applicable to all," she said.

Climate talks involving every country and many negotiators — while frustrating — were essential to achieving a plan that was cost-effective and durable, said Ms. Figueres, adding that climate change was a universal problem to which every country could contribute in some way.

The expanding numbers of ministries and sectors giving input to the process has also raised the complexity of the talks, she noted, explaining that climate change was no longer a small environmental issue involving only environment ministers. "This is a development challenge the likes of which the world has never seen."

While climate change could wipe out decades of development progress and threaten future sustainability, it also pushes us towards improved ways of living and doing business in our best interests, she noted.

"There is barely any measure you can take to address climate change that does not make sense to our development," she told the audience.

Sources

- www.eco-business.com
- www.abccarbon.com
- www.cdm.unfccc.int

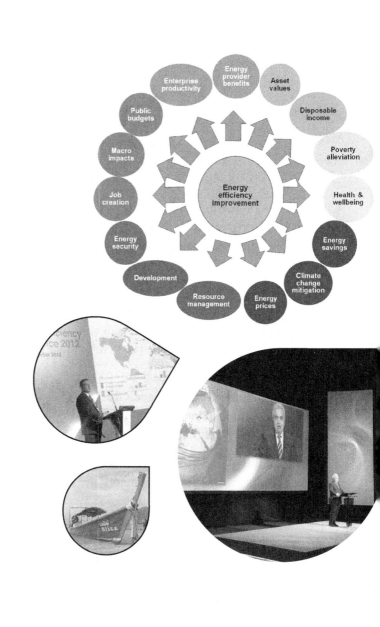

Making
Energy Efficiency
Sexy

Section 2

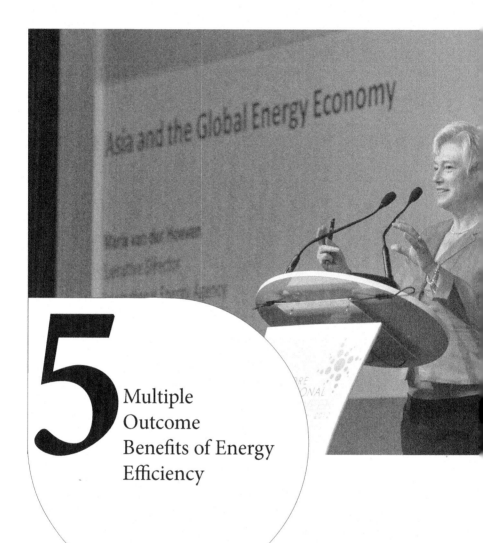

5

Multiple Outcome Benefits of Energy Efficiency

The presentation by Ms. Maria van der Hoeven, Executive Director of the IEA was a highlight of the Singapore International Energy Week opening day, but it was not as well reported as it should have been with its relevance to Singapore. The week-long series of conferences, meetings and a full scale exhibition in October 2012 was well worth attending as there was a wealth of worthwhile papers and exhibits to enthuse over. This article was expressly written for the NEA Energy Efficiency website…

Cutting Costs Amounts to More Than Energy Savings Alone

The failure to properly evaluate the benefits of energy efficiency will likely result in under investment in energy efficiency, so the multiple outcome benefits represent the "opportunity cost" of failing to adequately evaluate and prioritise energy efficiency investments.

This was the important message in the keynote address at the Singapore International Energy Week 2012 opening ceremony from Ms. Maria van der Hoeven, Executive Director of the International Energy Agency (IEA). She shared her perspective on "Shaping a New Energy Landscape" and drew particular attention to the "multiple outcome benefits" of energy efficiency.

She invited the audience to "have a look at what energy efficiency could bring in", noting that "significant technology changes" will have to be made in the transport, building and industry sectors.

Photo of Ms Maria van der Hoeven, Executive Director of the IEA, taken at the Singapore International Energy Week (2012): www.flickr.com/photos/singaporeinternationalenergyweek/8112421900/in/photostream/.

IEA has established that energy efficiency accounts for more than half of the carbon reductions needed to achieve sustainability. But reduced energy consumption is not just a question of emissions.

"They also have implications for energy security by reducing import dependence," Ms. van der Hoeven said, "as the most secure barrel or kilowatt will always be the one we don't use."

She made it quite clear that energy efficiency and the switch to low-carbon fuels will also be crucial for the Asian building and industry sector.

"So while energy efficiency may not be as politically enticing as new construction projects, it is often the most affordable and most effective tool to achieve policy goals."

Ms. van der Hoeven made special mention of a range of other "silent" benefits which are often not included in the debate, but which usually rank high among the concerns of policy makers.

These, the IEA describes as the "multiple outcome benefits of energy efficiency", graphically shown in the chart on the chapter opening pages, which appears on both the NEA and IEA website and set out in full in the IEA report *Spreading the Net: the Multiple Benefits of Energy Efficiency Improvements.*

The Executive Director of IEA pointed out that by better understanding the different benefits arising from energy efficiency, it should be easier for policy makers to prioritise for the most significant outcomes, in addition to energy savings, in optimising energy efficiency policy designs.

Although the rebound effect can result in energy efficiency measures producing less energy savings than expected, IEA pointed out that it should still be considered in light of the variety of other benefits which are generated.

As can be seen in the chart, outcomes are produced at different levels of the economy: at the individual level (individuals, households and enterprises); at the sectorial level (by the various sectors of the economy such as transport, residential, industrial and commercial sectors); at the national level (including macroeconomic benefits, and benefits to national budgets); and at the international level (reflecting the international public good of these benefits).

In many cases, a ripple effect emerges when energy efficiency improvements take effect at the individual level, triggering benefits for a household and/or enterprise that have a multiplier effect on a specific sector and possibly the whole economy.

Ms. van der Hoeven drew attention to just a few of the benefits which at the individual level include health and well-being impacts.

This mainly relates to the public health improvements observed as a result of improved heating and cooling of buildings, and better air quality from more efficient transport and power generation, and less demand for both.

Other benefits at the individual level include:

- Poverty alleviation: energy affordability and access; and
- Increased disposable income.

In the economic sectors — industrial, transport, residential, commercial — IEA identifies these benefits:

- Industrial productivity and competitiveness;
- Energy provider and infrastructure benefits; and
- Increased asset values.

At the national level, multiple benefits include:

- Job creation;
- Reduced energy-related public expenditures;
- Energy security; and
- Macroeconomic effects.

At the international level, there are benefits seen in:

- Reduced greenhouse gas emissions;
- Moderating energy prices;
- Natural resource management; and
- Development goals.

The IEA pointed out that the failure to properly evaluate the benefits of energy efficiency will likely result in underinvestment in energy efficiency. The multiple benefits therefore represent the "opportunity cost" of failing to adequately evaluate and prioritise energy efficiency investments.

At the Singapore International Energy Week, Ms. van der Hoeven's words — and presentation — were very well received, as she drew attention to the need for Asian countries and businesses to not only invest in renewable energy but also in energy efficiency, where there are multiple outcome benefits.

She made it clear that with estimates of GDP growth resulting from energy efficiency converging around 1%, energy efficiency should be considered as part of mainstream economic policy rather than an energy issue only.

―――――◄○►―――――

Sources

- www.e2singapore.gov.sg
- www.ema.gov.sg
- www.iea.org

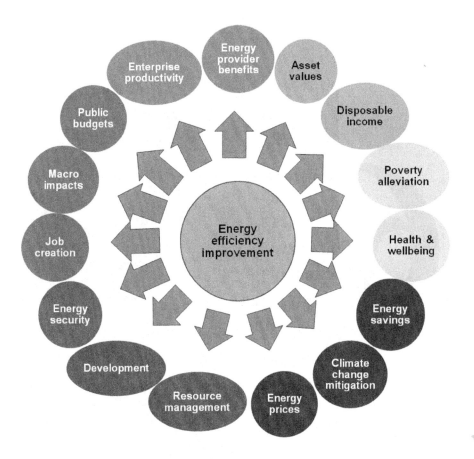

Photo Credit: Spreading the Net: Capturing the Multiple Benefits of Energy Efficiency Improvements, © OECD/IEA 2012.

6 Energy Efficiency as a Business Opportunity

Besides attending and reporting on the National Energy Efficiency Conference for two days, I was also the moderator for the closing plenary session, which turned out to be a lively affair. I also helped promote the event and managed to get some additional media attention, including Channel News Asia, which decided to talk to me about the conference subject matter, as well as Ram Bhaskar, head of energy efficiency for NEA. This article, which covered as much of the conference proceedings as physically possible, first appeared on www.e2singapore.gov.sg where you will also find continuous coverage on the world of energy efficiency...

Singapore Sees the Soft and Sexy Side of It

Soft and sexy is not how you would perhaps see energy efficiency, which has something of a hard, boring, technical and non-sexy image, unlike renewable or clean energy, where solar, wind and other forms of non-fossil fuelled power look and sound exciting and, well, sexy!

But how to make energy efficiency sexier and how to focus on the soft side to get more people on board the energy efficiency drive was an important focus of the National Energy Efficiency Conference (NEEC) in Singapore in September 2012.

Besides technology and equipment, businesses need to focus on getting their people on board, by communicating effectively and encouraging management and staff to think and behave in ways that save energy — one of the six key learnings from the two days.

Here's my report and the highlights of the event:

Where was the best place in the world to be in September 2012 to gain the upper hand in energy efficiency? To hear world-class speakers who have experienced first-hand the trials and tribulations — and successes — in changing the way their businesses are run to achieve significant energy savings?

The second NEEC was held on 19 and 20 September 2012. Under the guiding hands of the National Environment Agency (NEA), the Economic Development Board (EDB)

and the Energy Market Authority (EMA), industry case studies and best practices came thick and fast at the 2012 NEEC.

Energy efficiency experts representing some of the world's biggest businesses like ABB, Siemens, Texas Instruments and DuPont, featured alongside presentations from globally respected thought leaders from the Rocky Mountain Institute (RMI), McKinsey and Accenture.

More than 200 delegates from Singapore and other Southeast Asian countries gained from the first-class advice and first-hand accounts from leaders in their respected fields, with local and regional success stories from NatSteel, Total, Petronas and Shell.

A recurring comment expressed by delegates, speakers and moderators alike was that energy efficiency has yet to achieve unequivocal recognition as a "sexy" undertaking, compared to other initiatives by industries. Yet the results and outcomes consistently demonstrate that it is the "low-hanging fruit" and the easiest and best way for businesses to cut emissions, save energy and save costs at the same time.

Six key learning takeaways that sum up the two-day conference:

1. Learn from the best — there are many excellent industry case studies and best practices from near and far to apply to your own business or industry.
2. Introduce ISO 50001 — this is designed as the approved energy management certification tool and is supported by Singapore agencies like NEA and SPRING.
3. Help is at hand to introduce energy efficiency measures — NEA will be setting up a one-stop centre to assist companies in identifying and implementing energy efficiency initiatives, as well as adopting energy efficiency best practices.
4. Concentrate on the "soft" side — besides technology and equipment, businesses need to focus on getting their people on board, by communicating effectively and encouraging management and staff to think and behave in ways that save energy.
5. The business imperative — energy efficiency makes perfect business sense. It enables companies to save money, even make money, and drives the bottom line.
6. National and global goals — energy efficiency fits into all strategies and targets by reducing fossil fuel use and greenhouse gas emissions, locally and globally.

Fastest and Cheapest Way of Cutting Energy Use

Two keynote speakers set the pace for Day One.

Jim Kelly, Head of Global Energy Efficiency business for ABB, a leader in power and automation technologies operating in 100 countries with 145,000 employees, spoke of how energy efficiency adds to productivity and cost savings.

Citing a recent study commissioned by ABB of nearly 400 utilities and industrial companies worldwide, he said more than 50% had not conducted a single audit on where energy was used and lost. This energy dislocation or the lack of alignment between awareness and action could be traced to, among others, a lack of confidence in the projected results.

"Improving energy efficiency is the fastest and cheapest way to reduce energy use and emissions while mitigating the need for power generation and resource acquisition to support economic growth," he told the delegates.

As industries account for about one-third of the world's energy demand, key industrial players in Singapore can successfully reduce their carbon emissions. Successful case studies are available that show clear return on investment with economic benefits to be reaped.

By leading in the energy efficiency space, Singapore would reinforce its attraction as a destination for industrial capital investments.

For Juan Aguiriano — DuPont's Worldwide Managing Director of Sustainable Solutions — it was important for businesses to set goals and targets for improvements in energy efficiency. Making these targets "public" was a key to ensuring success.

In DuPont's own experience as the owner and operator of over 150 diverse production facilities worldwide, a highly significant portion of 40% or upwards of the total energy efficiency improvement opportunity can be realised through relatively minor, low-cost or no-cost continuous improvement energy projects. Often, many of these are rooted in effecting a change in culture.

Mr. Aguiriano drove home the message on the importance of dealing with the "soft" side of managing energy efficiency, taking the position that 70% of energy efficiency can be driven by a company's culture and capability building. He acknowledged, however, that changing cultural mind-sets can be tough.

The New Business Imperative

Some highlights from Day One on the conference theme of *Energy Efficiency as a Business Opportunity*:

– In the session *Driving Energy Efficiency — Public and Private Sector Perspectives* with speakers from EDB, Texas Instruments, GSK and Accenture, a supportive corporate culture was recognised as a key to driving energy efficiency as every energy management system must consist of people, processes and technology. In addition, proper processes and systems had to be in place to set efficiency targets and to track performance. Energy efficiency is a data-driven activity — you cannot manage what you cannot measure. It is important to invest in software as well as hardware.

– A breakout session involving Actsys, KBC and Tuas Power on *Benchmarking and Optimisation* showed that top-class industrial plants were able to find scope for greater energy efficiency through improvement retrofits. Further synergies were achieved by integrating energy and water usage across neighbouring plants. In the case of power supplier Tuas Power, thermodynamic performance monitoring enabled early identification of the cause for any energy efficiency loss, and allowed for a predictive maintenance programme to maximise generation efficiency.

– How big is your energy bill? Understanding why you consume energy was the big question raised in the breakout session on *Energy Management Tools*. Speakers from McKinsey, Petronas, Accenture and Siemens confirmed this: Rigorous and accurate data collection is fundamental to effective energy management, along with the use of meaningful KPIs and benchmarks from which stretched targets can be derived. Ownership creation is essential, so is open and transparent communication between all departments involved.

– In the session on Energy Efficiency Transformation, barriers to industrial energy efficiency in Singapore were explored by speakers from

National University of Singapore (NUS) and McKinsey. The main motivation of industries for energy efficient improvements is to drive down costs. Getting the desired results would make the greatest impact to ongoing efforts. By putting in place an integrated energy strategy, companies would have the certainty of capturing 20–30% in energy savings.

- System Energy Efficiency was the topic for panellists from Greenpower Asia, SDC, ABB and Siemens. Discussions at the breakout session emphasised that the drive for energy efficiency has to be a continuous process. Companies also need to look beyond surface limitations to discover innovative solutions. As buildings play a major role — being responsible for 40% of the world's energy consumption — energy efficiency can be achieved through both physical facilities and professional attention. A case study on the Fuji Oil Co-generation project was presented to show the opportunities for energy savings.

Teaming Up for Energy Savings

The first plenary session on Day Two addressed the topic of *Developing Singapore's Energy Efficiency Capabilities*. James Scott Brew from the renowned RMI drew on a bold vision with ambitious targets. Called "Reinventing Fire", this business-led transition in the US is designed to grow the economy, improve energy efficiency, adopt renewable energy, reduce fossil fuel use and mitigate CO_2 emissions. He affirmed that through this, energy security has been enhanced and the natural environment improved, while the substitution of energy sources from oil, coal and nuclear with renewable energy could be permanent and create huge business opportunities. From the National Research Foundation, Tsoi Mun Heng expanded on the Singapore approach which is to leverage research, development and demonstration to solve complex national challenges of climate change and energy efficiency — with global relevance. Elspeth Thomson of Energy Studies Institute moderated this session.

Continuing the discussion on *Developing Singapore's Energy Efficiency Capabilities* at the second plenary session were speakers from NUS, McKinsey and NEA, with moderator Professor Michael Quah from

NUS. With a strong emphasis on education, they pointed out that promoting energy efficiency had to address market barriers, including people and cultural factors. In support of R&D, there must be meaningful education, involving technologies and systems, as well as practice and application. McKinsey's planned Green Campus will help build up sustainable energy efficiency transformation capabilities, while legislation like the Energy Conservation Act and other programmes such as the Singapore Certified Energy Manager Programme would help spur industries and result in improvements of lower energy costs.

Sharing in Success: How You Can Do That

Best Practices and Success Stories made up two breakout sessions. Moderated by Nanyang Technological University's (NTU) Nilesh Jadhav and NEA's Ram Bhaskar, here is a sampling of the key case study findings by speakers from participating companies:

- Total: Process improvement is achieved through utilisation of waste heat; continual improvement is important and energy efficiency definitely enhances profitability; the initial step even with the EASe grant had been a hesitant one, but following successful implementation, energy efficiency was viewed differently.
- NatSteel: Improvement in the energy efficient performance of key equipment such as the furnaces, has led to substantial energy reduction and a significant improvement in profit margin.
- Shell: Leadership played a vital role in setting an urgent pace on energy efficiency; grants such as GREET help to improve the economics of energy efficiency projects.
- ABB: Barriers for industries include the requirement for high reliability and integrity of industrial processes forbidding breakdowns; the uniqueness and confidentiality of industrial processes, and limited capital due to the secondary priority for energy efficiency.
- SSW: As LED technology gets more advanced and evolves to deliver better lumens per watt performance, boasting longer life, lower running cost, the solutions present significant energy efficiency advantages over traditional lighting products.

Getting Hot on Green

Two breakout sessions deserved more time as they attracted the delegates' attention — *Integrative Design for Energy Efficiency* and *Data Centre Energy Efficiency*.

With contributions from The Green Asia Group and Texas Instruments, and moderated by NUS's Chandra Sekhar, this *Integrative Design for Energy Efficiency* session highlighted that an integrative design process and approach reduces both capital and operational expenditure (CAPEX and OPEX), as well as construction risk.

As it is important to consider life-cycle and procurement costs, energy efficiency should be an early part of the design process. Good communication and the integration of various working groups of different disciplines are key factors in making the entire facility energy efficient instead of just some of its components or systems. The scalability of an integrative design also means it can work for smaller single-family houses as well as mega facilities.

There was very good reason for the speakers, including the moderator — NTU's Professor Toh Kok Chuan, to draw on their vast knowledge on *Data Centre Energy Efficiency*, given that data centres consume 1.3% of energy worldwide, a figure that is continuing to grow. According to Dieter Brack, Director of Solution Design at Green Datacenter AG, digitisation and increasing demands on IT are driving a 10% expansion of data centre space yearly. With fewer power conversion steps, data centres could operate more energy efficiently with less cooling requirements. Consolidating and having fewer components, lower operating cost and smaller footprint could translate to 20% energy savings. Emphasis was placed on a reduction of complexity and the enhancement of reliability which translates well into genuine cost-cutting outcomes.

Robert Pe of Hewlett-Packard revealed that the soon-to-be-released Data Centre Benchmarking study in Singapore had found the implementation of air management practices lacking. Over 60% of data centres in Singapore are running at temperatures of 21°C or less, which is a lot cooler than needed. He cited the Ashrae temperature criterion for green data centres at between 24–27°C. The same study also showed that only 22% of the sites audited had the capability to implement energy management and conversion programmes without external help. Only 13% of sites audited were actually tracking and trending their energy usage.

Here's the report from Rachel Kelly for Channel News Asia (20 September 2012):

Countries Should Explore Ways to Maximise Use of Water and Energy

SINGAPORE: China is looking to expand its power capacity to meet future needs and the target is no mean feat.

By 2030, it plans to add more than the total installed power capacity of the US, UK and Australia combined.

Meeting this goal will add pressure on resources such as energy and water.

To meet China's growing need for power, experts said, it will need to harness more coal resources.

But currently, HSBC estimates that almost half of the coal reserves in the country are located in water-scarce regions.

To meet its target for power capacity, China will need greater efficiency in the use of water and energy.

Experts agree with some having said that energy efficiency is a low-hanging fruit that can be implemented by most companies and achieve significant savings.

Chairman and CEO of Sustain Ability Showcase Asia, Ken Hickson, said: "It is the easiest thing to address, the thing that you can make such a difference in a relatively short time, payback for any investment you are making in two years, and energy reduction of 50% by being smart in the way you use energy."

"So it is a no brainer for the industry and business to do that and there are plenty of examples from companies around the world as to why they doing this and how they are achieving remarkable results."

But China should not be alone in making these efforts.

Experts said that other countries should also explore new ways to maximise their use of water and energy.

To assist companies in identifying and implementing energy practices, Singapore's NEA will be launching a one-stop online centre — the energy efficiency office will help to link companies to relevant parties.

NEA said more information on the Energy Efficiency Support Office (EESO) will be announced when ready. This is part of ongoing efforts by NEA.

NEA's Director of Energy Efficiency and Conservation, Ram Bhaskar, said: "Last year, the NEA formed the energy efficiency national partnership as a platform to support companies in their efforts for energy efficiency. We have three main areas that we are covering — the first one is in energy management systems (where) we believe that companies should set up energy management systems so that energy efficiency becomes a sustainable business practice and the norm in their normal daily operations."

NatSteel Holdings was recently recognised by NEA and awarded Outstanding Energy Manager of the Year.

It reduced its CO_2 emissions by about 7.5% over the past two years by bringing onboard a number of streamlining measures such as scrapping preheating using waste-off gas, hot charging from steel mills directly into rolling mills, sidewall oxygen lance and a carbon injection system.

———<o>———

Sources

- www.channelnewsasia.com
- www.abccarbon.com
- www.nea.gov.sg
- www.e2singapore.gov.sg

7

Mobilising Investment in Energy Efficiency in Southeast Asia

Based on an insightful report from the Washington-based WRI, this article endeavoured to show the investment opportunities in Southeast Asia, and Thailand in particular, where the government has introduced a number of incentive schemes including the Energy Conservation Promotion Fund, for energy efficiency. It first appeared on NEA's Energy Efficiency website…

World Resources Institute

Developing nations can learn from Thailand with regard to energy efficiency programmes, in particular, to see how investment can be mobilised to fund this important means to cut greenhouse gas emissions, according to a report by the World Resources Institute (WRI).

Entitled "Mobilising Climate Investment", the report incorporates a case study on Thailand which demonstrates how strong government leadership combined with strategic support from international climate finance can drive the transition toward an energy efficient economy.

Developing countries will need about US$531 billion of additional investments in clean energy technologies every year in order to limit global temperature rise to 2°C above preindustrial levels, thus preventing climate change's worst impacts.

To attract investments on the scale required, developing country governments, with support from developed countries, must undertake "readiness" activities that will encourage public and private sector investors to put their money into climate-friendly projects.

In the early 1990s, as Thailand's economy was growing rapidly at 10% per year, the power sector was growing even faster; the government recognised that conserving energy would provide a low-cost way to meet its citizens' rising demand for energy.

It responded by passing the Energy Conservation Promotion Act in 1992 that required

Photo by Neitram (2006) taken from WikiMedia Commons (CC BY-SA 3.0):www. commons.wikimedia.org/ wiki/File:Thailand_koh_phi_ phi_long_boat.jpg.

large energy users to conduct energy efficiency audits and develop and submit plans for energy efficiency improvements, and established an Energy Conservation Promotion Fund, which raised funds for energy efficiency projects by taxing petroleum products.

The government also introduced a demand-side management plan, using about US$40 million in climate finance from the Global Environment Facility (an international climate fund) and the Australian and Japanese governments. This plan included public awareness campaigns, setting energy efficiency standards for buildings and appliances, and demand-side planning to better manage the timing of consumer energy use.

The state energy generation utility successfully implemented the demand-side management plan, with impressive results: The utility achieved 15,700GWh of energy savings by 2012, in excess of its own targets. Key to the plan's success was the close coordination with the private sector, designed right from the start and carefully tailored to the Thai context. The plan was also widely disseminated through public awareness campaigns, resulting in strong support from industry and the public. Furthermore, the utility underwent considerable readiness activities — such as staff expansion and training — to ensure adequate capacity to effectively implement the plan.

Financing Energy Efficiency Projects

While the demand-side management plan garnered encouraging results, a significant barrier remained: Thailand's local banks had a limited understanding of and experience with energy efficiency projects, making it difficult for potential developers to obtain financing for such projects.

In order to overcome this barrier, the Thai government established an Energy Efficiency Revolving Fund in 2002, offering credit lines — initially at no interest — to local banks so that they could provide financing to developers for energy efficiency projects. The Revolving Fund familiarised commercial banks with energy efficiency projects, and by 2010, it had financed projects worth a total investment of US$453 million, resulting in energy cost savings in the region of US$154 million each year.

The financial incentives to banks, combined with the enhanced awareness of energy efficiency, were key to the success of the Revolving Fund. Another critical factor was that the government had a reliable source of funding from the Energy Conservation Promotion Fund to invest in the Revolving Fund, so it did not need to rely on international support.

Lessons from Thailand

The initial policies laid down by the Thai government has enabled the nation to transition smoothly from readiness activities — such as capacity-building, awareness-raising, and demonstration — to large-scale investments. It is currently embarking on a 20-year energy efficiency development plan funded through the Energy Conservation Promotion Fund with approximately US$560 million over five years, which aims to reduce the country's overall energy consumption by 20% by 2030.

Other countries can learn from Thailand's experience of combining strong national leadership with strategic use of climate finance for carefully targeted readiness activities. However, building an enabling environment for investment in energy efficiency and clean energy is an ongoing process. As Thailand moves forward with its 20-year energy efficiency development plan, it must continue undertaking readiness activities — such as training programs to address remaining skill gaps — to ensure it has the right conditions in place to scale up low-carbon development.

WRI, based in Washington, US, was launched in 1982 as a centre for policy research and analysis to address to global resource and environmental issues. It focuses on the intersection of the environment and socio-economic development. It goes beyond research to put ideas into action, working globally with governments, business, and civil society to build transformative solutions that protect the earth and improve people's lives.

Sources

- www.e2singapore.gov.sg
- www.wri.org

8 Profile —
Fatih Birol:
The "Fuel" to
Make a Difference

*I attended the Southeast Asia launch of the World Energy Outlook organised by the EMA on 4 December 2012 and listened enraptured to the considered words and excellent presentation by Dr. Fatih Birol. I had met him on a previous occasion and he is a very impressive figure who commands respect for his findings and views. While I clearly heard him offer some praise — for the industrial sector in the US, as well as China, Japan and Europe — for making some positive moves to capitalise on the benefits of energy efficiency, he also had a lot of harsh words, directed at those who failed to recognise the opportunities of energy efficiency. My report first appeared in **abc carbon express**, followed by the slightly subdued version on E2 Singapore...*

An economic sin. An epic failure of international energy policy.

Harsh words from the chief economist of the International Energy Agency (IEA), Dr. Fatih Birol, on why only a third of economically-viable energy efficiency measures are actually achieved globally.

He said this in Singapore at the Asian launch of the World Energy Outlook (WEO) 2012 organised by Energy Market Authority (EMA) on 4 December 2012. He clearly had some praise too: for the industrial sector in US, China, Japan and Europe, for making some positive moves to capitalise on the benefits of energy efficiency. What did he have to say on seizing huge energy efficiency opportunities?

Focus on energy efficiency as it's where the most can be achieved in the shortest time.

Eloquent and energetic. Mostly diplomatic, but very direct.

He doesn't mince words when revealing the fateful omissions of countries who fail to exploit opportunities to cut greenhouse gas emissions by effectively adopting energy efficiency measures.

Here's a man with his finger on the pulse of the global energy scene and his mind tuned to the bottom line of energy: what it costs to produce and what costs the planet has to bear.

He is undoubtedly an energy economist with a heart — one he proudly wears on his sleeve.

Cool and calculating, he tells the world, in this case a sober Singapore audience of 200 plus, that it is "an economic sin" that only a third of all economically-viable energy efficiency potential is being realised.

That means two thirds of economically viable energy efficiency opportunities are missed. Lost forever.

In terms of international energy policy implementation this is — in his words — "an epic failure".

He also made clear that this year the "fuel" IEA decided to focus on in its WEO was not coal, or gas, or renewables, but was energy efficiency. The fuel we often forget about. It goes to waste.

The gains promised by energy efficiency are within reach and are essential to underpin a more secure and sustainable energy system.

He covered what unlocking the purely economic potential for energy efficiency could do for energy markets, the economy and the environment.

Some of his strong words and impressive points:

- Energy efficiency can delay "lock-in" of CO_2 emissions permitted under a 2°C trajectory (set for 2017) until 2022, buying 5 extra years.
- Cumulative investments in energy efficiency of US $12 trillion are more than offset by fuel savings and trigger economic growth of a cumulative US $18 trillion.
- Industry is the one sector where most of the energy efficiency opportunities have been realised — that is because the industry recognises the business case — proof that energy efficiency works.

Here's an important extract from the WEO:

A Blueprint for an Energy Efficient World

Energy efficiency is widely recognised as a key option in the hands of policy makers but current efforts fall well short of tapping its full economic potential. In the last year major energy consuming countries have announced new measures: China is targeting a 16% reduction in energy intensity by 2015; the US has adopted new fuel economy standards; the EU has committed to a cut of 20% in its 2020 energy demand; and Japan aims to cut 10% from electricity consumption by 2030.

In IEA's New Policies Scenario, these help to speed up the disappointingly slow progress in global energy efficiency seen over the last decade. But even with these and other new policies in place, a significant share of the potential to improve energy efficiency — four-fifths of the potential in the buildings sector and more than half in industry — still remains untapped.

"Our Efficient World Scenario shows how tackling the barriers to energy efficiency investment can unleash this potential and realise huge gains for energy security, economic growth and the environment. These gains are not based on achieving any major or unexpected technological break-throughs, but just on taking actions to remove the barriers obstructing the implementation of energy efficiency measures that are economically viable. Successful action to this effect would have a major impact on global energy and climate trends, compared with the New Policies Scenario. The growth in global primary energy demand to 2035 would be halved."

This scenario shows how tackling barriers to energy efficiency investment can unleash this potential and realise huge gains for energy security, economic growth and the environment, Dr. Birol said.

IEA recognises industry as a sector where most energy efficiency opportunities can be realised: because the industry recognises the business case.

Energy Efficiency: The Fuel to Make a Difference

Report for E2 Singapore

It's called the WEO 2012, but in fact it is the blueprint for action with a 25-year frame of reference from 2010 to 2035.

The "fuel" the IEA decided to focus on in this WEO was not coal, or gas, or renewables, but energy efficiency.

The fuel we often forget about. But where, in the opinion of IEA Chief Economist and WEO lead author, Dr. Fatih Birol, "the most can be achieved in the shortest time".

"The focus on energy efficiency is one of the very few valuable options to reduce emissions in the short term and perhaps for some time after," he said to an audience in Singapore — the first in Southeast Asia to get a first-hand account of the WEO.

He pointed out that IEA studied all countries, sectors and energy saving opportunities.

The gains promised by energy efficiency are within reach and are essential to underpin a more secure and sustainable energy system.

In the WEO, 6 types of policy action are proposed. If widely implemented, they can make the IEA's Efficient World Scenario reality. They include:

1. Increasing the visibility of energy efficiency through strengthening its measurement and disclosing its gains;
2. Prioritising efficiency by integrating it into the decision-making process in the government, industry and society;
3. Increasing its affordability by creating appropriate business models and financing instruments;
4. Making efficiency mainstream by incentivising the most efficient technology options and discouraging the least efficient ones;
5. Making it real by implementing monitoring, verification and enforcement activities; and
6. Making it realisable by increasing governance and administrative capacity at all levels.

He talked about the benefits of unlocking the purely economic potential for energy efficiency and what it could do for energy markets, the economy and the environment. These benefits include:

– Delaying "lock-in" of CO_2 emissions permitted under a 2°C trajectory — set to happen in 2017 — until 2022, thus buying 5 extra years.

In the WEO, Dr. Birol explains that the climate goal of limiting warming to 2°C is becoming more difficult and costly with each passing year. Almost four-fifths of the CO_2 emissions allowable by 2035 are already locked-in by existing power plants, factories and buildings. If action to reduce CO_2 emissions is not taken before 2017, all the allowable CO_2 emissions would be locked-in by energy infrastructure existing at that time. Rapid deployment of energy-efficient technologies (as in IEA's Efficient World Scenario) would postpone this complete lock-in to 2022, buying time to secure a much-needed global agreement to cut greenhouse gas emissions.

– Offsetting US$12 million of cumulative investments in energy efficiency through fuel savings and triggering economic growth of a cumulative US$18 trillion.

Energy efficiency is widely recognised as a key option in the hands of policy makers but current efforts fall well short of tapping its full economic potential. But Dr. Birol has high hopes, as in the last year, major energy-consuming countries have announced new measures:

- China is targeting a 16% reduction in energy intensity by 2015;
- The US has adopted new fuel economy standards;
- The EU has committed to a cut of 20% in its 2020 energy demand; and
- Japan aims to cut 10% from electricity consumption by 2030.

In the IEA's New Policies Scenario, these help to speed up the disappointingly slow progress in global energy efficiency seen over the last decade. But even with these and other new policies in place, a significant share of the potential to improve energy efficiency — four-fifths of the potential in the buildings sector and more than half in industry — still remains untapped.

Gains for energy security, economic growth and the environment do not require a major technological breakthrough. Action is needed to remove barriers preventing the implementation of economically viable energy efficiency measures. Only then will gains promised by energy efficiency, essential for a more secure and sustainable energy system, be within reach.

More, however, must be done to improve energy efficiency and ensure the global energy system stays on a more sustainable path, said Dr. Birol.

He noted that the central scenario of WEO 2012 shows that several conflicting trends persist — energy demand and CO_2 emissions are rising; energy market dynamics are increasingly determined by emerging economies; fossil fuels are still dominant as sources of energy; and the world is lagging in providing universal energy access to the under-privileged.

"Without a concerted policy push, two-thirds of the economically-viable potential to improve energy efficiency will remain unrealised through to 2035."

———◁◇▷———

Sources

- www.siew.sg
- www.ema.gov.sg
- www.worldenergyoutlook.org
- www.iea.org
- www.e2singapore.gov.sg
- www.abccarbon.com

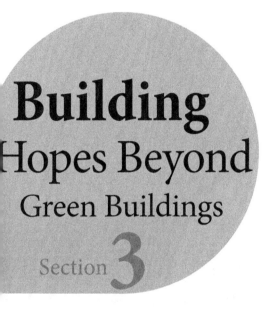

Building
Hopes Beyond
Green Buildings

Section 3

9

Reinventing Fire: Amory Lovins on Energy Efficiency and Retrofits

While I have read much and learned a lot from Amory Lovins and the RMI before, I met him for the first time at two events in Singapore in November 2012. I had the pleasure of talking to him as well as listening to his penetrating presentation, which clearly showed that he is a man with limitless energy himself, full of innovations and soundly researched ideas. This article is written expressly for the E2 Singapore website…

There's not much Amory Lovins doesn't know about energy efficiency, whether for buildings, industry, transport or homes. He lives in a super-smart home which produces and saves more energy than it uses. He knows that energy efficiency is a business imperative and is profitable for business.

Even though much of his work revolves around policies and projects in the US, his message is clear. And Singapore is in his "line of fire". Reinventing fire, that is.

Apart from his book "Reinventing Fire", you soon realise he is trying to reinvent the way the world works. The way energy is used or abused.

The National Environment Agency (NEA) hosted a seminar in the Environment Building, Scotts Road (15 November 2012), featuring Lovins and his work with Rocky Mountain Institute (RMI).

Amory Lovins is introduced as a consultant physicist and innovator in energy and how it links with resources, security, development, and the environment. He has advised the energy and other industries for four decades as well as the US Departments of Energy and Defense, lately serving the leaders of Coca-Cola, Deutsche Bank, Ford, Holcim and Interface.

He is a man with limitless energy himself, full of innovations and soundly researched ideas. To get a measure of this man with a mission, here's a glimpse at what he had to say on building energy efficiency into new and old structures:

Photo by Robert Paul Young (2005) taken from WikiMedia Commons (CC BY 2.0):www.commons.wikimedia.org/wiki/File:Empire_State_Building_Dec.2005.jpg.

Old Buildings Better Than New

Buildings in the US consume 42% of the nation's energy and 72% of its electricity. An energy efficiency revolution could revive the real-estate sector, create jobs, revitalise the national economy, and reduce fossil fuel use.

"Negawatts", Lovins' emphasises, stands for the watts/electricity not used when a building is designed and managed to save energy.

He calls for change which is more than incremental and disruptive technology which he sees as "integrative design". This approach involves renewable energy for the built environment and encompasses combined heat, cooling and power systems, energy efficient designs for refrigeration/air conditioning, and all appliances and systems.

Old buildings can be better than new. There is the temptation to tear down and start afresh, but Lovins knows that smart retrofitting can mean up to 75% savings on energy use.

A way to enhance energy efficiency is to reduce power loss/waste in transmission from source to end user. Co-generation, with smaller, local grids, and localised renewable energy, e.g. solar or wind, can greatly reduce energy lost in transmission. He said as much as 90% of energy produced in the US is wasted in this way.

He provides some US case studies: the iconic Empire State Building, a Federal Office building in Colorado and Ford Motor dealerships.

Empire State Building

In 2008, a team of 5 key players (Clinton Climate Initiative, Empire State Building, Jones Lang LaSalle, Johnson Controls and RMI) created an integrated sustainability programme, including retrofit measures for New York's Empire State Building. This achieved a 38% energy use reduction (mainly through super smart windows to reduce heat loss/gain but maintain effective natural light, and more efficient chiller/heater systems), acting as a model of a deep retrofit project in a large multi-tenant building.

A design partner and technical peer reviewer for property owners RMI brought a whole-systems approach to the project. It facilitated workshops, gave design input, conducted the life-cycle cost analysis, contributed to presentations to ownership, and assembled various outreach efforts (e.g. create the project storyline and a project website).

Byron G. Rogers Federal Office Building

This building in Denver, Colorado is on track to become one of the most energy efficient office buildings in the US, due to be completed in 2013. It will result in a 70% reduction from existing energy use through efficiency measures alone — a staggering feat for a historic building. With the incorporation of cutting edge technologies like chilled beams and LED lighting, the retrofit will position this building 5 to 10 years ahead of schedule towards reaching Net Zero energy goals by 2030.

Ford Motor Company

RMI was invited to help Ford create a compelling green dealership programme that they could offer to their dealers. The first step was to build a strong business case for comprehensive efficiency upgrades by partnering with pilot dealerships in different climate zones throughout the US. The team conducted deep energy audits and assembled an interactive bundle of measures that could be cost-effectively replicated across the entire chain.

Over half of the pilot store energy cost savings could be replicated across the entire chain with minimal corporate administrative time, minimal design and analysis. The team anticipates savings of roughly 30–50% of the energy cost in stores, with a five-year simple payback or less.

Lovins left a few parting shots:

- Singapore should approach energy efficiency with the same ingenuity and dynamism it has dealt with water and transport.
- Architects and engineers are paid for what they spend not for what they save.
- Old buildings can become *better than new* through smart retrofitting.
- Governments must see climate protection as a business opportunity.
- Turn stumbling blocks into stepping stones! Obstacles are business opportunities.

———— ⟨○⟩ ————

Sources

- www.rmi.org
- www.e2singapore.gov.sg

10

Initiatives to Keep Singapore Ahead in International Green Buildings

Attending conferences and collecting useful papers — and meeting excellent speakers and enthusiastic delegates — is something I do a lot of, so the International Green Building Conference 2012 proved to be a great source of all of those gifts — thanks to the BCA, the SGBC and all those involved. This article, written primarily for www.e2singapore.gov.sg, shows clearly that Singapore has come a long way along the green building journey and has some initiatives to share...

Photo by Lee Xin Ying.

W hen an international green building event is held in Singapore, you would expect that the greatest value would come from all the imported speakers, delegates and exhibitors — experts in their own right — introducing new techniques, ideas and systems to achieve greater energy efficiency and integrated design for building performance.

But, if anything, the 2012 International Green Building Conference was a sign of Singapore's coming of age, as time after time, local initiatives unintentionally upstaged the foreign ideas and systems expounded.

These included announcements of advances relating to the greening of data centres, introducing new valuation guidelines for green buildings, new tools to calculate carbon footprints of properties, moves to target tenants of buildings to operate premises more efficiently, as well as a renewed emphasis on supermarkets and the retail sector to get to grips with energy efficiency measures.

That's not to say Singapore audience was ignoring the best from abroad, but in many cases the ideas and systems are already being incorporated in the work of the Singapore Green Building Council (SGBC) and the Building & Construction Authority (BCA), the two key players in the organisation of the event and the implementation of green building practices in Singapore.

While there were many wise words from notable speakers — and we draw attention to three who stood out on the Singapore stage — as well as displays by companies represented at the concurrent Build Eco Xpo (BEX) exhibition, it all reinforced the fact that Singapore is "up with the play", and while ever ready to learn new tricks, is already implementing measures for green buildings and energy efficiency that is on a par with — or in some cases ahead — of international trends.

Singapore can certainly continue to justify the "international" tag to its green building events and efforts. But maybe from now on Singapore will be the place to come to not only get good advice and products, but check out where new green building practices and processes are being put to the test and gain first-hand understanding of the early adoption of technology and techniques.

Here's the selected highlights of the International Green Building Conference 2012, held alongside the annual BEX Asia 2012 — Southeast Asia's premier business platform for the green building and construction industry:

–   **The Singapore Institute of Surveyors and Valuers (SISV) and building regulator, the BCA, announced new green building valuation guidelines which will be included in a revised version of the SISV's industry guide to provide information on how to evaluate the cost benefits of green features such as energy and water efficiency.**

    (www.bca.gov.sg/newsroom/others/pr12102012_IGBCA.pdf)

–   A new carbon tool was presented to help architects plan for low-carbon industrial estates from the beginning of the design process. Available on the BCA website, the Green Mark Carbon Calculator allows builders to quantify the carbon impacts of each carbon-related Green Mark criteria based on information from local agencies. For example, water consumption figures use carbon emissions data for water treatment from Singapore's water agency — Public Utilities Board, and emissions data for electricity consumption from the National Environment Agency.

    (www.eco-business.com/news/counting-the-carbon-new-and-improved-tools-for-singapore/)

–   The new Green Mark for Data Centers, which the BCA said took two years to develop in partnership with the Infocomm Development Authority (IDA), is aimed at encouraging businesses to make their data centres more energy efficient.

    (www.bca.gov.sg/newsroom/others/pr10102012_IGBCA.pdf)

- Targeting energy consumption by individual tenants rather than entire buildings was the intention of three new Green Mark schemes introduced by BCA, directed not at developers and building managers, but at tenants with heavy energy consumption. At the same time, four green supermarkets and three green retail outlets were recognised under the BCA schemes — Green Mark for Supermarkets and BCA Green Mark for Retail respectively.

(www.bca.gov.sg/Newsroom/pr11102012_IGBC.html)

- **Our greatest challenge is to green existing buildings. Typically, a building cooling system consumes about 30–50% of the building total energy consumption and the typical lifespan of the building cooling system can be as long as 15–20 years. To capture this opportunity for energy efficiency when buildings replace their chillers, BCA mandated minimum environmental sustainability standards for existing buildings.**

(www.bca.gov.sg/Newsroom/pr10092012_BCA.html)

To demonstrate that Singapore is still willing to learn from others, attention is drawn to three speakers — one each from Europe, Asia and America — who made a significant contribution at the conference and offered some specific examples of what can be achieved by cities when they plan for the adoption of green building and energy efficient practices:

- Professor Jacqueline Cramer, Director of the Utrecht Sustainability Institute and previously Netherlands' Minister of Housing, Spatial Planning and the Environment, demonstrated the good work not only of the institute she runs but the way innovations have been put into practice in the city of Utrecht, with a population of over 300,000. Public private partnerships were the answer, but so was public engagement on a large scale. She called it a "collective approach", involving not only the local government, industry and citizens, but also the financial community drawn in the fund projects, including street-or community-wide solar panel installations.

(www.uu.nl/university/internationalstudents/en/sd/Pages/jacquelinecramer.aspx)

– Ms. Yuko Nishida, Planner for the Policy Planning Division, Bureau of Environment, Tokyo Metropolitan Government, outlined the impact of Tokyo's cap-and-trade programme, the city's ground-breaking initiative to introduce a market-based approach to emissions reductions at the urban scale. She said reports on 1,159 building facilities show collective emissions reductions of 13% over base-year figures; this was due to the active implementation of more than 5,700 measures by building owners to reduce energy use and corresponding emissions. Cited as a "world-leading policy" by the World Green Building Council (WGBC), Tokyo's emissions reduction programme for buildings provides a compelling example for other cities to follow as it demonstrates that C40 Cities are at the forefront of climate action, achieving verifiable and consistent monitoring of urban emissions and implementing innovative actions for tackling the problem.

(www.c40cities.org/c40blog/spotlight-on-tokyo-world%E2%80% 99s-first-urban-cap-and-trade-program-yields-promising-first-year-results)

– Hilary Beber, Policy Advisor in the NYC Mayor's Office of Long-Term Planning and Sustainability, outlined how the Office is charged with implementing PlaNYC, the City's 25-year sustainability outline. Besides setting out the results of the city's 2011 energy and water benchmarking results for non-residential properties — released for the first time in September 2012 — she also described the steps New York has taken in energy efficiency for buildings, including the iconic Empire State Building. As New York is a dense city of buildings — almost a million of them in an area of little more than 300 square miles — it makes sense to concentrate on the buildings if New York City wants to tackle its environmental issues.

(www.nyc.gov/html/gbee/html/home/home.shtml)

The next International Green Building Conference and accompanying BEX show is scheduled for 11–13 September 2013.

Sources

- www.e2singapore.gov.sg
- www.bca.gov.sg
- www.sgbc.org

11

Flying Machines and Robots Bring Productivity to the Building Industry

*Flying machines and robots were not on my mind when I first ventured to the SEC in April 2013. I couldn't get out of my amused and inspired mind — "Up down, flying around" — as I watched with intrigue how these controlled mini-helicopters. Yes, this was happening right here at a serious-minded seminar involving very serious architects, engineers and scientists from all over the world. Here was a former aviation writer — now a sustainability consultant — witnessing technology and good old-fashioned inventiveness coming together in the appropriately named CREATE building in Singapore. So I wrote about it all in **abc carbon express** after an eye-opening visit…*

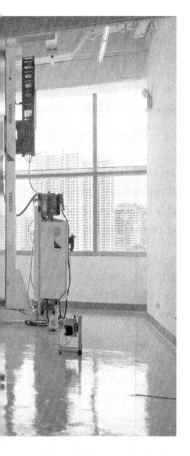

Photo Credit: Gramazio&Kohler, Architecture and Digital Fabrication, Singapore ETH Centre; Photo by Bas Princen.

W hile the construction and property industry has made great advances in the introduction of green and sustainable materials with "green buildings" becoming the norm, it has not significantly improved its productivity for 40 years — unlike the automotive industry, where for every 10,000 workers there are 700 robots.

Which all goes into making more automobiles more productively, more sustainably, using recycled material, using less energy, less water — and most importantly — less men and women. Could things change as a result of the work of the Future Cities Laboratory (FCL) of the Singapore-ETH Centre for Global Environmental Sustainability (SEC)?

"Up, down, flying around,
Looping the loop and defying the ground.
They're all frightfully keen,
Those magnificent men in their flying machines."
– From the 1965 film and song of the same name, "Those Magnificent Men in the Flying Machines".

The words wouldn't get out of my amused and inspired mind — as I watched with intrigue as small radio-, or more correctly, computer-controlled mini-helicopters lifted and correctly positioned blocks to build a multi-storey construction.

Yes, this was happening right here at a serious minded seminar involving very serious architects, engineers, and scientists from all over the world at the FCL of the SEC.

Admittedly, it was a video-taped demonstration shown to the room, but also on hand was one of the real little flying machines to show their size and shape.

Robots in action to build buildings — and high-rise ones at that — are not some figment of an imaginative architect but being put into practice — admittedly in test beds and research centres at this stage — in Singapore and Switzerland.

And for good reason. The construction industry worldwide has been very slow to adopt automation. If you could find robots anywhere on a building site, they are literary dwarfed by high-rise cranes — hundreds of them — in an industry obsessed with getting more and more men doing more menial tasks.

Compare construction with the automotive industry, where automation plays such a major role. Robots do practically every task on the car production line, once manned by busy manual workers.

For every 10,000 workers in automotive industry there are 700 robots. Which all goes into making more automobiles more productively, more sustainably, using recycled material, using less energy, less water — and most importantly less men and women.

At the same time, the human mind is still well utilised. The cars of today and tomorrow are still designed by real people, but the same designers are making greater use of computers and automation.

Why hasn't the construction industry adopted some of these practices? Admittedly architects and engineers are well practiced in the use of Computer Aided Design (CAD) designs, Building Information Modelling (BIM) systems and go through building simulation and computerised assessment of materials and methods.

But for all that — as an industry leader told me recently — the construction and property industry has not significantly improved its productivity for 40 years. Forty years of advances in technology have not made their presence felt on the construction site, even as buildings have gone up higher and higher. They take just as long to make now — and involve just as many men per square metre — as 40 years ago.

80

Race for Sustainability

That has to change. And the FCL, with its architects and engineers driving it, are moving towards significant changes. With robots and mini-flying machines to the fore.

It was an experience to visit the Laboratory and talk to the scientists there, including Professor Ralph Eichler, President of the Swiss Federal Institute of Technology (ETH Zurich) as well as Professor Gerhard Schmitt, the director of the Singapore centre. Also on hand to deliver the most impressive presentation on robotic fabrication was Professor Fabio Gramazio.

On the day of the visit, ETH had this to say:

"The world today faces a rapid growth in urban population — the UN estimates that nearly 75% of the world's population will reside in urban areas by 2050. Cities, as we know it, will become even denser than they are now. Innovation is needed to create an environment that can cope with the growth of urbanisation in a sustainable way and increases liveability."

So the work of the FCL, set up by Singapore's National Research Foundation and the Swiss Federal Institute of Technology (ETH) Zurich, incorporates research of digital fabrication to investigate the implications of robotic processes on the design and construction of high rises.

A panel discussion on the day focused on the pace of urbanisation in Asian countries, agreeing that high rise buildings will continue to play a critical role in high-density cities, especially in cities like Singapore, where land area is limited.

"High rises are here to stay, and while we have gotten used to their presence in our cities, it is now pertinent for us to start investing in innovative, sustainable and more importantly, integrated ways of constructing these high rises," said Professor Gramazio, who leads the robotics team at FCL.

As we noted earlier in this article and as ETH confirms, "robotic and automatic productions have taken over large parts of many industrial sectors. However, the potentials of robotic fabrication are not fully exploited if it is only used for the execution of purely repetitive mass fabrication processes."

As we observed, robots can be controlled individually and thus offer the potential for variety, differentiated assembly and mass customisation — at a large scale.

Professor Gramazio further emphasises: "It is time to think about customised robotic processes, products and planning methods for architecture at larger scales."

Reinforcing Professor Gramazio's sentiments, Professor Eichler added that the accelerating rate of urbanisation is a great global challenge.

"In high-density urbanisation, robotic fabrication of high rises will certainly play an innovative and efficient role." The ETH Zurich President also concluded that the collaboration of top scientists and engineers within the FCL and together with the universities based in Singapore is a unique opportunity to deliver ground-breaking research.

⸻◦⸺

The final words come from a fact sheet produced by the FCL.

Architecture and Digital Fabrication:
Design of Robotic Fabricated High Rises

Robotic and automated production processes have taken over large parts in many industrial sectors. In architecture and building, attempts to deploy robotic processes remain the exception.

Many applications have been confined to prototype and, at larger scales, have often resulted in failure. This is because the general approach has been to either automate existing manual processes or the complete production process. However, the potentials of robotic fabrication are not fully exploited if used solely for the execution of purely repetitive mass fabrication processes. Robots can be controlled individually and thus offer the potential for variety in design as well as for differentiated assembly.

As Singapore's land area is limited, high rises represent the most common building typology. In order to investigate and develop customised robotic processes, products and planning methods for architecture at such a large scale, three robotic facilities were installed at the FCL in Singapore. These facilities allow the fabrication of 1:50 scaled models of up to 50-storey high buildings.

The research module carefully investigates specific design logics and construction processes to identify potentials for robotic application and to develop new high-rise typologies. The aim is to define strategies for the production of formal differentiation and functional diversification in generic urban contexts, and to test the integration of robotic technologies into the design, construction and fabrication of high-rise buildings.

———◁○▷———

Sources

– www.futurecities.ethz.ch
– www.abccarbon.com

12

Profile — Lee Eng Lock: Engineering Energy Efficiency Excellence

This article is based on an interview I did with the award-winning engineer who knows buildings and energy efficiency from the inside out. The greatly admired and awarded Lee Eng Lock doesn't mince words and I have heard him speaking his mind a number of times. He was no different with his presentation at the 2012 International Green Building Conference...

Lee Eng Lock is entertaining and engaging. He is respected. He is listened to not only at home but aboard. He wins awards.

The latest being the prestigious "Champion of Energy Efficiency Award" from the American Council for an Energy-Efficient Economy (ACEEE), presented at its 17th biennial Summer Study on Energy Efficiency in Buildings in August 2012.

The four winners were selected by a committee of ACEEE's Board of Directors from a worldwide pool of more than 120 nominees, in recognition of leadership and accomplishment in the field of energy efficiency.

"To Eng Lock Lee, Trane Singapore," the inscription reads, "for world-leading Heating, Ventilation, and Air Conditioning (HVAC) design and engineering that shows the rest of the world how much energy can be saved through good engineering, innovative design, and attention to details."

For the past quarter century, Eng Lock's life has revolved around HVAC — the mechanical systems that provide thermal comfort and air quality in an indoor space, including central air conditioners, heat pumps, furnaces, boilers, rooftop units, chillers, and packaged systems.

He has been conducting energy audits, retrofits, designing and building extremely energy efficient buildings and mechanical systems, and he is regarded as the pioneer in very accurate long-term measurement and monitoring for mechanical plants.

Way back in 1985, he was involved with the HVAC system for AT&T Consumer Products in Kampong Ubi, which achieved what is believed to be the world record for combined air and water side performance, at lower than 0.70 kW/ton for air handlers, fan coils, chillers, pumps, and cooling towers.

At the time, visiting US scientists from the Lawrence Berkeley National Laboratory were extremely impressed with the very precise monitoring and trending at one-minute intervals for all parameters, using software written in Singapore, with laboratory grade instrumentation, and hand calibration of sensors using internationally recognised fundamental standards for thermometry.

In 1994, he was awarded the Association of Energy Engineers USA's Energy Project of the Year for the Western Digital factory in Kuala Lumpur, benchmarked as the most efficient disk drive factory in the world, including all services such as vacuum, compressed air, class 10 clean rooms, process cooling, and chiller plants.

He is a passionate advocate of change. He is the acknowledged energy efficient expert — a perfectionist, yes — but when pressed he can give out some deserving accolades to buildings where valuable results were achieved. He knows what was done, because he was directly involved and from what was achieved, he can fully verify the results.

One of the big problems he sees in the industry and in achieving real results is the lack of transparency: "Some will say that they can achieve certain energy savings, or they have already done so, but they cannot verify that. No one knows for sure."

"We Must Have Total Transparency."

"We are not going to get anywhere unless we get total transparency." That's his campaign call.

In his talk at the recent International Green Building Conference 2012 attended by industry regulators, industry developers, building managers, and energy managers — he made several points of criticism:

- Energy consumption readings being taken cannot be trusted;
- Correct tools are needed if accurate measurements are to be made;
- Wrong data leads to wrong decisions;

- There is too much acceptance of lower standards;
- Data must be shared; and
- Admission of mistakes must happen in order for lessons to be learnt.

He reminded the audience that professionals in the building industry needed to be more like doctors who learn medicine by cutting up bodies! Is that what we should be doing to fix buildings? Maybe.

But whatever it is, Eng Lock knows we must not bury our mistakes.

"We must be more transparent. We have to see what works and how it works."

Reducing Energy Consumption Does Cut Greenhouse Gas Emissions

When asked for examples and case studies of where energy efficiency has been put into practice and shown improvements, he will give some examples.

"Of course there's the Grand Hyatt in Singapore, but that was a few years ago. Yes, we have some good information on that."

The Green Energy Management (GEM) project, which won the Bronze Award in the 2004 Asian Innovation Awards, involved the hotel spending almost S$2.6 million, covering the heating, ventilating and air-conditioning system. The redesign produced annual savings of more than S$1.1 million, paying for itself in just over two years. Most of the savings are in reduced use of electricity and water, which means less CO_2 is being pumped into the air.

"Then there was the SingPost building. That worked." It won an ASEAN Energy Award in 2008.

He explains that the main objectives of this project were to reduce energy consumption by 20% without compromising comfort and the service level provided to the tenants and occupants. The key focus of this initiative is in the central chill water plant room. In fact, it achieved a 23.17% energy savings year on year.

In addition to the energy cost savings, this project also saves an estimated 2,694 tons of CO_2 per year being discharged by the power plants into the atmosphere.

This project clearly shows that commercial buildings can cut greenhouse gas emissions by reducing energy consumption.

Besides the technology and equipment that was installed to bring about improvements in energy efficiency, SingPost also embarked on an education programme to inculcate the correct practices of energy conservation.

Members from higher management were appointed into an Energy Conservation Committee as a visible sign of corporate commitment for genuine change. To align day-to-day operations to energy conservation goals, metrics were embedded into department KPIs. Other initiatives included organising talks to raise widespread awareness, and publishing articles and materials focused on the topic of energy conservation.

The latest that he is most proud of is the United World College new campus at Tampines. It has been touted as one of the best examples around of integrated design and application to achieve genuine results. And it is being measured and managed in real time when results can be monitored, where mistakes can be detected and fixed.

According to Eng Lock, there are positive moves underway from all quarters. The Building & Construction Authority (BCA) has come up with higher standards and better management of the Green Mark process. Property developers are paying greater attention to "genuine greening" of their buildings and better systems are being introduced to measure and manage energy.

For more insight into Eng Lock's approach to buildings and energy efficiency, it is worthwhile viewing the 2009 video on YouTube, "Negawatts for Buildings: Observations from the Past 25 Years", which is based on a talk he gave at the Lawrence Berkeley National Laboratory, where barriers, success stories as well as failures associated with the Negawatt revolution were discussed. "Negawatts" is a term employed to show that energy efficiency is cheaper, faster, cleaner, more sustainable and more profitable than building more power plants of any kind.

Sources

- www.youtube.com/watch?gl=SG&hl=en-GB&v= hFWXMmmiihk
- www.e2singapore.gov.sg
- www.aceee.org/press/2012/08/american-council-energy-efficient-ec
- www.bca.gov.sg
- www.trane.com

The Sun
Shines on
Renewables

Section 4

13

Is Solar the Renewable Energy of Choice in Asia?

This was originally provided by me as a "quick overview" of clean energy in Asia on request from Amit Jain, Energy Access Specialist at the Asian Development Bank (ADB) to promote its "Energy for All" campaign. It was first published in the RTF Mirror Volume 1, Issue 2, January–March 2012 for the Regional Task Force (RTF). The ADB supported the creation of the RTF as an international knowledge platform in the form of a non-profit organisation to promote Public Private Partnerships for global green innovation, including renewable energy smart grids, electric vehicle development and energy efficiency enhancement…

The sun doesn't always shine through the clouds in tropical Asia or in the colder regions of North Asia, but quite clearly the sun is going to be driving the most encouraging trends for the clean energy revolution in Asia.

Solar energy, mostly through photovoltaic cells, will be the predominant renewable energy source in the future in Asia, as it is projected to be in the rest of the world, as it weans itself off its fossil fuel dependency.

While this cannot possibly be a comprehensive survey of all clean energy development in Asia, it does provide a quick overview to show that Asia is moving ahead with a high degree of determination to "come clean" in energy production, distribution and use. It also shows that the private sector is not backward in coming forward.

Photo adapted from Pjk (2010, CC-BY 3.0) and Lou Hernandez (2010, public domain), both from WikiMedia Commons:www.commons.wikimedia.org/wiki/File:Beijing_bird_nest.jpg; www.commons.wikimedia.org/wiki/File:Defense.gov_photo_essay_100302-F-PY930-002.jpg.

India

In India, for example, the Ministry of New and Renewable Energy (MNRE) announced on 3 December 2012 that it is aiming to add 6,300 MW of photovoltaics (PV) and 2,700 MW of Concentrated Solar Power (CSP) to the energy mix in India between April 2013 and March 2017. According to the latest numbers from Bridge to India in its latest India Solar Compass (www.bridgetoindia.com), as at the end of 2012 there was already 1,096.5 MW of solar PV installed throughout India, but only 5.5 MW concentrated solar power. Obviously a lot of room to move, but moving in the right direction.

It has been well known for some years that India was also doing a lot with biomass — energy from rice waste — looking at energy production from planting *jatropha* and other highly productive plants, as well.

Hydro and wind also has potential to grow, and we know Atlantis Resources is looking into a tidal energy project in India to add to its portfolio that includes Canada and Scotland.

China

We all know that China has taken a leadership role in the production of solar PV panels as well as wind turbines, but what about the mix in terms of its own energy use?

In a survey by Goldman Sachs late last year (www.goldmansachs.com/our-thinking/topics/environment-and-energy/sustainable-growth-china-cohen.pdf), China still has a long way to go to come clean, particularly as it graduated to the top energy consumer spot in the world in 2010, surpassing the US. Consequently, energy use increased by more than 150% during the past ten years.

Coal remains the dominant source of energy in China, which accounted for roughly 70% of the country's energy use in 2011. China's Five-Year Plan (2011–2015) included a target to increase the proportion of non-fossil fuels in energy consumption to 11.4% by 2015 and to 15% by 2020, from 8.3% in 2010. These goals are extremely ambitious, with some estimates indicating China would need to add 320–480 GW of non-fossil fuel energy over the next decade to meet the 15% by 2020 target. This is estimated to equal roughly one-third to one-half of total new global non-fossil energy capacity over the next ten years.

In terms of solar energy in China, the capacity is currently a small portion of the generation portfolio but the government has announced targets for installed capacity to grow nearly six-fold to reach 20 GW by 2015. Similar to wind technology, grid connectivity will also be a key issue for solar expansion.

Malaysia

With a goal to achieve 40% cut in carbon emissions by 2020, the Malaysian government plans to increase the share of renewable energy in the

Race for Sustainability

total energy mix to 5.5% by 2015. The government had created support mechanisms and launched a feed-in-tariff (FIT) scheme which pays a premium rate for generating electricity through renewable sources, Prime Minister Najib Razak has announced. Renewable energy would make investments worth RM70 billion ($23 billion) and support 50,000 jobs by 2020. More on this at www.cleantechnica.com.

Technologies to improve the economics of solar power, technologies to store energy (e.g. batteries for electric vehicle application) and new crops for renewable energy are just a few of the niches that can be explored.

The release of a new 20 MW quota for small-scale PV installations in Malaysia was postponed until Q1 2013. The FIT quota is for installations smaller than 500 kW and was scheduled to be released on 17 December 2012.

In September 2012, the Sustainable Energy Development Authority Malaysia (SEDA Malaysia, www.seda.gov.my) — announced details on the 2,000 Solar Home Rooftop Programme.

Thailand

The Natural Energy Development Co. Ltd. (NED), www.ned.co.th, owner of the largest thin film solar power plant in the world, is interested in sharing its expertise in solar energy with the Philippines.

The Thailand-based solar firm, which operates a 224-ha solar power plant, believes that solar technology such as theirs will be viable in a country like the Philippines.

Chaiwut Saengpredekorn, plant manager of the Lopburi solar power plant, said that solar technology is sustainable. NED's 73 MW solar power plant in Thailand took 1.5 years to build.

NED installed more than 545,000 thin-film solar PV panels for its solar power plant, the biggest installed in Asia.

To date (end 2012), the company is expanding by another 11 MW that would bring its solar plant to a total of 240 ha by the first quarter of the next year. According to NED, the new frameless glass-on-glass thin-film solar cells are optimal for use in a high-temperature climate as compared to crystalline solar cells.

Philippines

The Philippines possesses enough renewable resources to satisfy current and future energy demand, according to the Clean Energy Solutions Centre (www.cleanenergysolutions.org). It is one of the leading countries in Southeast Asia in the development of renewable energy resources. Renewables, including hydro, accounted for around one third of the country's 16.8 GW of generation capacity in 2009.

The Philippines has developed 2 GW of geothermal generation, making it the second largest generator of electricity from geothermal energy in the world. In addition, the island nation has 3.3 GW of installed hydropower and 33 MW of grid-connected wind power.

However, developed renewable energy sources are dwarfed by the size of the Philippines' untapped potential. Across a country made up of more than 700 islands, there is an estimated 76 GW of wind capacity, 10 GW of hydropower and good solar potential. Biomass potential is abundant too: The Philippines is the world's tenth largest producer of sugarcane and the largest producer of coconut oil, and those industries create enough waste biomass to generate 230 MW of electricity per year.

In January 2009, the Philippines enacted what was then the most comprehensive renewable energy policy package in Asia, the Renewable Energy Act. The act calls for a renewable portfolio standard, which would require power suppliers to include a percentage of energy from renewable sources.

A FIT provision would provide renewable energy generators with a guaranteed market and a guaranteed price for their power, in addition to tax credits for developers and value-added tax and duty-free importation of renewable technologies.

Singapore

Described as "renewable energy challenged", Singapore doesn't take its imported fossil fuel dependent state lying down. It is driving energy efficiency programmes like no one else, and it has set up leading edge centres to research alternative fuels and test bed clean energy projects.

The Solar Energy Research Institute of Singapore (SERIS) brings together leading solar researchers from around the world to look into improvements in solar technology and its applications. It even considers how solar can "partner" with energy efficiency to bring about improvements in the energy performance of buildings in the tropics, where air conditioning is the greatest energy guzzler.

Electric vehicles are on trial and Singapore is seen by many as the ideal urban environment to reduce the use of "dirty fuels" to get people around the island state, which is already starting to see the strains of private vehicle use on its air quality and traffic congestion.

But energy efficiency is the way Singapore has chosen to go, along with predominant use of natural gas as the cleaner option.

It was also the "fuel" the International Energy Agency (IEA) decided to focus on in the World Energy Outlook (WEO) 2012. Not coal, or gas, or renewables, but energy efficiency.

The fuel we often forget about. But where, in the opinion of IEA Chief Economist and WEO lead author, Dr. Fatih Birol, "the most can be achieved in the shortest time".

Cookstoves

The Global Alliance for Clean Cookstoves — a public-private initiative to save lives, improve livelihoods, empower women, and protect the environment by creating a thriving global market for clean and efficient household cooking solutions — is active in Asia.

Besides its work in many Southeast Asia countries, it also organised a Clean Cooking Forum: igniting change, fuelling markets and sparking adoption in March 2013 in Phnom Penh, Cambodia.

The Alliance's "100 by 20" goal calls for 100 million homes to adopt clean and efficient stoves and fuels by 2020.

The Alliance will work with public, private, and non-profit partners to help overcome the market barriers that currently impede the production, deployment adoption, and use of clean cookstoves in the developing world. For more, go to: www.cleancooking2013.org.

Solar Lamps

The private sector is playing its part to introduce clean energy in the developing countries. In 2012, CarbonSoft Corporation, the carbon credit aggregator, has signed an agreement with Eureka Forbes Ltd (EFL), the Mumbai-based supplier of sustainable household goods, to provide carbon credit revenue to support the distribution of EFL's new line of innovative Eurodiya solar lamps, made by US-based Nokero, throughout southern India.

The programme is at the leading edge of a worldwide movement to reduce the burning of kerosene for lighting and is part of the objectives outlined by UN Secretary General Ban Ki-Moon as he launched the International Year of Sustainable Energy for All in 2012.

More than 1.3 billion people worldwide live without electricity and often burn kerosene fuel for lighting. These lamps are dangerous, expensive and release approximately 190 million tonnes of CO_2 into the air each year — the equivalent of 30 million cars — according to Nokero.

With this new programme, Eureka Forbes aims to sell 158,000 of their economical, durable and environmentally friendly lights to households in Karnataka, Andhra Pradesh, Tamil Nadu and Kerala, southern India. The contract will run for seven years, to 2018.

CarbonSoft has calculated that this project will prevent more than 80,000 tonnes of CO_2 emissions being released into the atmosphere, generating the same number of carbon credits. This will subsidise the cost of the lights for end-users, making them more affordable to the poorest households.

Carbon Soft is also working on introducing the clean solar lamps in Indonesia and the Philippines. For more, go to: www.carbonsoft.net/.

The Clean Energy Fund

Also announced mid-2012 was the setting up of the Armstrong South East Asia Clean Energy Fund, the first of its kind in the region, which has secured US$65 million in its first funding round. Overall, it aims to raise $150 million for small-scale power generation, including solar, in Southeast Asia. It is believed the region will become a "highly attractive" small-scale project market.

Andrew Affleck, managing partner, Armstrong Asset Management (www.armstrongam.com) said, "To date the team has originated a strong pipeline of potential deals and detailed negotiations are underway. We are hopeful of completing one to two key deals soon. Small-scale solar and mini-hydro are two priority sub-sectors the team is currently focused on."

The Clinton Climate Intitiative

Promoting electric vehicles is essential to advancing carbon-neutral transportation technologies.

C40-Clinton Climate Initiative (CCI) Cities has brought together 15 of the world's largest cities, including Hong Kong, New Delhi and Seoul, in collaboration with four leading electric vehicle manufacturers, to make major cities more electric vehicle friendly. They form the "C40 Electric Vehicle Network" and collectively will address four areas of municipal action that are critical to the successful introduction of electric vehicles.

————◀◉▶————

Sources

- www.enertgyforall.info
- www.rtf.sub.jp
- www.abccarbon.com
- www.clintonfoundation.org/cci

14

Harnessing the Tropical Sun's Energy for Efficient Buildings

Written after I attended the seminar on Energy Efficient Façades and Fenestrations in the Tropics organised by SERIS in January 2013, this article reviews what was a fascinating introduction to the possibilities of using materials to enhance a building's capacity to make the best use of the sun to do more than provide solar energy. I saw the light. Energy efficiency achieved by letting in the light. It first appeared on the E2 Singapore website...

Photo provided by SERIS.

L etting the sunlight into buildings to illuminate their interiors naturally, but blocking the solar heat gain and thereby reducing the building's energy consumption. That is the aim of many designers and engineers working on greening buildings in the tropics.

That's where the Solar Energy Research Institute of Singapore (SERIS) comes in. As the national institute on the development of solar energy technologies for a sustainable energy supply, you would expect SERIS to look for the best ways to capitalise on what the sun offers. However, they are also devoting a lot of attention on how buildings can maximise the light and minimise the heat impact on buildings.

How can buildings be more energy efficient? How can air-conditioning systems, which account for about 70% of all energy used in Singapore's buildings maintain a comfortable temperature inside offices and homes while benefitting from solar light and heat?

SERIS doesn't yet have all the answers, but they are working on everything from the best materials to use in building façades, to positioning of windows and shading for buildings, as well as how the right sort of air conditioning can actually utilise some of the sun's heat to run more efficiently.

In a seminar at National University of Singapore, SERIS's Director of Solar Energy Systems Thomas Reindl made it very clear that buildings can be much better designed to capitalise on the solar energy and reduce the amount of heat absorbed without losing the usable light.

"Energy Efficient Façades and Fenestrations in the Tropics" was the title of the seminar. While most in the audience could understand what façades were all about, the word "fenestrations" was a challenge. Simply put, it refers to "the design and placement of windows in a building".

SERIS makes it very clear that substantial savings are possible — in energy and money — through utilising high performance building envelopes and building services, particularly in the tropics. As you would expect, on-site energy generation through renewable energies can further reduce the dependency on fossil fuels as well as produce added efficiencies.

There are 3 areas which SERIS focuses on in its R&D on relating to energy efficiency and these were covered at the seminar.

Façade Technologies

As façades account for almost 50% of the thermal loads in buildings in the tropics, it is advisable to incorporate optical and thermal properties inherent in materials used in construction and in positioning buildings for sun and shade. This is particularly applicable for windows and fully glazed curtain wall systems, given the trend for fully glazed buildings.

Creating a model of a building and putting it through solar tests is an ideal way to measure the effects of the sun. Based on the sun's path, the effects of lighting and thermal absorption of the building can also be studied, along with optimising the natural light to reduce the use of electrical lighting at times.

The Sandcrawler Building, housing the LucasFilms' Singapore headquarters, is an example of a building designed with the sun in mind. A two-layered exterior allows daylight penetration without soaking up solar heat gain, while draping plants provide shade.

A study on a new building under construction in Singapore (Market Street) by global engineering firm Arup demonstrated the value of incorporating a double skin façade, with greenery between skins in parts. This reduces the building's thermal absorption, while overhangs provide shading.

A "cool void" — an induction funnel through the middle of the building to draw cool air from above — reduced cooling load, while "sunpipes" increased natural lighting.

Race for Sustainability

Building Integrated PVs and Energy Simulation

Integrating solar PVs into roofs or façades can reduce the electricity consumption significantly. Newly developed semi-transparent modules can even replace architectural elements made of glass, such as windows and skylights. The cost of installing and maintaining solar panels in Singapore is now on par with that of using conventional electricity.

SERIS research shows that with analytical performance monitoring, utilising performance ratio, measuring yields and energy losses on site, annual electricity savings can be accurately monitored with daily energy demand and supply matched.

With the new see-through solar cell modules designed to act as architectural glass in walls and roofs, a building can optimise both the optical and thermal properties of solar. The Palmenhouse in Munich has incorporated this feature into its architectural design successfully.

Solar Assisted Air Conditioning

The SERIS work also focuses on the dehumidification of air in buildings, which is particularly useful in a tropical, humid climate like Singapore. It is possible to power dehumidification systems via solar, or waste heat, to reduce the electricity demand for air-conditioning systems significantly.

So whether it is by design and alignment to natural sunlight — thereby reducing the electricity needed for inside lighting — or from the choice of building materials and their responses to solar heat, much can be gained by taking into account the power of the sun.

Solar energy can be a cheaper source of power for a building. Solar cells can also be incorporated into the building's structure, in the walls, glass and roofs, to generate energy without taking away the natural lighting.

The sun can provide not only a substantial source of energy but significantly improve energy efficiency for buildings as well.

Sources

- www.seris.nus.edu.sg
- www.e2singapore.gov.sg

15

The Price Is Right! Renewable Energy Is Cheaper than Fossil Fuels

When Andrew Affleck first passed me a paper on the prospects for renewable energy in Southeast Asia, I recognised it immediately as a thoroughly researched report that very conclusively revealed that renewable energy was cheaper to produce than bulk grid power from imported gas and oil. I welcomed the opportunity to edit this version of the article by Edward Douglas, Investment Director, Armstrong Asset Management, which I published in *abc carbon express* and it also appeared in eco-business. com…

Green School in Bali, Indonesia, taken by Paul Prescott.

I t's a fact. Renewable Energy (RE) is cheaper than imported gas and oil. What's more, RE offers Southeast Asia clean and secure power at fixed long-term prices which are lower than the price for power generation from marginal fossil fuel on an unsubsidised base.

This came out in a recently released report (May 2013) by Armstrong Asset Management called "Entering a New Phase of Growth: Renewable Energy in SE Asia", which clearly shows the opportunities for investment and the cost advantages of coming clean.

That was my introduction in **abc carbon express**.

Here's the edited version of the article by Edward Douglas:

RE offers Southeast Asia clean and secure power at fixed long-term prices which are lower than the price for power generation from marginal fossil fuel on an unsubsidised basis.

As part of its ongoing analysis of the potential in Southeast Asia for RE, Armstrong Asset Management has produced a report "Entering a New Phase of Growth: Renewable Energy in SE Asia" which shows that there are a rising number of high quality solar photovoltaics (PV), wind, hydro and biomass/biogas investment opportunities in all of the key markets with interest from both debt and equity providers to invest in them.

Let me provide an overview of our findings and highlight in particular what we see as the opportunities for investment in the RE sector in Southeast Asia. Some key points first:

- It is now cheaper to produce RE in some Southeast Asia countries than bulk grid power from imported natural gas and fuel oil;
- The cost advantage of RE continues to grow in Southeast Asia as pricing, environmental and security risks associated with imported fossil fuels are more accurately evaluated;
- Southeast Asia has excellent renewable resources but relies on a high level of fuel oil for power generation, due to their sprawling geographies and inadequate grid infrastructure;
- ASEAN-5 (Thailand, Indonesia, Philippines, Vietnam and Malaysia) will need to install between 168 and 192 GW of new power generation capacity by 2025 to maintain its projected economic growth rate of 5.8%;
- Governments in all Southeast Asian markets are significantly expanding their commitment to RE as a proportion of the energy mix.

According to a recent study from Centre of Strategic & International Studies (CSIS) on Sustainable Energy Futures in Southeast Asia in December 2012, the ASEAN-5 will need to install between 168 and 192 GW of new power generation capacity by 2025 to maintain its projected economic growth rate of 5.8%.

As with the rest of the world, where nearly 50% of newly installed electricity capacity in 2011 (208 GW) was RE, it offers clean and secure power at fixed long-term prices which are now lower than the price for power generated from marginal fossil fuel supplies on an unsubsidised basis.

From 2000 through 2006, the emerging markets of ASEAN-5 generally adopted a cautious approach to the development of RE due to its perceived high cost.

But the commitment to RE really took hold and became a significant component of national power development plans across the breadth of ASEAN-5 against the background of: (i) the rise in oil prices; (ii) the declines in RE costs; and (iii) the level of concern surrounding energy security.

Over the past seven years, the impetus behind RE has continued to build in the region and the factors necessary to support private investment have been established.

We believe the increase in the quality and quantity of RE project development and construction witnessed over the past 36 months is confirmation that the sector is already in a phase of robust and sustainable growth.

Cost Competitiveness

The first and primary driver of recent growth is cost. In a growing majority of situations, RE is simply cheaper than the alternatives and so utilities, distributors, independent power producers (IPPs) and end consumers are demanding more. In the case of solar, wind and hydro, it is a cost that is essentially fixed for 25–40 years.

Investors in fossil fuelled power plants on the other hand, must accept significant long-term fuel pricing and environmental risks which are increasingly being factored into policy and buyer decisions.

Southeast Asia has excellent renewable resources which, when combined with reductions in RE system costs, have resulted in RE now being cheaper than bulk grid power from imported natural gas and fuel oil — in many cases, significantly cheaper.

Policy Traction

Even good government policy takes time to implement and invariably evolves before gaining traction and achieving a critical mass. In Southeast Asia, significant RE policies were first implemented between 2004 and 2006, due to the rising economic, political, environmental and social case for a greater emphasis on its deployment.

The high cost (as a proportion of GDP) and dependence on fossil fuel imports had become a rising headwind to economic growth and a key security concern for all Southeast Asian governments.

Energy policy rose to the top of the government agenda and policy makers started paying particular attention to the advances being made elsewhere in the world with regards to RE.

As RE costs have come down and the future pricing and security risk of imported fossil fuels better appreciated, policy support in Southeast Asia has continued to strengthen to the point where government targets and commitment are very much in line with those in Europe and other leading international advocates of greater RE adoption.

Thailand, the Philippines and Indonesia have committed to RE targets from 2025 to 2030. The successful installation and operation of projects following early initiatives, the maturing of supply chains and the readiness of private financing sources has allowed governments to commit more aggressively to a competitively priced and credible path of RE growth which would see these targets reached.

Lowering of Non-Economic Barriers to Investment in RE

We also consider how the strengthening regulatory and policy frameworks are helping RE developers and investors in Southeast Asia to overcome both economic and non-economic barriers and thereby accelerate the growth of RE capacity.

In its 2010 working paper "Deploying Renewables in Southeast Asia — Trends and Potentials", the International Energy Agency states:

"Substantial non-economic barriers, such as infrastructure and grid-related problems and regulatory and administrative hurdles, continue to be a major impediment to the deployment of renewables. These barriers can have high economic impacts by increasing the return on investment required by financiers, especially if their impact is primarily in the earlier investment-intensive project cycle phases. Investors are likely to require a high-risk premium to accept the possibility of policy changes affecting RE project development."

Support from policy makers can be broken down into four main categories:

- Tariffs which better reflect the risks and are therefore able to attract capital;
- Implementation of special fast track administrative and regulatory processes for RE;

- Removal or reduction in subsidies extended to traditional energy (fossil fuels) or power generated from them (which strengthens budgets and make funds available to upgrade energy infrastructure); and
- Implementation of measures and incentives which align the interests of incumbent utilities and grid operators with RE developers and investors.

Supply Chain Readiness

The quality of development and the subsequent execution risks of green field construction of RE projects are very much tied to the availability of experienced firms and individuals. As early policy initiatives took hold and the fundamental drivers of RE continued to improve, a critical mass was reached in solar, wind and small hydro which allowed supply chains to mature to the point of sustainability.

Experienced and proven project development groups, world leading RE equipment suppliers and a wide range of internationally recognised service providers now have local operations in Southeast Asia, serving the growth in the Thailand, Indonesia and the Philippines markets.

Private Capital Availability

The economic attractiveness, policy support and supply chain development has allowed many sources of both equity and debt to get comfortable with the risks associated with the construction and operation of RE power assets. There is now growing interest from a wide range of financing sources to invest in the sector. On the equity side, these include PE Funds, corporates, and increasingly, family offices.

Growth of New Constructions Accelerating

There has been significant and sustained growth in the construction and development of solar, wind and hydro projects across Southeast Asia over the past five years. The quality of the resource and the increasing strength of policy support are driving the deployment of each technology in each market. Policy support means both financial incentives and the removal of technical (non-economic) barriers to entry.

Breadth and Depth of Opportunities

The accumulated investment into RE globally is now paying dividends globally as it translates into a positive feedback loop of volume, experience, costs and investment.

Southeast Asia is moving into its own phase of positive feedback where the larger and more established the broader Asia market becomes, the higher the quality of projects and management teams, which further lowers the cost of RE, which further drives growth. Asia's rising prominence as a focus for RE investors is detailed in a number of recent reports and market data releases including:

- **Global Trends in Renewable Energy Investment 2012 from UNEP's Collaborating Centre for Climate and Sustainable Energy Finance, which cites a 21% growth in investment from US$71 billion in 2010 to US$86 in 2011, making Asia second only to Europe as a region for RE investment;**
- Meeting the Energy Challenge in Southeast Asia: A Paper on Renewable Energy, July 2012 from IPSOS Business Consulting which illustrates a growth of RE in ASEAN from 9.8 GW of installed capacity in 2010 to a projected 53.8 GW by 2030 based on a consolidation of official government data; and
- Market research from IHS, the global energy research firm, which projects Asia as the largest solar PV market globally in 2013, compensating for the slow-down in Europe.

For the reasons listed above, the depth and breadth of RE investment opportunities have improved significantly over the past three to four years. There is a rising number of high quality solar PV, wind, hydro and biomass/biogas investment opportunities in all of our key markets with interest from both debt and equity providers to invest in them.

Although the fast improving economics and compelling low-risk characteristics of solar PV have made it a recent focus for many RE investors looking at Southeast Asia, small hydro and wind remain the lowest cost sources of RE and therefore of high interest to policy makers.

Due to recent rises in feed-in-tariffs (FITs) and implementation of supportive regulations, developers are now making good progress in developing the excellent but under-exploited hydro and wind resources of the region. We therefore expect the rate of growth of these technologies to be a major boost to the sector.

We also see increasing opportunities in biogas and biomass power generation where higher tariffs and the maturing of the sector are presenting attractive opportunities for investment.

We have looked in some detail into three key Southeast Asian Markets — Thailand, Philippines and Indonesia — and produced country reports.

Here are a few edited highlights on a country by country basis:

Thailand

Thailand now has more than 2800 MW of installed RE energy and has successfully achieved all of its main policy milestones to date, on its path to a RE target of 25% of energy use by 2021.

Thailand is expected to announce a significant increase in the FIT for biomass based power generation from approximately THB 3.8/kWh to THB 4.5/kWh to further stimulate development of the sector.

Philippines

The Philippines is Southeast Asia's most liberalised and highest priced power market where many small- to medium-scale independent power producers already sell power to cooperatives/distributors and industrial off-takers under power purchase agreements (PPAs).

Following the steep drop in the system costs of solar PV and the increasing availability of development funding for run-of-river hydro and wind projects, developers and IPPs are increasingly looking at small-scale RE solutions to meet the power needs of their off-takers.

Indonesia

Indonesia has had a regulatory framework for RE in place since 2006 under which the state utility (PLN) is obliged to purchase electricity generated from generation facilities with a capacity of more than 1MW and up to 10MW.

In 2009 (Ministry of Energy Regulation No. 31), a new tariff was introduced for mini-hydro projects, together with measures to help deal with non-economic barriers (including a standard form PPA). This applies to projects with a capacity of more than 1 MW and up to 10 MW.

About Armstrong Asset Management

The Armstrong Southeast Asia Clean Energy Fund is a private equity fund that invests in small-scale RE and resource efficiency projects in Southeast Asia. This strategy is driven by the high energy demand and strong market fundamentals in the region. Armstrong Asset Management will seek to provide investors with a gross return in excess of 20% per annum.

The geographic focus of the Armstrong Fund is principally in three countries: Indonesia, Malaysia and Thailand. As Manager, it can allocate up to 25% of the funds gross assets outside these primary countries, but within Southeast Asia, including the Philippines and Vietnam.

To request the full report on "Entering a New Phase of Growth", go to www.armstrongam.com/market-research.

Edward Douglas, Investment Director, Armstrong Asset Management

Edward has more than 20 years' experience as an engineer and investment professional in the RE, power generation and utilities sectors.

Prior to joining Armstrong Asset management, he was the senior Investment Director with FE Clean Energy Group Inc., a leading private equity fund manager specializing in RE which, between 2006 and 2011, closed investments in Asia totalling over $150 million.

He has board experience across a variety of active companies and, from 2007–2011, served as Managing Director of an integrated bio-ethanol and bio-energy agriculture operation based in Thailand. Edward previously held management positions with Siemens, Cummins Power and SP International, the power investment arm of Temasek Holdings, where he managed the development of natural gas power and energy efficiency projects across the Asia Pacific region. He combines applied understanding of a wide range of energy technologies with hands-on experience of leading the engineering, plant construction and operations of small energy businesses in Asia.

He is a Chartered Engineer and holds a BSc Honors degree in Mechanical Engineering from the University of Dundee and an MBA from Imperial College, London.

———◄○►———

Sources

- www.abccarbon.com
- www.eco-business.com
- www.armstrongam.com
- www.csis.org
- www.iea.org
- www.unep.org
- www.ihs.com
- www.ipsos.com

16

Profile — William Armstrong or Robinson Crusoe? Serendipity Reality Check

*Call it serendipity or what you will, but I feel compelled to tell a tale which has some very interesting, fortuitous and coincidental consequences. What follows is based on my personalised account of a "serendipitous encounter" as the Last Word in Issue 189 of **abc carbon express** in April 2013. Usually, I reserve that spot in my fortnightly newsletter for a penetrating report or a revelation relating to climate change communication, sustainability reporting or something intriguing from the media at large. This time literary and creative juices were running freely, so much so that we end up profiling two heroes, one from fiction and one very real historical figure…*

Photo adapted from: a) Oliver Newbury (2009) for Armstrong's house — the first to be powered by hydroelectricity from WikiMedia Commons (CC BY 2.0): www.commons.wikimedia.org/wiki/File:North_front,_Cragside_-_geograph.org.uk_-_1189249.jpg; b) and c) Photographic reproduction of 2D art on Armstrong and Crusoe, public domain: www.commons.wikimedia.org/wiki/File:William_george_armstrong.jpg; www.commons.wikimedia.org/wiki/File:Slavery_Good_White_Man.jpeg

M y serendipitous encounter involved real people, a bit of history, and two books. And, as you would expect, a clean energy message from clean energy pioneers.

It also illustrates the clear advantage of keeping an open mind, meeting interesting people and engaging in some of the age-old practices of picking up and reading a "real book" and not being so over-dependent on what I must call — for want of a better description — "digital engagement".

You wouldn't imagine there would be any commonality between Daniel Defoe's "Robinson Crusoe" (first published in 1719) and a book by Henrietta Heald about William Armstrong, "Magician of the North", who lived from 1859–1900. Armstrong was a real living man and Crusoe a figment of Defoe's vivid imagination.

But both had something in common. They utilised clean energy powered by water for very useful purposes. To survive on his fictional island, Crusoe invented a process to mill corn using the energy from a flowing river. I read about this not in the original story by Defoe but in a fascinating book on literary heroes (and other fictional characters) in "Sebastion Faulks on Fiction".

Being a great admirer of the writing skills of Mr. Faulks — Birdsong, Charlotte Gray and even a James Bond book (as invited by the Ian Fleming Trust) called "Devil May Care" — I was so pleased to pick it up in a Singapore Change Alley bookstore called

Precious Words (a bookstore with a difference, as they offer books for lease as well as sale!).

And here's where the serendipitous bit comes in. I was on my way to meet Andrew Affleck of Armstrong Asset Management. Yes, you guessed it. Named after the same Armstrong — William — and subject of the book, which I found lined up in the bookcase in Andrew's conference room.

I had certainly heard about Armstrong from Andrew before as to why he had chosen the name for his company. The Englishman was a great admirer of the very inventive and industrious William Armstrong. And as I flicked through the book, waiting for the meeting to start, I came across the reference to Armstrong's invention of hydroelectricity.

Tapping the energy of a river on his Newcastle on Tyne property in 1880 to produce the power to light his house, history records that his was "the first house in the world to be lit by hydroelectricity".

At the time, Armstrong was recognised and revered as highly as the Stephenson's — Robert and George — with their locomotives and railway line; Michael Faraday, with his electromagnetism discoveries; Brunel, with his railway and bridge engineering, and Charles Darwin, with his *Origin of the Species*. But history has "shamefully neglected" Armstrong, according to the novelist and thriller writer Len Deighton, an expert in military history, who welcomes the publication of the first comprehensive biography of this remarkable man.

Armstrong went on to be associated with ship building, armaments, cars and aircraft, but it was his first pioneering work in clean energy that I was most interested in. Hydro power to electrify lights.

So imagine my surprise — yes, obviously I had not religiously read Robinson Crusoe so well as a boy — to discover that Mr. Defoe had his hero use the energy from a flowing river to work its magic and drive a mill to grind his grain to help feed him in this remote place. The author didn't have to invent this out of his creative mind, as using water to drive a mill had been around for centuries.

But for me, reading — all within an hour or so — about the fictional hero of water energy on a remote island and the historic figure of the

English early industrial age with his hydroelectrical powered lights made me think.

How sad it is that when the world had access to clean energy so long ago, it turned instead to fossil fuels to drive its industrial age and in the process, severely damaged not only the environment on earth but produced excessive amounts of CO_2 — and many other nasty greenhouse gases — which we are now doing our best to reduce, and eliminate if possible, to save the planet.

It was another historic figure — a contemporary of Armstrong's — the Swedish Nobel prize winner in chemistry in 1903, one Svante Arrhenius, who released his landmark work in 1895. He talked about the "greenhouse effect" and what would happen if industrial emissions grew enough to double the amount of CO_2 in the atmosphere. He predicted a warming of about 5°C.

But he was wrong in that he predicted it would take 2,000 years for that to happen. Latest predictions by climate scientists are that the earth is on track to reach that landmark 5°C warming by 2050. Arrhenius should have said 200, not 2,000 years. But he had no way of knowing the extent to which industrialisation, along with the digging up and burning of coal, along with the exploitation of oil and gas, would do so much damage.

And I doubt if his contemporary William Armstrong — the magician of the north (England) — really foresaw what would happen to hydro-generation, which has become a major source of energy for any country, lighting for homes, streets and buildings, or his other clean and not so clean inventions.

But we can but take hope from the fact that these men — Armstrong in particular — is now the inspiration for a movement to fund clean energy production and distribution in Southeast Asia.

Hydroelectricity might well figure among some of the to-be-funded projects. But more likely is solar, which is not only taking the world by storm — in the nicest possible way — but based on forecasts will be responsible for by far the majority of all the world's energy well before the end of this century. Shell's latest forecast is that by 2070, solar PV panels will become the world's largest primary source of energy.

Solar, by way of PV panels on roofs of buildings everywhere. As well as solar thermal, by way of large arrays of mirrors to reflect the heat of the sun onto towers to heat salt to produce steam to drive turbines to produce electricity 24 hours a day. This is happening in Spain and California now and there are plans for massive use of solar thermal in Australia and in the Sahara.

Advances in solar technology are considerable. Thinner and more effective solar cells. The work of the Solar Energy Research Institute of Singapore centre in Singapore to utilise solar cells in the windows and façades of buildings. Or the work of special glass now installed in the Empire State Building. Or the work of companies like Phoenix Solar — in Singapore and around the world — to install solar panels on many buildings as an alternative to fossil fuel power.

Interesting to note that the first solar power plants in the world were in France. We noted in an article a few months ago after friends reported on visiting the world's first modern solar furnace — and the world's largest — at Mont Louis, near Odeillo. It is believed to have been built in France in 1949 by Professor Félix Trombe. The Pyrenees were chosen as the site because the area experiences clear skies up to 300 days a year.

France has been doing other work on solar thermal — the THEMIS solar power tower is a R&D centre focused on solar energy and is located near the village of Targassonne, in the department of Pyrénées-Orientales, 3 km from the world's solar furnace in Odeillo.

We must not ignore one of the latest advances in solar from the UK. Eight19, which takes its name from the time it takes sunlight to reach the earth — 8 minutes and 19 seconds — is a developer and manufacturer of third generation solar cells based on printed plastic.

Originating from technology initially developed at Cambridge University in the UK, these flexible, robust, lightweight solar modules benefit from high-speed manufacturing and low fabrication costs. With a fraction of the embedded energy of conventional solar modules, printed plastic solar modules are particularly well suited to consumer and off-grid applications.

What is the world coming to? Printed plastic solar modules. Solar cells incorporated in glass windows.

And we end with the work of another genius — Sir Harry Kroto, of Cambridge, another Nobel Prize winner in Chemistry, for his work with C_{60} — the wonder carbon.

Could this open the door to genuinely cheap, clean, low-carbon energy?

Could this be the 21st century equivalent to Armstrong's innovations, and that of his fellow Victorian inventors?

Keep your eyes and ears open. Read and meet real people. Recognise serendipity when it hits you!

Notes: The first noted use of "serendipity" in the English language was by Horace Walpole (1717–1797). In a letter to Horace Mann (dated 28 January 1754), he said he formed it from the Persian fairy tale *The Three Princes of Serendip*, whose heroes "were always making discoveries, by accidents and sagacity, of things they were not in quest of". The name stems from Serendip, an old name for Sri Lanka (a.k.a. Ceylon).

———◁◦▷———

References

- "Faulks on Fiction", by Sebastian Faulks, BBC Books, 2011, www.sebastianfaulks.com.
- "William Armstrong: Magician of the North", by Henrietta Heald, Newcastle: Northumbria Press, 2012, www.williamarmstrong.info.
- Armstrong Asset Management, Singapore, www.armstrongam.com.
- Solar Energy Research Institute Singapore, www.seris.nus.edu.sg.
- Phoenix Solar, Singapore, www.phoenixsolar-group.com.
- Eight 19, www.eight19.com.

Source

- www.abccarbon.com

Industrial nd Innovative Solutions

Section 5

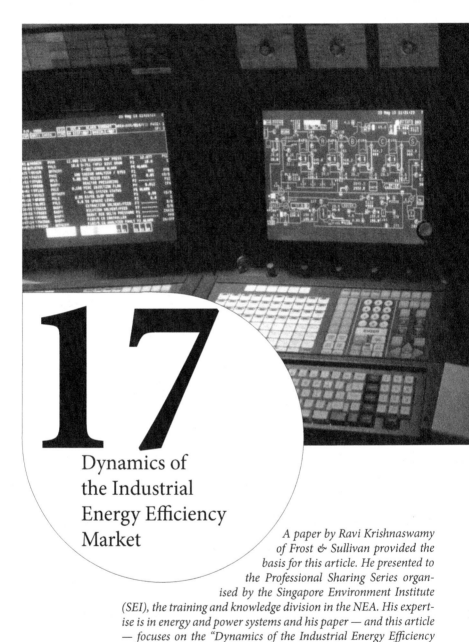

17

Dynamics of the Industrial Energy Efficiency Market

A paper by Ravi Krishnaswamy of Frost & Sullivan provided the basis for this article. He presented to the Professional Sharing Series organised by the Singapore Environment Institute (SEI), the training and knowledge division in the NEA. His expertise is in energy and power systems and his paper — and this article — focuses on the "Dynamics of the Industrial Energy Efficiency Market in Singapore"…

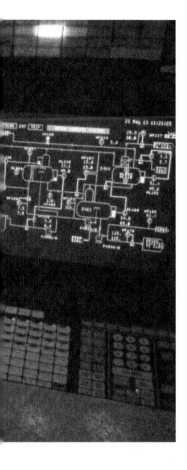

What are the current trends for energy efficiency in Singapore's industries? What are the market levers and impediments towards greater industrial energy efficiency? What is the market potential for the different industrial sectors?

All these concerns, and more, are addressed by Mr. Ravi Krishnaswamy, Vice President and Global Leader of Energy and Power Systems Practice (Asia Pacific) for Frost & Sullivan in his paper: "Dynamics of the Industrial Energy Efficiency Market in Singapore".

The global push towards greater energy efficiency in the face of climate change has led to targets by the Singapore government for a reduction in energy intensity by 20% and 35% by 2020 and 2035 respectively.

As the industrial sector makes up 34.3% of Singapore's electricity consumption share, there exists vast opportunities for energy efficiency improvements. The market potential for industrial energy efficiency till 2015 is estimated at US$397 million to US$739 million, depending on policies and demand push, according to research done by Frost & Sullivan.

The following industries have the best potential for energy efficiency improvements:

Chemical

The largest consumer of electricity amongst all industries. The chemical industry has a market potential of $251 million, focusing mainly on process heating and cooling (80% of energy consumption), and motor systems (15%).

Pharmaceutical and Biotech

The industry has a typical payback period of 3 years and a market opportunity of $278 million. Focus areas are heating, ventilation and air conditioning (HVAC) which forms 65% of energy use, and plug loads, e.g. centrifuges and incubators — which consume 25% of the energy.

Electronics

This industry has a market opportunity of $178 million, with areas of focus in HVAC which consumes half of the industry's energy, and process tools which form 30–40% of energy use.

Environment and Water

This industry has a market opportunity of $178 million. A large proportion of the energy in this industry is consumed by pumps. As Singapore increases the use of seawater desalination as its water source, the energy intensity of this industry is due to increase.

These sectors present great opportunities for energy service companies (ESCOs) to offer their services in identifying and implementing energy efficiency solutions, especially in areas such as process heating and cooling, HVAC and pumps and motors, which tend to be the biggest energy users in industries.

Levers and Impediments

Besides services provided by ESCOs, Singapore's industrial energy efficiency market is also boosted by levers such as the increase to the bottom line of companies through reduced energy cost, and the positive public perception developed by projecting a "green" image.

Financial incentives, such as the Grant for Energy Efficient Technologies (GREET) and Energy Efficiency Improvement Assistance Scheme (EASe) support the industrial energy efficiency in Singapore.

At the same time, impediments to the growth of the industrial energy efficiency market in Singapore remain. The lack of awareness, focus and trust on solutions or efficacy suppresses uptake by industrial

companies. Complexity of audits and considerations of downtime also act as deterrents to investments in energy efficiency.

In companies where procurement policies and KPIs are aligned for initial cost minimisation, investments in energy efficiency face difficulties in getting approvals due to their high initial costs.

The Singapore government has introduced policies to drive energy efficiency improvement. Mandatory energy management requirements came into effect in April 2013 under the Energy Conservation Act (ECA). Energy users consuming more than 54 TJ (terajoules) of energy yearly must appoint an energy manager, monitor and report energy use and emissions, as well as submit improvement plans.

The Energy Efficiency National Partnership was also introduced by the National Environment Agency, Energy Market Authority and Economic Development Board in 2010 to help companies reduce energy use.

Looking Further into the Asia Pacific Region

Energy efficiency advisers and auditors in Singapore are well positioned to tap into the Asia Pacific market, as a greater awareness of the importance of energy efficiency develops in Malaysia, Thailand and Indonesia.

While, the industrial energy efficiency market in Singapore still offers great growth opportunities, there are still considerable impediments to overcome in order to fully develop it, and this is where policy support and incentives from the government will greatly help.

———◄◦►———

Sources

- www.nea.gov.sg
- www.e2singapore.gov.sg
- www.frost.com

18

For Halcyon Agri, Sustainability Makes Business Sense

This article has been assembled from two primary sources. Howard Shaw, Senior Vice President (Corporate Social Responsibility) for the Halcyon Group prepared and published an article as Green Commentary in the Group's newsletter Halycon Days (September 2012). I am well aware of Howard's excellent work on the ground in Indonesia dealing with local issues and opportunities in the community where the company's rubber works are located. But first we incorporate the words of the Chairman and CEO of Halcyon Agri, Robert Meyer, which was the preface to their first sustainability report (in July 2013)…

Robert Meyer makes it clear that "Halcyon Agri believes a sustainable business makes for sustainable profits. Developing and implementing the best practices in corporate social responsibility and sustainability make perfectly good business sense".

As Halcyon Agri's vision is: "To be a leading natural rubber producer in terms of quality of production, sustainability and profitability," the company's chairman and CEO says, "It is wonderful to have a vision but it's even better to put into practice what we believe in. To measure and to manage our progress to show we are making significant improvements in the way we conduct our business as we travel on the very important sustainability journey."

In its first sustainability report, the company spells out how far it has come, and demonstrates its commitment to change and progress, benchmarked against internationally accepted sustainability guidelines. Its reporting is aligned with the principles and framework of Global Reporting Initiative's 3.1 Reporting Guidelines as well as the Singapore Exchange (SGX) guidelines for sustainability reporting.

In the group Annual Report for 2012, Mr. Meyer made it clear that "we believe a sustainable business makes for sustainable profits. Developing and implementing the best practices in corporate social responsibility and sustainability make perfectly good business sense."

"Of course, we have a commitment to wider environmental and societal issues, like working to prevent pollution and conserve Indonesia's natural resources, as well as to ensure we are reducing our own impact on the environment. We are exploring ways, for example, where we can reduce our emissions of greenhouse gases and use non-fossil fuel sources of energy, like the potential use of biomass."

"We also believe our people and our stakeholders are essential partners in our sustainability progression."

Mr. Meyer at Halcyon believes that sustainability goes beyond environmental factors to the way it looks after its own people and its involvement in the local and wider community. "I am pleased to see that we have adopted some very positive measures in terms of staff welfare, health and safety. We continue to contribute to community development initiatives and local infrastructure improvements."

"We have set six strategic priorities in terms of social and environmental factors impacting our industry and our business. They include: staff welfare; staff health and safety; adherence to customer requirements and quality standards; production efficiency; environmental compliance; and good housekeeping."

A critical component of this is Halcyon's stakeholder engagement — how it treats and factors in its partners.

Halcyon takes into account that its international customers are increasingly demanding responsibly managed supply chains. That provides additional pressure on the company as a supplier, but it also reinforces its commitment to do things right by the environment and society, to be more productive and sustainable in all its operations.

"Our processing facilities are already ISO 9001-certified for quality management systems but we want to — we need to — raise our operating standards even more by aiming for ISO 14001, the international benchmark for environmental management," Mr. Meyer reports.

Halcyon also needs to be conscious of, and committed to, improving its upstream stakeholder engagement. Even if contact to date with rubber farmers has been limited, the company needs to recognise its ability to play an influential role in advocating sustainability issues.

Halcyon has made some efforts, such as providing rest areas for rubber raw material suppliers. Moving forward, the company plans to expand these areas and use them as venues for communication and obtaining feedback.

It also intends to engage its stakeholders upstream to identify social and environmental issues and understand how best to address them. This is best done, Halcyon believes, through a combination of individual and collective effort through industry memberships.

"We can also be a power for good in the wider rubber industry as well as the community at large," Mr. Meyer says, "as we are engaged and working closely with organisations like the Rubber Association of Indonesia (GAP-KINDO), the International Rubber Study Group and the Singapore Chinese Chamber Rubber Association to explore and initiate collective action on ensuring that sustainability has an important place in the natural rubber business as it does for us."

"Naturally, I am pleased to see that the demand for natural rubber is projected to increase," he says. "But with greater growth and increased business opportunities comes added responsibility. The overall vision and strategy for our company over the short, medium and long term is to effectively manage key challenges in the industry and to address all social and environmental impacts while sustaining economic growth."

Halcyon is committed to sustainability as it is to being an industry leader in productivity and profitability. "We look forward to continuing on the sustainability journey in partnership with our people and all our stakeholders."

For Mr. Meyer, reporting on sustainability is one important step. "We are ready to take the next step to implement actions to show that we mean business and to demonstrate that sustainability is a business imperative."

Green Commentary

What would be more appropriate to say — "transplanting" or "translating"?

Probably a bit of both, writes Howard Shaw in the Halcyon Days newsletter:

Sustainability initiatives embrace economic, environmental and social aspects, with economic sustainability being the linchpin determining the successful implementation of the overall concept.

Spurred by accelerated deterioration of the human environment and natural resources and the consequences of deteriorating economic and social development, the UN coined an internationally accepted definition of sustainable development (SD) as development that meets the needs of the present without compromising the ability of future generations to meet their own needs.

SD concepts remained restricted within the arena of government to government discussions throughout the 80s and it wasn't till the early 90s, probably born out of the frustration of the status quo, that the private sector took on their own initiative to address sustainability as part of their CSR.

Early movers included Hewlett-Packard, who imposed standards throughout their supply chain and reaped economic gains through improved efficiency and closing the manufacturing loop.

American carpet manufacturing giant, Interface Inc, led by then CEO Ray Anderson, transformed his business from selling modular carpets to providing carpeting services, resulting in a closed loop system that achieved zero landfill and facilitated the creation of energy and recycling businesses.

The last decade has seen increased pressures on soft commodity sectors to get onto the sustainability bandwagon, especially in timber and palm oil industries.

The natural rubber (NR) industry, not withstanding, finds itself on the same path and faced with the same complexities. A "Drag and Drop", or transplant, approach to the transformation of the NR industry has been fraught with challenges due to geopolitical, cultural, and institutional differences that exist between sectors. Nevertheless, sustainability models that have worked for other agricultural commodity economies do serve as a useful template for stakeholders of NR to translate and learn from.

A common core across other commodities in approaches to developing sustainability schemes is the formulation of standards and criteria in a clear and measurable way. It is important that that there are clear guidelines that differentiate which parts of criteria apply to which parts of the value chain and to what extent.

In the NR industry there would be obvious sub-sets of criteria that differ greatly between farmers, processors, and consumers with intersects of common criteria. For example, in the case of farmers/smallholders, specific criteria linked to impact on biodiversity may exist, whereas this may be down scored or deemed not applicable to a processing operation. Common criteria may include metrics such energy and water usage per product unit.

Simple as this may sound, the NR industry, which is still in a nascent stage of implementing sustainability schemes, faces many complex challenges ahead. A key process will require stakeholders to establish operational baselines which will give rise to the development of better management practices (BMPs) and KPIs to facilitate continuous improvement through ISO type management systems.

However, before any of these steps can take place, there is the issue of reliable data, data management, and the need to get granular with those aspects that are significant and measurable. For instance, in the case of NR processing operations, sub-metering of electrical machinery and data logging can be considered a low-hanging fruit and a step in the right direction.

Monitoring and verification by an accredited third-party is essential to the credibility of an industry-wide scheme and indeed one of the greatest challenges here is differentiating requirements for farmers/ smallholders, ensuring that they have management skills and internal controls.

Led by the International Rubber Study Group, an Industry Advisory Panel meeting was held in February 2012 to prioritise a work programme for the ongoing construction of a Road Map, which was further discussed at the World Rubber Summit 2012 held in May.

On both supply and demand sides, gathering of statistics and identification of indicators for sustainable rubber were ranked as top priorities, followed by the need to address planting policies and their impact on

NR production on the supply side, and tyre legislation and its impact on rubber demand on the demand side.

As the Road Map takes shape, it will surely be met with some scepticism from various stakeholders who perceive developments as instruments that will increase costs and retard economic development. However, there are also those that are able to look beyond the visible horizon and see that the sustainability route is one that the industry is ultimately bound for, both for the health of the industry and the broader altruistic needs of social and environmental development.

Already, though still fragmented, businesses along the NR supply chain have implemented BMPs and have proven to be positive drivers reaping economic benefits from better yields/revenue, reduced production costs, reduced wastage and storage losses, improved access to reliable inputs and improved access to markets.

On the environmental front, efforts to preserve natural assets and improve soil quality have given rise to healthier trees, increased productivity and longer production periods. Within the processing sector, there exists opportunities to replace traditional fossil based energy sources with the abundance of biomass available in NR-producing regions. Already some operators have made a one-on-one switch to palm kernel shell to replace coal and other forms of bio-waste are being tested at pilot stage. Up-scaling and consolidation of such clean energy projects could eventually warrant registration for carbon credits.

Corporate social responsibility and addressing the social bottom line may be less quantitative, but a more qualitative component of the sustainability mix, yet investment in improved sanitation and health of workers and communities, as well as training and education, is crucial to community and worker relations and bolsters a sustainable workforce.

On a closing note: The NR industry can have its cake and eat it. Nevertheless, the cake was never meant to be eaten in one chunk, but a series of bite size morsels that are digestible and palatable.

There is an urgent need for adoption of a new paradigm. To quote author Paul Hawkens in *Ecology of Commerce*, conducting ourselves in a business as usual manner and tackling sustainability issues the way we are doing now is equivalent to "bailing out the Titanic with a teaspoon". On an optimistic note, we should all hope there are many teaspoons at hand.

―――◄○►―――

Source

– www.halcyonagri.com

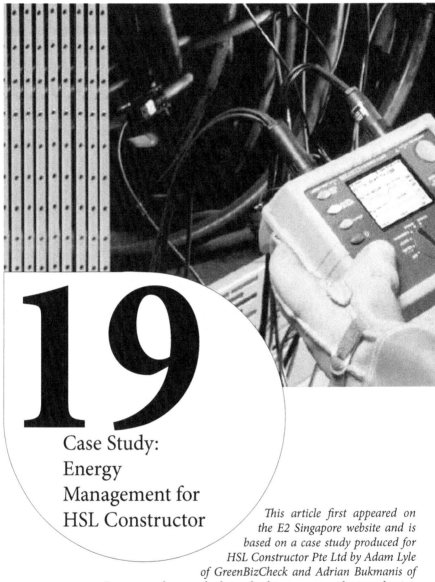

19

Case Study: Energy Management for HSL Constructor

This article first appeared on the E2 Singapore website and is based on a case study produced for HSL Constructor Pte Ltd by Adam Lyle of GreenBizCheck and Adrian Bukmanis of Energenz, who were both involved in managing the introduction of the energy management programme. The construction company was among the first in Singapore to be certified under the new standard, ISO 50001…

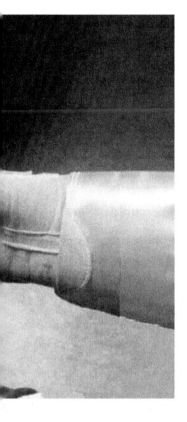

Improving energy performance, reducing consumption of electricity, improving overall energy efficiency and advancing its knowledge on energy uses might all sound like a tall order for any company.

But these objectives were achieved by a Singapore civil engineering firm which at the same time managed to achieve annual energy cost saving of 26% and gained an internationally accepted energy management certification award in the process.

HSL Constructor Pte Ltd, a family-owned and family-run Singapore-based construction company involved in civil engineering, marine structures and mechanical piping works, became one of the first organisations in Singapore to receive the ISO 50001 energy management certification.

Route to ISO 50001 Certification

First, an assessment of what the problem was in the first place. HSL, with its head office at Gul Lane with a workshop area, outside yard and training facility, also has temporary construction project sites which contain office space, diesel storage facilities and generators, and other types of energy equipment.

In mid-2011, the energy consumption of HSL was rising, and had been since 2009.

Electricity and diesel consumption had escalated unexpectedly, indicating that efficiency savings could be made.

In 2011, HSL spent over S$100,000 on electricity and over S$1 million on diesel. With an environmental management certification to maintain and a public corporate social responsibility programme, the organisation chose to take action to cut costs and drive forward its environmental programme.

HSL commissioned energy efficiency consultant Adrian Bukmanis of Energenz to carry out an energy survey of the head office in Gul Lane. Among the recommendations adopted was to establish an ISO 50001 standard energy management system (EnMS) to address the whole scope of the organisation's energy uses.

HSL took advantage of Singapore government's SPRING funding to in turn pay for the consultancy services provided by GreenBizCheck.

Adam Lyle of GreenBizCheck designed a three-phase programme delivered through a series of workshops, coaching sessions, tools, document templates, and internal audits, all supported by expert advice on energy performance from Energenz.

The programme commenced in late March 2012 and from preparation to certification took seven and a half months.

In November 2012, after undergoing a two stage audit process undertaken by the certifying organization, Lloyd's Register Quality Assurance (LRQA), HSL was awarded the ISO 50001 energy management certification.

Since commencing action to improve energy performance, HSL has seen its electricity consumption at its Gul Lane site fall to within 1% of its 2009 level with an expected 26% annual cost saving in 2012, compared to business as usual projections.

Action Required for ISO 50001 Certification

To prepare for the ISO 50001 certification project, HSL had to identify an energy management representative, energy management team, and project sponsor at board level.

The new team received training on energy management systems and the ISO 50001 standard.

A further challenge for HSL was identifying how to integrate the EnMS with their existing integrated system for quality, health and safety, and environment. The existing systems manager was therefore a crucial part of the new team.

The first major step in designing the EnMS was to use an assessment process to identify the most significant energy uses which would help to focus the efforts of the team. The process of assessing significance was based upon an analysis of energy data and organisation factors such as the scope for improvement of the energy use.

The resulting set of nine significant energy uses (SEUs) was felt to appropriately reflect the reality of the organisation's energy performance at this time.

Once the SEUs had been identified it was time to set objectives and targets to improve performance. In order to do this, the organisation needed to fully analyse its current energy performance.

This exercise included establishing the current efficiency with which SEUs were functioning, including the factors affecting their energy performance, and establishing energy saving opportunities so that HSL could set challenging yet realistic targets based on an assessment of likely energy savings, efficiency improvements and process improvements.

Energy Management Action Programmes

A lively action planning workshop, as part of the three-phase programme designed by GreenBizCheck, resulted in the development of a number of Energy Management Action Programmes (EMAPs) designed to achieve the new objectives and targets.

HSL wanted a set of targets that addressed the whole scope of their energy management system. Targets were therefore set to address energy performance, procurement, organisation culture and the management of the new EnMS.

Targets were backed by robust monitoring and measuring processes. A monitoring and measuring plan with tools was developed. It was difficult at this early stage to identify the exact resources that would be needed to implement the new EMAPs, therefore, the programmes contained actions to complete feasibility studies and obtain quotations for improvements which could then guide decision making in the future.

To complete the design of the EnMS, HSL developed a training programme to add to the internal competencies of staff and identified which competencies they would obtain externally. As a result, a number of staff were trained on the use of air compressors and attended local energy conferences.

The team designed a communication programme informed by the results of a staff survey on environmental and energy issues. New policies and operational controls were written to address procurement where it has an ability to affect energy performance, such as when renting new diesel equipment, to address energy in design issues, and to manage each of the SEUs.

An energy auditing programme was designed and documents from the existing integrated management system (IMS), such as the document and records control procedures, as well as addressing non-conformances, providing correction, corrective and preventive action, were amended to incorporate the new EnMS.

As a result of all this, HSL now better understands where, how, and why it is using diesel and is in a position to compare the performance of key items of equipment and performance across project sites. HSL will use this knowledge to enhance their operational controls and identify improvements.

Moving Forward Beyond Certification

HSL also plans to progress its EnMS by working with its suppliers, vendors and sub-contractors to raise awareness of the need to improve energy performance and find mutually beneficial ways to improve it.

HSL is currently in the process of building a large new facility, the Penjuru Lane Complex, where they shall relocate in late 2013 and for which they hope to receive a Green Mark Gold rating.

The move to the new Penjuru Complex will pose challenges for re-setting the organisation's baseline and using the building in a way which maximises energy efficiency and achieves the efficiency that the building is designed to achieve.

To learn more about ISO 50001, visit: www.iso.org/iso/home/standards/management-standards/iso50001.htm.

———◦———

Sources

- www.e2singapore.gov.au
- www.hsl.com.sg
- www.greenbizcheck.com
- www.energenz.com

20

Profile — Mann Young: Sustainability and Innovation in Construction

*Mann Young and I were both on the same platform at the National Sustainability Conference in Singapore in July 2010. We have met many times since and I have interviewed him for the book on Lend Lease's 40 years in Singapore — **Forty: Building a Future in Singapore** — so two relevant extracts from the book appear here. There was also a report in **abc carbon express** in May about Mann as the recipient of the Green Advocate of the Year Award for 2013. I also sat in on two interviews Mann did in Singapore with Nobuko Kashiwagi, Chief Correspondent, United Brain Networks. The full interviews can be seen on the web-based channel but I include some of the conversation here...*

Mann Young with CLT panels, a Lend Lease photograph from the book *Forty: Building a Future in Singapore*.

Mann Young of Lend Lease, recipient of Singapore's Building & Construction Authority's (BCA) Green Advocate of the Year Award, talked on UBrain TV about his background — arriving in Australia as a refugee from Vietnam — how he was given a start in his career with Lend Lease and he got involved in the world of sustainability. He also talks of world leading sustainable buildings in Singapore and the potential of cross laminated timber (CLT) in the building industry.

To Mann, sustainability and innovation are embedded in Lend Lease's way of operating — in its DNA — and he adopted this as his mantra as well. As construction engineer, he could appreciate the importance of not just building a building, but "creating the best places and leaving a positive legacy".

Sustainability is not complicated. It is about doing things better. He believes we need to simplify and communicate its value.

"We need to rethink and reconnect", which was his experience in working with tenants at the Lend Lease shopping centre — 313@ somerset — which became the first Green Mark Platinum retail mall in Orchard Road. Green leases were adopted and training was offered to tenants to understand and implement sustainability measures like waste management and energy efficiency.

"We have the tools and the technology. We must effectively use the technology, be smart, connect the dots and do good," says Mann, who admits he never stops learning.

He sees the introduction of CLT as the latest innovation for Lend Lease to introduce into Asia and one that demonstrates leadership in the construction industry.

He now takes on the job of Head of CLT Business for Asia for Lend Lease and sees it as an opportunity to be "smart about how we design and build buildings", with less impact on the environment and with important productivity gains.

<hr>

In May 2013, I reported in **abc carbon express**:

Lend Lease is honoured to win two awards at the annual BCA Awards 2013. Mr. Mann Young, Head of Sustainability, Asia, Lend Lease will be awarded the Green Advocate of the Year Award while Jem®, a mixed-use development in Jurong Gateway, is one of the recipients of BCA's coveted first Universal Design (UD) Mark Award for its exemplary UD features.

Mr. Mann Young said at the time: "At Lend Lease, the community is at the heart of everything we do. We want to kickstart a revolution in the building industry by focusing on innovative technology and programmes that ultimately produce an inclusive and greener built environment. This is in line with our vision of Creating the Best Places, as we create designs that revolve around people to leave a positive legacy for generations to come."

Congratulating Lend Lease, BCA CEO Dr. John Keung commented: "We are proud to work with partners like Lend Lease, who are renowned for placing sustainability at the top of their priorities. Their projects are an example of how one can optimise project outcomes that are not only sustainable but also take into consideration the commercial and business aspirations of all key stakeholders. This is the way forward, as we embark on our journey together to develop a truly sustainable and inclusive city."

Mr. Mann Young was conferred the Green Advocate of the Year at this year's BCA awards ceremony on 16 May 2013 in recognition of his commitment and passion for environmental sustainability.

Responsible for driving Lend Lease's sustainability philosophy of "Every Action Adds Up", he constantly introduces innovative technology to the building sector, hoping to see a positive revolution in the industry.

Lend Lease's Jem®, 313@somerset and Parkway Parade are leading examples of his notable project contributions in Singapore, with all three awarded the BCA Green Mark Platinum status. He also contributed to help Setia City Mall be the first mall in Malaysia to win the BCA Green Mark Gold Award.

His other industry advocacy roles in the sustainability arena include the Chairperson of Asia Pacific Real Estate Association (APREA) Sustainability Committee, a committee member of the UN Environment Programme Finance Initiative (UNEP-FI, Property Working Group) and the World Green Building Council Regional Manager of the Asia Pacific Green Building Council Network.

These industry recognitions on both an individual and project-wide level are strong testaments to Lend Lease's continual strong commitment to sustainability and alignment to BCA's vision to have the best built environment for Singapore, our distinctive global city.

The profile on Mann Young as it appears in the book — "Forty: Building a Future in Singapore":

Here's a young man who has already been places. And with Lend Lease, he continues to grow and take on more responsibility. Mann Young was, up until end May 2013, Regional Head of Sustainability for Asia.

He is now the Head of CLT Business for Asia, with the exciting responsibility for introducing CLT as a sustainable alternative to reinforced concrete and structural steel for multi-storey constructions. He is used to wearing more than one hat. When he first came to Singapore in January 2008 — re-joining Lend Lease after five years with Jones Lang LaSalle as national director of Asia Pacific — he was involved in major retail operations.

But it wasn't long before he took on the added role of sustainability, making sure the retail projects, like Parkway Parade and 313@somerset, met the firm's high sustainability standards. He talks with passion about sustainability and makes sure everyone he meets — on and off the job — understands the importance of sustainability, not only through the way a building is constructed, but how it is operated to save precious resources, like energy and water.

The energy efficiency measures — and benefits — which he advocates, are as much for the shopping centre tenants and customers as they are for building owners and managers. All a far cry from his first job when he joined Lend Lease in Sydney in 1993 as an onsite Project Manager, fresh from the University of New South Wales with first class honours and a Bachelor of Building degree. He was keen on retail, so it wasn't long before he was retail operations director for Lend Lease looking after a number of shopping centres, including the iconic Sunshine Plaza in Queensland, Australia.

Queensland was home for Mann Young in his formative years. Few knew — or needed to know — that he was a refugee from Vietnam who settled with his family to make a home in Queensland. His father was given a job on a sugarcane plantation. This is after the terrifying ordeal of fleeing his war-ravaged homeland as a seven-year-old.

He recounts from his memory of the journey in a rickety fishing boat and ending up on an island on the east coast of Malaysia. Eventually, the boy and his parents were flown from Kuala Lumpur to Brisbane — by Singapore Airlines, he proudly recalls — and settled in the town of Ayr. By courtesy of an aunt, Mann got to Sydney to finish his schooling so he could go onto university.

He thinks he's lucky that he managed to secure a job straight from University with a company he had come to admire, led by the visionary Dick Dusseldorp. That a very determined and passionate Mann Young has seized opportunities in the firm but also followed in the sustainability footsteps of past masters at the game, is as much a credit to him as it is to Lend Lease for spotting and growing talent, no matter from where it originates.

Lend Lease Introducing Innovative and Sustainable Building Methods to Singapore and Asia

The next big innovation for Lend Lease is CLT, successfully introduced in Australia and now approved for its first pilot construction project in Singapore after stringent testing.

Mann Young, Head of CLT Business for Lend Lease in Asia, is taking responsibility for managing the introduction of CLT in Singapore.

This is seen as a landmark development in construction and property development.

World leading and landmark CLT projects, predominantly completed in the UK and Europe, have led to the recent completion (in December 2012) of the world's tallest residential timber structure, the ten-storey Forté project in Melbourne, Australia, which has been designed and built by Lend Lease.

This major achievement has been reached through a coordinated transfer of knowledge to the Australian market which has set a precedent for introductions to other new markets at a global level.

The Forté CLT project will be used as a case study at the Sustainable Building Conference in September in Singapore with the theme "Realising Sustainability in the Tropics".

Mann Young will report to the conference on progress on the introduction of CLT in Singapore and the recently completed Australian project to demonstrate the product and its system capabilities.

CLT is seen as an innovation that would improve construction productivity significantly and bring a much needed paradigm shift to the building industry. In Asia, Lend Lease is taking a strategic lead in collaboration with Singapore's academic institutions and government agencies to be the first to introduce this innovation into Singapore and use it as a test bed for other parts of Asia.

The introduction of CLT is very timely given Singapore's long-term growth aspirations of creating cost-effective, liveable, sustainable and resilient urban environments and as a regional R&D showcase hub in Asia.

Sources

- www.lendlease.com
- www.ubraintv.com
- www.abccarbon.com
- www.bca.gov.sg

Gold

Standard for Sustainable Events

Section 6

21 Taking Sustainability Seriously for Events in Asia

Written by request for CEI Magazine, this article appeared in their January 2013 issue. I also acted as moderator for a CEI roundtable on sustainability for events in Singapore (reported in the May 2012 CEI issue). I drew on my SASA experience in managing the sustainability programme for i Light Marina Bay (see Chapter 22) and also what I knew of the ISO 20121, the new gold sustainability standard for events, starting with the London Olympics in mid-2012. I have also been in discussions with events organisations and appropriate government agencies, like the Singapore Tourism Board, about how sustainable standards can be introduced for events…

ck on ity

any,
h

estination, resort and more

It's not rocket science to create and manage events in a sustainable fashion, but now there is a scientifically devised and certifiable standard to help the events industry do things better, cleaner and greener.

"Twenty Twelve One" — or alpha-numerically ISO 20121 — is the new standard which is taking the event world by storm. It first saw the light of day with the 2012 London Olympics — the first major event to introduce and earn the certification. The process itself evolved out of BS8901 and now a number of venues and events have gained the Olympic gold standard.

Less is not more in Asia. So far only Thailand has officially submitted itself to the certification standard. The Thailand Convention and Exhibition Bureau announced in July 2012 that it is collaborating with SGS to introduce ISO 20121 to the Meetings, Incentives, Conventions and Exhibitions (MICE) players. The new standard aims to elevate Thailand's MICE industry to meet world standards.

Australia has embarked on the ISO 20121 process with a practiced hand. There is the experience offered through the Sustainable Events Alliance, and one of its founding members, Green Shoot Pacific, has worked on the implementation of ISO 20121 for its client, Sydney Festival.

In Europe, there are plenty of examples of venues and events which quickly latched onto the scheme, understandably maybe as this evolved from the accepted British standard, BS8901.

The Millennium Stadium in Cardiff — the venue for Rugby World Cup matches — was one of the early adopters, as was Dublin's Croke Park, achieving ISO 20121 certification after an audit by SGS Ireland in May 2012, describing the award as "the Event Sustainability Management System International Standard".

In June 2012, Coca-Cola Great Britain achieved ISO 20121 with SGS United Kingdom Ltd, ready for the London 2012 Olympic and Paralympic Games. The company's certification covered all its London 2012 operations, including the Olympic Torch Relay, Venue Operations, Showcasing, Hospitality and Licensed Merchandising activities.

Closer to home, Singapore is having a serious look into the best way to introduce and manage standards for sustainability in the event industry. There are some big events in Singapore — conferences, exhibitions, festivals — as well as major venues like Marina Bay Sands, which have started to embark on the sustainability journey and subject themselves to the verifiable event standard.

It might be a sensitive issue, but there is no reason why the Formula One motor racing event, which Singapore has committed to for another five years, should not go through the ISO 20121 process.

No event is perfect, as the event industry has to acknowledge. In fact, staging an event of any sort in "inherently un-sustainable", as pointed out by Phil Cumming and Fiona Pelham, authors of "Making Events More Sustainable: A Guide to BS 8901".

We can see where some of the global events Singapore has scheduled in the year ahead are "ripe for sustainability". We have already suggested this for the big first time World Engineers Summit, which takes place at Marina Bay Sands in September 2013, and not just because its theme is "Innovative and Sustainable Solutions to Climate Change"!

By adopting a sustainability programme or approach, the organisers can reduce an event's impact on the environment, for example, if they take into account the factors and opportunities (see the ten tips highlighted by the London Olympics' sustainability team).

It can work just as well for a major conference or exhibition as it can for a smaller MICE event.

Getting the right advice and support means any member of the MICE industry can seriously take sustainability on board. It is the future and it is the way the world of events is moving.

While there might be a cost to embark on this process, it is one that will pay off as showing leadership in sustainability is as important as showing you are professional and creative in the way you approach events.

And an important point to remember — as many major international companies have recently discovered — sustainability can produce some direct benefits to the bottom line. Reduced energy use, cutting back on paper and waste, introducing recycling programmes, can all directly give you cost savings for your events and your business.

So making events sustainable makes sense — very good business sense — and in the process it's good for the planet, people, as well as profit!

—— ◀◉▶ ——

Top Ten Tips for Events

Just what does the new event standard really require? The London Olympics sustainability committee puts it simply as a ten-point process of questioning and application, which in turn becomes ten tips for any event organiser, venue, country or company to apply:

1. Access: Ensure good communication methods and physical access to facilities so everyone is welcome.
2. Local area: Look after your local community. Try to reduce congestion, litter and noise.
3. Energy and water: Think of inventive ways to reduce your energy and water usage.
4. Transport: Walking, cycling and public transport are healthy and more environmentally friendly ways to travel to an event.
5. Reduce and reuse: Think about what you really need — buy only what is needed and hire/reuse everything else.
6. Responsible sourcing: Try to support local businesses and socially responsible organisations.
7. Food and beverage: Try to showcase local, seasonal and Fairtrade produce and provide free drinking water.
8. Keepsakes: Ensure giveaways add to the customer experience, are useful, reusable and/or recyclable.
9. Make it easy to recycle: Try to provide recyclable packaging and provide recycling and general waste bins.
10. Health, safety and security: A safe environment is a happy environment. Assessing the risks in advance can help ensure that everyone can enjoy the event.

Sources

- www.sustainable-event-alliance.org
- www.sustain-ability-showcase.com
- www.greenshootpacific.com
- www.cslondon.org
- www.iso.org
- www.sustainableeventsltd.com
- www.cei.asia

Race for Sustainability

22

Case Study: Asia's First and Only Sustainable Light Art Festival

Confession time: I have been very close to this event for the best part of two years. My company SASA was appointed as the sustainability consultant to i Light Marina Bay 2012 to work with URA and Pico, the event managers. So the case study was written by me and I have also given presentations to event organisations SACEOS and ISES. A very full report on the sustainability management of the event was provided to URA and an illustrated presentation on the event can be found on our SASA website...

Photographs of light art installations, featured at i Light Marina Bay 2012, from the official website www.ilightmarinabay.sg.

S ustainability doesn't mean you have to "dumb-down" an event or make it less exciting. It is possible to demonstrate — as has been shown with i Light Marina Bay — that a major event designed for enjoyment and entertainment can be managed in a sustainable fashion. This case study tells the sustainable event story:

The second edition of the highly successful light art festival, first held in Singapore in 2010, i Light Marina Bay 2012 covered 24 days and nights — 9 March to 1 April 2012. The festival featured 31 art installations located around the Marina Bay, from both local and international artists, attracting a total of 560,000 visitors.

"Asia's first and only sustainable light art festival" was presented by Urban Redevelopment Authority (URA) with Smart Light and managed by Pico. Sustain Ability Showcase Asia (SASA) was appointed the sustainability consultant for the event, responsible for a rigorous but pragmatic sustainability management process.

With all stakeholders' committed, the event was organised with the key objectives of promoting Marina Bay as a forward-thinking, culturally vibrant, sustainable urban district, as well as to raise and promote awareness of new sustainable lighting technologies to professionals, building owners, tenants and the public.

Drawing on the accepted international standard for sustainable events BS8901 — the forerunner of ISO 20121 — as the primary guide, a sustainability action plan was formulated, focusing on four guiding principles:

- Accessible and inclusive;
- Minimisation of negative impact on the environment;
- Leaving a positive legacy; and
- Encouraging sustainable behaviour.

In practice, the sustainability action plan involved the four M's:

- **Meeting** all relevant stakeholders to achieve maximum involvement and commitment;
- **Measuring** everything that could possibly be measured in accordance with the agreed objectives and principles;
- **Metering**, for the first time, the art installations for energy use, which were the obvious and visible public features of the festival; and
- **Managing** all elements of the process and festival with sustainability in mind throughout.

Highlight: Art Installations

As the public and visual face of the festival, the art installations were designed to demonstrate sustainability and energy efficiency to the visitors. Each artist was provided a Recommended Approach for Creation of Art Installations that outlines the energy use, material composition and disposal method for the installation to enable effective management.

Also, for the first time, all 31 art installations were metered for their energy usage, which over the period of 24 nights amounted to 6568 kWh — or 3.40 tonnes of CO_2 equivalent (CO_2 e).

"Switch Off, Turn Up" Campaign

A major achievement of the 2012 festival was having 47 properties surrounding Marina Bay and beyond to join in the energy saving "Switch Off, Turn Up" campaign. This led to a total saving of 210,424 kWh — equivalent to 109 tonnes of CO_2 — over the 24-day period. This was nearly three times the number of properties in 2010 (16 properties) and five times the energy saving (41,377 kWh).

The amount saved was more than enough to offset the emissions attributed to the festival, which included the installations, freight,

artists' flights, and associated emissions from contractors, suppliers and partner events — a total of 80 tonnes of CO_2 e.

The sustainability achievements can be attributed to the time and effort put in to securing the commitment of the various properties to adopt energy saving practices.

Meetings were held with the property managers to explain the festival and campaign objectives to secure their commitment. Walkthroughs of the properties were also done to point out the areas where energy savings can be made.

These were followed by data collection through a detailed template provided by SASA and follow ups were made to check and confirm the figures provided. Information sheets were provided to the properties to educate their tenants on the purpose of the campaign and to encourage participation.

Contacts with the properties were also made throughout the festival period to check on their energy saving exercises as well as to provide feedback. A final check was made at the end of the festival to confirm the energy savings of the properties.

In a post-event survey, 81.8% of the properties indicated that they are "very likely" to participate again, with 15.9% indicating "likely". 77.3% of properties will also be maintaining some of the sustainability/energy efficiency practices introduced during the campaign, while 52.3% will be introducing additional energy saving measures.

Sustainability Initiatives

In addition to the sustainability measures taken above, a number of other initiatives were also implemented during the three week-long festival. These included:

- Workshops and competitions;
- Education and communication;
- Introducing eco products and displays;
- Sponsorship by Power Seraya; and
- Recycling and managing waste.

With all the sustainability measures undertaken through the planning, implementation and management of the festival, i Light Marina Bay 2012 can justifiably be recognised as Asia's first and only sustainable light art festival, at the same time setting a new benchmark for sustainable events in Singapore by:

- **Making a positive contribution to the environment and the community, through energy saving measures and effective use of resources;**
- **Using the festival as a means to educate and inform all stakeholders and the general public; and**
- **Demonstrating that it is possible to manage a major event designed for enjoyment and entertainment in a sustainable fashion.**

2012 Downtown Pinnacle Award

A few months after the 2012 i Light Marina Bay was held, Cheryl Tay reported in Property Guru (also on Yahoo) and the *Straits Times* reported on 23 September 2012 that the event had won an international award. Here's Cheryl Tay's report:

The URA has clinched the 2012 Downtown Pinnacle Award from the International Downtown Association (IDA), in recognition of i Light Marina Bay 2012, Asia's first sustainable light art festival.

Washington DC-based IDA, an international association that promotes vital and liveable urban centres, presented the award to the URA on Saturday, 22 September, during the 58th IDA Annual Conference in Minneapolis, USA.

i Light Marina Bay 2012 featured over 30 unique light art installations around the bay, as well as a host of interactive activities for three weeks. Over 500,000 local and international guests participated in the festival.

Commenting on the award, Ng Lang, Chief Executive Officer of URA noted, "The success of this event is due to the strong support shown by our programme and community partners, sponsors and stakeholders, and we look forward to working closely with them to present another exciting edition in 2014."

He added that the award highlights URA's efforts to make Marina Bay "a vibrant and energetic waterfront destination that the community can enjoy".

The URA won one of two Pinnacle Awards for the Events and Programming category, which recognises organisations for: focusing on programmes and events that improve the image and vitality of the downtown with events that promote the downtown and attract visitors and delivering projects that communicate the vision, mission, function, and achievements of the downtown or business district association.

"URA's project received this prestigious award for demonstrating excellence in downtown management," said David Downey, President and CEO of IDA.

"Each year the IDA Awards Jury honours the very best programmes and projects in each category to recognise great work and most importantly to set the standard for best practice in our industry. i Light Marina Bay is a wonderful example for all downtowns to emulate."

The IDA Downtown Achievement Awards comprises the Pinnacle and Merit Awards across seven categories for sustainable projects worldwide.

In March 2014, 7 to 30, i Light Marina Bay returns.

———— ◁◦▷ ————

Sources

- www.ilightmarinabay.sg
- www.ura.gov.sg
- www.pico.com
- www.abccarbon.com
- www.sustain-ability-showcase.com

Race for Sustainability

23

Can a Luxury Hotel and Convention Centre be Sustainable?

When writing about MBS, you cannot fail to take note of its size. It is an imposing property and one that has in a very short time become an icon for Singapore. So pleasing then for an observer and advocate of all things clean and green, to see that MBS has embraced sustainability: It is working hard to make its venues and the MBS experience as sustainable as possible. I have attended so many events at MBS and experienced first-hand how it has done things. MBS was very involved with i Light Marina Bay, acting as a host for many of the art installations as well as media events, and identified with the sustainability initiatives of the festival. I have talked to Kevin Teng many times and recommended him for an interview on UBrain TV to talk about the sustainability commitments at MBS...

How can a luxury hotel be environmentally friendly? That was the actual question posed by Nobuko Kashiwagi, Chief Correspondent, when she interviewed Kevin Teng, Director of Sustainability for Marina Bay Sands (MBS) Singapore for UBrain TV in June 2013. A month before MBS played host to Sir Richard Branson and the Carbon War Room's "Creating Climate Wealth" event, which drew attention to the sustainability commitments of the venue and its management.

As MBS is the recipient of the Singapore's Building & Construction Authority's (BCA) Green Mark Gold Award and has taken many steps to green its property and its events, Kevin Teng is the driver in the sustainability hot seat.

So Kevin extended his answer to go beyond the hotel to the important MICE — Meetings, Incentives, Conventions and Exhibitions — segment of the property, as well as broaden it to go beyond environmental to the full sustainability spectrum.

Just as he answered Nobuko, he also tells me and others:

- Sustainability is one of the core values for the company and the property;
- Sustainability and hospitality go well together;
- Guests want to stay in a place that is managed efficiently and responsibly; and
- The company wants to ensure it is doing things right for the environment and society.

It was back in March 2012 that MBS gained a significant accolade for its green efforts. Singapore's *Business Times* reported on the occasion:

MBS has made history by being the largest single building in Singapore to be awarded the prestigious Green Mark Gold Award for its sustainability efforts.

This national recognition — awarded by the BCA — is MBS's first green accolade here since opening its doors nearly two years ago.

The BCA's Green Mark scheme was launched seven years ago as an initiative to drive Singapore's construction industry towards more environment-friendly buildings. There are a thousand BCA-certified green buildings to date.

At the time, the director of sustainability, Kevin Teng, said that energy conservation and efficient water usage were high on the agenda even during the integrated resort's design and construction phase.

'We knew that we were going to have to deal with all these higher operating costs later on if we didn't invest the capital at the design and procurement stage of the building,' Kevin said.

Most other developers, he added, are "not accountable" for the buildings they construct because they lease it out upon completion, leaving the tenant to worry about the energy bills.

The reasons for MBS clinching the award are plentiful, said Mr. Teng.

He shared how about two out of every three lights installed at MBS are energy efficient. While these lights may cost two or three times more than traditional ones, they consume only a seventh of the energy and can last at least twice as long.

"We have the most guest rooms of any property in Singapore and we have made them as environmentally friendly as possible. From the beginning, we knew we had to get it right because the impact is multiplied by 2,560 rooms — which is about five times the number of a standard hotel," he said.

But while there is plenty of buy-in from the management, one of the biggest challenges is to get the support and attention from the 9,000-plus staff at MBS to make the green movement a success.

"We have all these internal activities to promote sustainability among our team members and we try to make them trendy, but we are also very aware that these cannot be facetious. They can't be silly," said Mr Teng.

"In the end, going green is a very serious issue. Our message to staff isn't about doing this for fun. Do it because it drives environmental savings, cost savings and more importantly, it's the right thing to do," was how he was summed it up in the *Business Times* report.

―――◄○►―――

Kevin Teng was appointed Director of Sustainability at MBS in January 2012, progressing into this role after being the integrated resort's Chief Engineer for Development and Capital (A&A) Projects since opening.

In his current role, Kevin is responsible for the entire property's green initiatives, spearheading many sustainability projects with both internal and external stakeholders.

One of his top priorities is to inspire and develop a green culture throughout the property operations, including improving operational practices, providing sustainable options for meeting planners, and extending the property's community outreach and education — consistent with the Global Sands Eco360 programme created by parent company Las Vegas Sands Corp.

His strong background of engineering, urban planning and project management started in 2004 when he managed development and design projects in China, Southeast Asia and the Middle East for EDAW|AE-COM. In 2008, he was appointed as Director of Corporate Development and Sustainability for Las Vegas Sands Corp., where he co-directed The Venetian Hotel's energy efficiency initiatives that went on to earn it the LEED-EB Gold Certification. (The Leadership in Energy and Environmental Design (LEED) Green Building Rating System is the nationally accepted benchmark for the design, construction and operation of high-performance green buildings in the US.)

Kevin has a Master of Science in Urban Planning from the London School of Economics, and Bachelor degrees in Electrical Engineering, Biomedical Engineering and International Studies from Duke University. He was also a 1999 Howard Hughes Institute grantee and a 2002 Fulbright

Scholarship recipient by the US State Department. In addition, he is a published writer for trade publications and a USGBC LEED Accredited Professional.

For Kevin, the focus of all he does now is to educate all on the MBS Green Initiatives — inside and outside the property — and see where things can be enhanced.

For MBS, protecting the environment requires a long-term commitment. Since its construction days, MBS has implemented eco-friendly operational processes to protect nature and to ensure that the property is an environmentally responsible, energy efficient and healthy place to live and work in.

It wasn't until February 2012 that MBS's sustainability efforts paid dividends. Once BCA awarded the integrated resort with the Green Mark Gold Award, MBS has ramped up its sustainability drive through Sands Eco360, a global sustainability strategy that crosses all of the Sands businesses.

It consists of four priorities: green buildings; environmentally responsible operations; green meetings; and sustainability education and outreach. MBS' first green accolade in Singapore follows the lead of Las Vegas Sands in the US, where The Venetian® and The Palazzo® jointly form the largest LEED®-certified building in the world.

In October 2012, Las Vegas Sands ranked 128th in the US and 239th globally on Newsweek's Green Rankings, which ranks the 500 most eco-friendly US and global companies. Its US ranking marks a 238 rank jump from 2011, the largest improvement for any company in 2012.

In May 2012, MBS joined EarthCheck in its internationally leading benchmarking and certification programme for environmental sustainability. With this programme, MBS takes a scientific approach to benchmarking and is committed to report its environmental footprint based on an internationally recognised standard.

Powering an eco-friendly building: At the core of MBS's green initiatives is a S$25 million intelligent Building Management System, which allows automated control over lighting, heating and water supplies for the entire integrated resort, thus conserving precious resources.

What does this mean? Here are five facts:

- MBS uses regenerative drives on its lifts, which require 40% less energy than comparative non-regenerative lifts;
- MBS has removed over 700 light bulbs in its heart-of-house and common areas to optimise lighting levels. This has reduced energy consumption by roughly 3,000 kWh per year;
- MBS has installed over 12,000 energy-efficient fluorescent and LED lights throughout the property;
- MBS has been recognised as a "Water Efficient Building" by the Public Utilities Board (PUB) in Singapore; and
- MBS has installed 461 fittings under the Water Efficient Labelling Scheme. These fittings yield water savings of more than 6,700 m^3 per year.

Towards a Greener Building

As one of the biggest properties in Singapore, MBS undertook several steps to cut waste to a minimum during its construction phase, including:

- Non-toxic eco-paints were used to reduce the amount of toxic fumes released into the air.
- These eco-paints frequently incorporate recycled or leftover paints, which would normally go to the landfill.
- Waste was segmented into organic and construction waste for proper disposal.
- Waste was minimised with recycling and reusing of wood, metal and excavated earth.
- As part of PUB's Keep Marina Bay Clean Campaign, MBS has adopted Marina Bay to help ensure that the bay is clean and provide an emergency response if needed, to minimise pollution.

Staff Awareness

MBS initiated a company-wide education programme to raise awareness of sustainability and encourage environmentally friendly behaviour.

Launched in February 2012, the programme includes paper reduction challenges, recycling drives, switch-off-the-light campaigns and home tips for energy efficient practices in the community.

The first staff recycling drive in April 2012 was a success. The amount of materials recycled was:

- 17,820 litres of paper recycled — equivalent to saving over 390 trees from being cut down;
- 24,660 litres of plastic bottles recycled — equivalent to saving enough energy to power 140,000 light bulbs; and
- 5,280 litres of cans recycled — equivalent to saving enough energy to run a computer for three years.

It's for these planning events, that the MBS green meetings plan, with its very own green meetings concierge, comes into its own.

It is possible to go paperless and hassle-free, MBS proudly announced earlier in the year.

It also enables organisations to promote their event at MBS with a fully customisable and hassle-free mobile app dedicated to the purpose.

The MBS customisable mobile app gives event organisers and managers the added advantage of going paperless for the event, helping eliminate some of the environmental impact and costs associated with paper-based materials.

MBS tells meeting organisers: "The app allows you to update your event schedules and make news announcements in real-time, providing your attendees with the most current information for the complete conference experience."

In addition, the MBS Green Meetings Concierge features:

- More than 30 fully customisable built-in features and components such as in-app messaging, exhibitor and speaker profiles, photo galleries and social sharing;
- Security, privacy and access settings;
- Branding and advertising opportunities; and

- iOS and Android versions (free for event attendees to download and use).

It all goes to show that MBS, with Kevin Teng in charge of sustainability, goes to great lengths to aim for the top — to be the best at event sustainability. The next step is to advance to the global gold standard. It wants to be the first property in Asia to secure the coveted ISO 20121 certification. It is well on the way.

―――◄ ○ ►―――

Sources

- www.marinabaysands.com
- www.ubraintv.com
- www.bca.gov.sg

24

Profile —
Sir Richard Branson:
Carbon War Room's
"Creating Climate
Wealth" Event

*I did get a word in with Sir Richard Branson when he visited Singapore in May 2013. Not a full-blown interview, but I asked a question and got a long, thoughtful answer. I produced a report of our meeting and what Sir Richard had to say for both UBrain TV (UK) and Eco Tv (Australia). I have also reported on the commitments and challenges presented by Sir Richard many times in my newsletter **abc carbon express**. More recently, I have become familiar with the work of the Carbon War Room. I've been an admirer of his work for a long time. He is prepared to stick his neck out and do the extraordinary. To achieve things against all odds. To put his money where his mouth is...*

War is not a nice thing, but a carbon war is the right thing because it's a call to arms… it is a war worth fighting. So says Sir Richard Branson, who was in Singapore to launch Carbon War Room's "Creating Climate Wealth" event.

He wants to spread the influence of the Carbon War Room to Asia and enhance its impacts by linking up with the UN's Sustainable Energy for All Initiative.

He also recognises the business imperative and mobilises his own businesses and others to act. The Carbon War Room is a classic example of this. He admits — as do other industrialists and business people — that he is contributing to the problem by adding fossil fuel derived CO_2 to the atmosphere through his airlines, trains and businesses. But he is doing all he can to reduce his business impact on the environment and getting others on board — not just onto his modes of transport!

For two days, I joined about 200 others in Singapore to explore options and to come up with solutions. Things which would work to better manage waste, for example. To see waste as a resource to be better managed and to produce energy instead of landfill.

Some great minds and some great business people got their heads together to look at shipping emissions and how to reduce them around the world. This is important for a country like Singapore with one of the busiest ports in the world.

Energy efficiency was uppermost in many minds — most importantly, top of the agenda for Singapore's Minister for the Environment and Water Resources Dr. Vivian Balakrishnan who said in his opening speech:

"Energy efficiency is, at this point of time, the only game in town. Given that every joule, every kilowatt hour of energy in Singapore comes from imported fossil fuels."

The good thing about Carbon War Room is that it doesn't organise talk-fests and waste people's time and money discussing things. It organises itself, and those it comes in contact with, to come up with workable solutions. Some will proceed in Asia and some will continue to be activated around the world.

Of course it helps that Sir Richard puts his name and brand to it, but he's also assembled a formidable group of people around the world to address these issues and opportunities.

A business-like approach to the problem.

And Sir Richard doesn't see his businesses as above the pressure to change.

I asked him about the aviation industry — an industry he is very much part of — and what he thinks airlines, like his own, should be doing about their impact on the environment and to reduce emissions of greenhouse gases.

He answered very directly and unapologetically, admitting that airlines provide a good example and have work to do.

"There are many things airlines can do — and some are doing — to reduce their carbon output. And save money."

"We built our spaceship of 100% carbon fibre." Aircraft can now be built of carbon fibre — as Boeing has done with its 787 — as this reduces the weight and therefore the amount of fuel used.

Sir Richard also was heartened to see airlines looking at alternatives to jet fuel (derived from fossil fuels) and looking into algae-based fuels and even a kerosene-like fuel from waste.

He said he has persuaded Air Asia to join the Carbon War Room and go for cleaner fuels.

Race for Sustainability

"We want every airline — and every business — to join the Carbon War Room."

He said he is encouraging businesses — including his own — to become aware of the problem and change the way they do things. To be more energy efficient and to look at cleaner fuels. To look at ways to reduce emissions.

———— ◄◊► ————

Jessica Cheam reported on Sir Richard's visit and the Carbon War Room for Eco-business:

Let's Do Carbon-Friendly, Not Carbon-Dirty Business

Carbon War Room, the non-profit backed by British billionaire Sir Richard Branson, is looking to expand in Asia and use Singapore as its base.

The founder and chairman of the Virgin Group told reporters this week that the outfit, which seeks to accelerate investment into carbon-cutting technologies, was "looking for business leaders in the Far East" to fight this war on carbon.

"We want to find groups of people who can help us in this region...we'd like to see Carbon War Room based in Singapore but helped by countries all around here. There's so much new business taking place here, and so many imaginative ways that we can do it in a carbon-friendly way instead of carbon-dirty way," said Mr. Branson.

Scientists have blamed the accumulation of carbon in the atmosphere for worsening climate change.

Speaking on the sidelines of Carbon War Room's "Creating Climate Wealth" summit — the first to be held in Asia on Monday — Mr. Branson said the building industry is one area that Carbon War Room is looking into, as dramatic savings can be achieved.

He conceded that his businesses "put out a lot of carbon" and this is why he started Carbon War Room in 2009.

"War is not a nice thing, but a carbon war is the right thing because it's a call to arms... it is a war worth fighting," he added.

Mr. Branson also went to lengths to explain his latest venture — Virgin Galactic — which is introducing rocket-powered space tourism flights by the end of the year.

When he asked the 250-strong audience at the summit who wanted to go to space, almost everyone held up their hand.

"It's an unusual business... but that's the answer. 90% of the world wants to become astronauts. There's nothing more captivating and enchanting and magnificent than to go up and look at our beautiful earth and have the experience of a lifetime," he said.

"I've talked to the Russians... and they said that with 50 million dollars, they'll be happy to have me. With that money, I'd rather build my own," he said to laughter in the audience.

When asked by Eco-Business later if this could be considered a "sustainable" business, he said it would have a minor impact on climate change.

"We have reduced the carbon cost of someone going into space from something like two weeks of New York's electricity supply... to less than the cost of an economy round-trip from Singapore to London," he explained to reporters at Marina Bay Sands.

"New technology can dramatically reduce the carbon output and that is the challenge we have set ourselves," he said.

More than 500 people have reserved seats on his space flight, and paid deposits on the $200,000 ticket price on the SpaceShipTwo (SS2). Its lightweight carbon-fibre body will also "reduce fuel burn dramatically", he said.

The SS2 is designed to be launched by a transport plane called White Knight Two and will be guided by a rocket motor before returning to Earth.

Speaking on the global climate crisis, Mr. Branson said that the "problem with climate change is you can't see it".

"Even though 98% of scientists say we have a problem, the 2% funded by the oil and coal industry have powerful voices and muddy the waters," he said.

"We have to make it advantageous for people to use solar and wind and develop really clean batteries that the little shift could make an enormous difference," he added.

Governments can play a role here by changing the playing field. Then, it's about business leaders "using our imagination, seeing how we can get our own house in order and save ourselves some money".

———◄○►———

The Energy for All Initiative

Around the same time Sir Richard was in Singapore and the Carbon War Room was actively engaging with many of its various projects, it was announced that Carbon War Room joined the UN Energy for All Initiative.

Washington DC, 21 May 2013: The Secretary-General of the UN, Ban Ki-moon, joined with the President of the World Bank, Jim Yong Kim, to convene the inaugural meeting of the Upper Level Advisory Board to the UN's Sustainable Energy for All Initiative (SE4All). The SE4All Initiative is a multi-stakeholder partnership between governments, the private sector and civil society.

Launched by the Secretary-General in 2011, it has three interlinked objectives to be achieved by 2030: provide universal access to modern energy, double the share of renewable energy in the global energy mix, and double the global rate of improvement in energy efficiency.

———◄○►———

Sources

- www.carbonwarroom.com
- www.ubraintv.com
- www.ecotv.com.au
- www.abccarbon.com
- www.eco-business.com
- www.sustainableenergyforall.org

Air
Pollution, Deforestation and Biodiversity

Section 7

25

The Burning Season in Indonesia: Where There's Smoke, There's Fire!

I have made the point when writing about the "haze", which badly impacted Singapore, Malaysia and Indonesia this year, that it is a real misnomer. It is air pollution, it involved destruction of forests and peatlands and it is bad. But we need to look at the wider issues. Both through my newsletter and through covering what others are saying, I tried to present the bigger picture. Hundreds of thousands of words have been written — and will continue to be written — about the problem and the work that is going on to address it, at high levels and on the ground. But I did ask Dorjee Sun, the producer of the film, The Burning Season, for his words of wisdom on the topic. I also selected a few other suitable commentaries. I will maintain a watching brief. This is obviously not the last word...

Photo by Keith Ramos (2013, public domain) from Wiki-Media Commons: www.com-mons.wikimedia.org/wiki/File:Big_tropical_forest_fire.jpg.

I t is air pollution — **impure** and simple — and it is dangerously unhealthy for people and the environment! To continue to call it haze is to belittle its impact. Haze and hazardous might have the same first three letters but the meaning is very different.

That's how I commented on the invasion of "haze" from Indonesia in my newsletter **abc carbon express** on 21 June 2013:

The thick smoke that blankets large parts of Southeast Asia — Singapore, Malaysia and Indonesia — comes from the illegal burning of forests and from farmers clearing the land in this most unsustainable and environment-ally damaging way.

When it comes close to home — and to your very own eyes, mouth, nose and lungs — you realise how much we value our clear air and clean environment. And how some people couldn't care less. But it should force us to think of the greater damage of environmental suicide coming from examples like this.

The long-term damage which results from deforestation — which alone accounts for around 20% of global greenhouse gas emis-sions — should convince us to change our ways. There are people out there who are destroying our health and the health of the planet. This cannot be allowed to continue.

The World Bank — as we announce in this issue — is committing billions of dollars to flood prevention, water management and other projects to help major Asia cities avoid the expected impact of climate change.

As a campaigner against deforestation and founder of Carbon Conservation, Dorjee Sun has been going on about the Indonesian Burning Season for a few years. Now, it is worse than ever for the health and environment of Southeast Asia. Deforestation is bad enough — it accounts for 20% of the world's greenhouse gas emissions — now the very health of its people is at stake. What does he think needs to be done to stop the burning?

Dorjee was the producer of the film "The Burning Season" and has considered all aspects of the "haze" issue. What can be done to end the burning and attend to the health and environmental consequences, not just for Singapore, but the rest of Southeast Asia and ultimately the world.

From Hong Kong, where Dorjee went to get away from Singapore's all pervasive air pollution from the Indonesian fires, he sent this considered report on 21 June on what he titles "HAZE 9-11":

HAZE 9-11

As a pragmatic environmentalist and a solution-oriented person, the current finger pointing and combative rhetoric by all parties is not the path to constructive long-lasting solutions, in my humble opinion.

Rather, we must build deep, open, honest and transparent collaborations for the next decade and beyond, and use this "HAZE 9-11" as a Pearl Harbour or black swan event that will never be forgotten but will be used as the motivation to find lasting solutions and that rarest of commodities: "long-lasting political will" in companies, communities and government to finally solve this persistent and recurring problem. "Lest we forget."

Carbon Conservation has been working on avoiding deforestation, stopping the haze and helping the industry towards a more sustainable business model for seven years and worked in Indonesia for nearly this whole period.

The sad fact is that behind the two super powers of America and China, Indonesia is the THIRD biggest emitter of greenhouse gases simply because of this forest clearing and burning.

So how do we solve this? Firstly, I believe that this is a man-made problem and thus is absolutely solvable. Let me repeat — "Yes we can solve this problem." I don't buy into the naysayers who say fires will always burn and I absolutely believe that where there is a will, there is a way.

Race for Sustainability

But to find the right solutions we need to be open-minded and collaborative with all stakeholders. We all just need to "stay calm and carry on".

We need to look at and evaluate all possible options — both "carrots and sticks". From "carrots" or payments to the people on the ground to value and protect the peatlands and forests, to exploring innovative ideas like incentivising forest stewardship and fire avoidance by rewarding those communities for the years where there are reduced or no hot spots and reduced or no haze.

This then could possibly be even parlayed into a regional carbon market hub in Singapore where companies buy carbon credits to offset their footprint by buying anti-haze community carbon credits.

We actually have a pilot project in Riau that would protect deep peat forest and could avoid the fires in the critical Kampar Peninsula peat dome area on the Sumatra island where the haze is originating. But were unable to raise sufficient financial support in 2009–2010. Now, with other industry partners, I hope to re-launch this effort and possibly build a bigger regional area of protection.

In terms of the viability of a Singapore-based regional carbon market for anti-haze carbon, please note that Shenzhen just launched a regional Chinese domestic carbon market this week and in 2009 the USA (under the Waxman Markey Bill) and the world came within inches of a market policy that would have included forest carbon within its trading boundaries.

Ironically and interestingly, the voluntary market report which was released just two days ago showed that voluntary markets are healthier than compliance markets with the average 2012 prices of US$5.90 per tonne, down only a fraction from US$6.20 in 2011, and traded volumes were actually up about 4% to 101 million tonnes.

Solutions could also involve the recognition of products carrying supply chain inputs from the burning areas and also identification of owners of the offending concessions. This would allow consumers to discern and decide where to spend their dollars.

The solutions might also involve encouraging the Indonesian Government to consider domestic "sticks" or enforcement of "zero burn" laws, which Indonesia has, but doesn't widely enforce. Or perhaps just allowing the ability for Singapore to mobilise water bombing efforts in circumstances of such serious haze. At what point can a country defend its sovereign right to clean air for its kids?

But before all of this, first, there needs to be the building of trusted and transparent sharing relationships where we come together to find mutually agreeable solutions. Unless we see the common win-wins of all our children enjoying fresh air and economic development, our efforts will be doomed to failure. And indeed the rift of "us versus them" or "rich dad, poor dad" will grow ever deeper, when in actuality we should all be prospering together.

The best example of global solutions was the Montreal Protocol and a bilateral example is where Australia will send firefighters to California to help fight their bush fires in the Australian winter. Unfortunately, the most notable failed example is probably the Kyoto Protocol and the Copenhagen UNFCCC summit.

But there is a silver lining in this terrible HAZE 9-11. Seven years ago, grisly images of burnt orangutans and devastated forest areas first moved my team and I to raise finance for forest carbon and motivated Carbon Conservation's first forest projects in Indonesia. What we lacked was the momentum, awareness and sustained interest of the society. We asked: "How could we rally the importance of this issue?"

Well, now environmentalists have the momentum, the attention and support of the society and so we must operate in pragmatic, realistic, achievable and transparent rational steps.

———◦———

We also reported what others were saying about the "haze", in this summary and headline in **abc carbon express**:

Fires from Slash and Burn Threaten Lives and Livelihood

The annual air pollution hazard — called simply "haze" by most — has once again descended on the island of Singapore and parts of Malaysia. A result of the slash-and-burn technique used for land clearing on neighbouring islands in Indonesia, the all-pervasive smoke has broken the previous high for dangerously unhealthy air recorded in 1997, leading to finger-pointing by the people and governments of Singapore and Indonesia. How bad will it get before companies and governments take real action against the culprits?

———◀◯▶———

Dangerously High Haze Levels in Singapore Limit Outdoor Activity

Julie Noce reports for *AFP News* (19 June 2013)

Smog from forest fires in Indonesia stayed at unhealthy levels in Singapore on Tuesday as the two neighbours blamed each other for the seasonal problem.

Singapore's Pollutant Standards Index stood at 115 as offices opened — still above the "unhealthy" threshold of 100 but down from the peak reached late Monday when the entire island was shrouded by a smoky haze.

Most commuters walked in bright sunshine on Tuesday without covering their faces despite the lingering smell of burnt wood in the business district.

The Ministry of Manpower has urged employers to issue protective masks to staff with heart and respiratory problems, and those working outdoors. The elderly and children have also been told to reduce strenuous outdoor activity.

The pollutant index soared to a peak of 155 late Monday, the highest since Southeast Asia's prolonged haze crisis in 1997–1998, but eased off overnight.

On Monday, Singapore urged Indonesia to take "urgent measures" to tackle its forest fires as smoke blown from Sumatra island choked the densely populated city-state as well as parts of Malaysia.

But the Indonesian forestry ministry said firefighters were already tackling the blazes and water-dropping aircraft would be deployed if local governors made a request.

A ministry official, Hadi Daryanto, also attempted to shift some of the blame onto Malaysia and Singapore, saying their palm oil companies that had invested in Indonesia were also responsible.

"The slash-and-burn technique being used is the cheapest land-clearing method and it is not only used by local farmers, but also employees of palm oil investors, including Singaporean and Malaysian companies," he said.

"We hope the governments of Malaysia and Singapore will tell their investors to adopt proper measures so we can solve this problem together."

But Vivian Balakrishnan, Singapore's minister for environment and water resources, kept up the pressure on Indonesia.

In remarks carried Tuesday by Singapore media, he said "commercial interests in Indonesia have been allowed to override environmental concerns."

He repeated an offer of help from Singapore, which has a modern military and civil defence system including firefighters.

The Singapore military came to Indonesia's aid after Aceh province was devastated by a tsunami in 2004.

—————◄◇►—————

Not Act of Nature but Man-Made: NEA Chief

By Zakir Hussain, Indonesia Bureau Chief In Jakarta, *Straits Times* (21 June 2013)

The haze triggered by fires raging across Sumatra is not an act of nature, but man-made, National Environment Agency (NEA) chief executive Andrew Tan said yesterday.

Hence, Indonesia needs to take more decisive action against errant companies, Mr. Tan told *The Times*, echoing remarks he made at a two-hour meeting held here yesterday afternoon between Singapore officials and their Indonesian counterparts.

Singapore, he added, could work together with Indonesia to map its satellite images of hot spots onto land concession maps of affected areas in Sumatra, and track those responsible.

"I urged Indonesia to take more decisive action, because the situation is likely to deteriorate in the next few weeks and at the onset of the dry season if no further efforts are taken," he said.

"We registered that given the weather conditions, the burning actions are man-made and therefore can and should be averted. We pressed them to take our concerns seriously."

The emergency meeting at Indonesia's Foreign Ministry followed telephone calls between foreign and environment ministers from both countries on Tuesday. In addition, Singapore's Environment and Water Resources Minister Vivian Balakrishnan is due to travel to Jakarta today.

Singapore's Pollutant Standards Index (PSI) hit a record high of 371 at 1pm yesterday, an hour before the Jakarta meeting began.

"On Singapore's part, we conveyed the very serious concerns that Singaporeans have over the deteriorating haze situation… how this was unprecedented and (how) PSI levels deteriorated very quickly," Mr. Tan said.

"(We) are now at a stage where air quality is at hazardous levels. So we can't take this lightly."

Singapore also proposed to bring forward a sub-regional ministerial meeting on transboundary haze set for August, he said.

Indonesian officials were asked to share if they have information about Singapore companies involved in illegal burning so that Singapore can act as well.

"We had a frank discussion with host agencies," Mr. Tan said.

The Singapore side was updated regarding a ministerial meeting yesterday morning that saw a national task force on haze being set up. Measures agreed on included stepping up firefighting efforts and enforcement against errant firms. Immediate steps included cloud-seeding to induce rain.

The task force, chaired by Coordinating Welfare Minister Agung Laksono, includes the ministers for foreign affairs, the environment and forestry. Mr. Agung told reporters that cloud-seeding would take place as soon as it was feasible, starting today. The salt is ready, the planes are in place, he said, but there must be clouds.

He noted that the burning was not always above ground. Some 850 ha of land had been ablaze in recent days, and fires in some 650 ha had been put out, he said.

The government is investigating which companies are responsible and will take action against those found culpable. "But there must be a process," he said.

———— ◀○▶ ————

Why Naming and Shaming Might Help Fight Haze

By Jessica Cheam in *The Straits Times* (21 June 2013)

Singapore, the clean and green garden city, turned hazy and grey this week when winds blew in the thick smog caused by more than 100 hot spots over Sumatra.

The haze that enveloped the Republic was the worst in history, hitting a record of 371 on the Pollutant Standards Index yesterday, curtailing outdoor activities across the island.

Indonesian officials say the huge tracts of land around the coastal city of Dumai — located on the coast of the Strait of Malacca that faces Singapore — have caught fire due to the early hot season.

Farmers are also using their "slash-and-burn" methods to clear plantations — an established practice for many smallholder farmers who regard it as the easiest, low-cost method although with exacting environment and public health costs.

Such a phenomenon is not rare in this part of the world, which has been plagued by transboundary haze pollution for many years, although the seriousness of the haze varies from year to year.

As the haze worsened, Minister for Environment and Water Resources Vivian Balakrishnan had tougher words for Indonesia. "No country or corporation has the right to pollute the air at the expense of Singaporeans' health and well-being," he wrote on Wednesday night.

The ASEAN bloc has tried to address the haze pollution for more than a decade with limited success. Each year, its ministers meet to discuss the issue and pledge cooperation on tackling it. There has been some progress such as in Jambi province, where Singapore and Indonesia worked together to implement steps to address forest fires.

But notably, the 2002 ASEAN Agreement on Transboundary Haze Pollution, which legally binds countries to prevent and control haze, has not been ratified by Indonesia, rendering it toothless because most of the burning originates there.

Indonesia has taken umbrage at suggestions it has not done enough, but over the years, it has been relatively ineffective in enforcing and prosecuting those who start the forest fires. Short of engaging ministers in more talk, Singapore and Malaysia have their hands tied as the burning is not in their territory.

Satellite technology pin-pointing the exact locations are also useful, but without being able to match the coordinates to land owners, culprits remain unexposed.

So, what options do we have?

If the authorities are unable to make progress, then commercial and public pressure could be the key to addressing the problem.

Singapore has now called on Indonesia to publish the concession maps that will show which companies own the burning spots. Indonesia has suggested that it was Malaysian and Singaporean palm oil companies behind the hot spots, and has since said it will check and "then we will coordinate".

This is a long overdue move, and governments, non-governmental organisations and wider society must put pressure for such information to be made transparent.

Minister for the Environment and Water Resources Vivian Balakrishnan hinted as much when he said: "I am sure consumers will know what to do."

In other words, the power to stop this lies with us.

When I say "us", I mean not just Singaporean consumers — as we are only a small country with limited buying power — but the wider international community, because the haze pollution knows no borders.

We might suffer most of it due to our proximity to the burning, but the larger concern is the huge amounts of carbon emissions the burning

is adding to the atmosphere, worsening climate change and destroying biodiversity.

As educated consumers, we have the capacity to demand that companies conduct their business responsibly and without detriment to the wider public. This includes ensuring that their entire supply chain is operated in a sustainable manner.

To some extent, this has already been demonstrated in campaigns by environmental groups against major palm oil players. A recent Greenpeace campaign targeting consumer giants like Unilever and Nestle, for example, has led to these companies dropping Singapore-listed Golden Agri-Resources (GAR) as a supplier.

The storm of public criticism had forced Unilever and Nestle to relook their supply chains and in turn, forced players like GAR to clean up their act. GAR has since engaged external parties such as the Forest Trust to look into their operations, and Unilever has also resumed buying from it.

It is unrealistic to expect these companies to clean up overnight, but at least there is a process of improvement.

Locals reports have since quoted Wilmar International as saying that they have a zero-burning policy, although it "cannot prevent local practices of slash-and-burn for agricultural and other purposes".

This is simply not good enough.

We need to apply more public pressure to ensure these companies are responsible for what happens on their land. Saying it cannot be controlled just shows that you simply aren't trying hard enough.

In the current era of technological innovations and crowd-sourcing, it is also difficult to withhold information from the public.

It is then up to us to demand these firms to do the right thing. After all, we are the shareholders who buy their stock and the consumers who buy their products.

Companies can no longer escape the public eye of scrutiny and think they can get away with anything less than responsible action.

The business practices of all palm oil companies who own forest land should be examined by the wider international community and we should mobilise people power to launch even more campaigns that will force companies to change the way they do things. Singapore is capable of that — witness the recent protests against the population white paper and the change in website licensing.

Sure, the issue is far more complex and involves challenges such as the size of forest land involved, and the ability to reach and educate smallholder farmers. These farmers are also trapped by the lack of alternative economic options, and there is an obvious absence of local law enforcement.

But that is precisely why action has to be taken sooner rather than later.

This is the only way to make progress on this problem. Sooner or later, the rain will wash away the smog and the skies will clear again. But even though we may no longer see it, the haze problem still exists.

And it will never go away until we take the necessary steps to address it.

Sources

- www.singapolitics.sg
- www.eco-business.com
- www.abccarbon.com
- www.sg.news.yahoo.com
- www.wildsingaporenews.blogspot.sg

Race for Sustainability

26

Clearing the Air on Health Impacts of Pollution

In July 2012, I attended the Clean Air Forum at the CleanEnviro Summit Singapore and reported on the event in my newsletter, mentioning the good work being done by the WHO, the SIIA and the NEA. While the country is determined to set high standards to keep its air clean and healthy, in spite of the "invasion" of hazardous haze from its neighbours, there are many other pollutants in the air which Singapore has to measure and manage. SIIA has been insistent in pointing these out...

T he World Health Organization (WHO) highlights the health threat posed by air pollution, especially in Asia, which bears 65% of global deaths.

At the Clean Air Forum in Singapore, delegates were told the pollutant posing the greatest risk is identified as particulate matter — fine particles that deposit in airways and can lead to increased acute morbidity, mortality, and decreased lung growth and function.

Action has been urged to clean up the air, especially from the industry, transportation and energy production. And diesel is seen as a significant contributor, too.

Asia's booming cities are experiencing mounting problems of air pollution and this is being borne out with the region having more than its share of deaths from environmental pollution, according to WHO.

While Singapore's air might be amongst the cleanest in Asia, attention is now turning to the very fine particles — less than 2.5 mm in diameter and labelled PM2.5 — which are believed to pose the largest health risks, increasingly accounting for cardiovascular and respiratory illnesses.

The Clean Air Forum jointly presented at the CleanEnviro Summit by the Singapore Institute of International Affairs (SIIA) and the National Environment Agency (NEA) set out to provide "innovative solutions to improve air quality among Asia's growing cities", but also drew sobering attention to the health and environmental impacts of indoor and outdoor pollution.

In a keynote address to the Forum, Nasir Hassan, PhD, Regional Adviser on Environmental Health for the WHO pointed out that globally, three million children under the age of five die every year due to environment-related diseases, with half of them — 1.5 million — from acute respiratory infections.

While outdoor air pollution is the most obvious problem and is identified as the cause of 800,000 deaths a year, nearly 50% of pneumonia deaths among children under five are due to particulate matter inhaled from indoor air pollution.

Asia is carrying an "uneven burden" from environmental pollution, says Dr. Hassan, as 65% of the world total of deaths and lost life-years occur in Asia.

He drew particular attention to the single most studied and the most important health-damaging pollutant: particulate matter (PM), which includes black carbon. Fine particles deposit in airways and can lead to increased acute respiratory morbidity (pneumonia, asthma), increased mortality (from all causes), as well as decreased lung growth and function.

While particles less than 10 mm in diameter (PM10) pose certain health concern, particles less than 2.5 mm in diameter (PM2.5), referred to as "fine" particles, are believed to pose the largest health risks. Because of their small size (less than one-seventh the average width of a human hair), fine particles can lodge deeply into the lungs.

Exposure to PM2.5 increases the risk of cardiovascular and respiratory illnesses, and reduces life expectancy.

As some of the largest contributors to urban outdoor air pollution are industries, power generation and transport, the WHO points to improvements in urban planning and public transport, stronger emissions controls for motor vehicles and regulations for the industry which have been shown to improve air quality and health.

May Ajero, the Programme Manager at the Clean Air Initiative for Asian Cities Centre, told the Clean Air Forum that the Centre's mission is to promote better air quality and liveable cities by translating knowledge to policies and actions that reduce air pollution and greenhouse gas emissions from transport, energy and other sectors.

"We need to put air pollution back on the agenda," she said, "as it is a major issue with severe impacts on public health and contributes to climate change."

While Asia has measures in place to help bring down pollution, Ms. Ajero believes there are still plenty of opportunities to bring down pollution further, identifying diesel exhaust as a major problem as it has been identified as a cause of lung cancer.

She drew attention to a report last month (June 2012) by the International Agency for Research on Cancer (IARC) which has for more than two decades classified diesel engine exhaust as a "probable" carcinogen — a cancer-causing agent — but until recently there was no clear evidence linking it to higher cancer rates.

This winter, however, two studies in the US were published based on research involving more than 12,000 mine workers done by the National Cancer Institute and the National Institute for Occupational Safety and Health, known as the Diesel Exhaust in Miners Study, or DEMS.

According to a CNN report — referenced by Ms. Ajero — industry groups and clean-air advocates alike say recent improvements in diesel engines are dramatic, but older engines are still in widespread use.

Dr. Christopher Wild, the IARC director, said that while the US and Europe already have "stringent" guidelines on diesel fumes, there is "relatively little information about diesel exhaust in developing countries". Other scientists warn that cancer takes years or even decades to develop, meaning that people exposed to fumes in the past are still at risk.

The Clean Air Forum also saw the launch of a new initiative by SIIA to further draw attention to the problems of air pollution. It has established the Clean City Air Coalition, a partnership of various stakeholders to raise awareness of the impacts of air pollution to inform policy makers and private corporations as well as change behaviours of individuals and the broader society.

Nicholas Fang, Director of SIIA and one of moderators at the Clean Air Forum, felt that more needs to be done to raise public awareness of this issue, especially pertaining to sources of pollutants such as PM2.5 and NO_x (nitrous oxides). In 2011, the annual PM2.5 level remained the same as the year before (2010) while the annual PM10 level increased slightly, with both exceeding the WHO's Air Quality Guidelines.

Nicholas Fang had a series of articles on clean air and air pollution published in the *Today* paper in Singapore in 2012 and these can be assessed on the SIIA website. Here is the concluding paragraph from one of these:

"Singapore's prized clean air is well-known and a major draw for residents and foreigners. However, the future of good air quality in the city-state will remain uncertain if there is an over-emphasis on carbon emissions alone. The discussion and policies regarding clean air should not simply be restricted to carbon emissions but must also encompass other pollutants like nitrogen oxides and particulate matter."

In working towards raising awareness, the SIIA will continue to write commentaries on the clean city air issue and also has ambitious plans to ramp up online initiatives to reach out to the general population.

Sources

- www.wpro.who.int/topics/air_pollution
- www.cleanairinitiative.org
- www.siiaonline.org
- www.nea.gov.sg
- www.abccarbon.com

Photo by Nanbeidadao (2009) taken from WikiMedia Commons (CC BY 2.0): www.commons. wikimedia.org/wiki/File:Xinhui_%E6%96%B0%E6%9C%83%E5%9F%8E_%E5%B2%A1%E5%B7% 9E%E5%A4%A7%E9%81%93_Gangzhou_Dadao_fog_morning_%E7%BE%8E%E8%8F%AF%E7% 99%BE%E8%B2%A8_department_store_ads.JPG.

BEES

Race for Sustainability

27

What's the Buzz?
Bee Populations in
Decline and Elephants
Feel the Sting

Kannan   Chandran   asked me to write something in 2012 with a sustainability theme for his magazine Storm. I had read about the real problem with bee population decline, particularly in the US. And I also came across the fascinating, real-life research project in Africa on elephants damaging farmers' crops. Bees provided a very sustainable solution. So this article came together, with some additional enlightening information on the value of bees. Kannan is doing some great work through the magazine and the forums he organises. I just attended one (July 2013) on his "Sustainability — Keep it Going" theme. And to top this off, I came across "BEES", which turns out to be the name of the Burm and Emily's Elephant Sanctuary in Thailand...

Image adapted from BEES.

W hat's this got to do with air pollution? You may well ask. We never hear about a shortage of honey, and hence, have never had to envisage a shortage of bees, but these little critters are, in fact, at risk.

Scientists call the phenomenon the "colony collapse disorder" and research conducted in US states and Canada found 121 different pesticides in 887 samples of bees, wax, pollen and other elements of hives, lending credence to the notion of pesticides as a key problem.

"Silent Spring" All Over Again?

Albert Einstein reportedly said many years ago: "If the bee disappears from the surface of the earth, man would have no more than four years to live."

I wrote about this in my newsletter and in an article for the *Storm* Magazine. But I also couldn't resist re-telling a delightful story about how bees were used in a very productive way to prevent elephants from damaging farmer's crops in Africa. Here are two stories with a definite sustainability message — and about the importance of keeping bad stuff out of the air and land. Give bees a chance. We need them.

Elephants Feel the Sting

In Kenya, bees are called upon to do more than pollinate flowers and produce honey. They're also used to scare elephants. Elephants frequently raid farms searching for food, such as ripe tomatoes, potatoes and maize. To protect their livelihoods, some farmers have resorted to extreme measures, including poisoning and shooting elephants.

Based on research that showed elephants avoided African honey bees, experts were called in from Oxford University and the charity, Save the Elephants, to test whether beehives could prevent elephant-human conflict on farmland boundaries. Bee stings cannot penetrate an elephant's hide, but bees can and do get elephants around the eyes and even get into their trunks.

The bees in Kenya (*apis mellifera scutellata*) are small with short tongues and swarm frequently, making them a real fear factor for elephants. The test involved suspending beehives on wires between posts, with a traditional Kenyan-style thatched roof to protect them from the sun.

The team created "bee" boundaries for 17 farms, incorporating 170 beehives into 1,700 m of fencing.

The interlinked beehive fences not only stopped the elephants from raiding the farms but the farmers profited from selling honey to supplement their low incomes.

In 32 attempted raids over three crop seasons, only one bull elephant managed to penetrate the novel defences.

Conservationists now hope to roll out the scheme in other farming communities — a sustainable solution all around.

The Bee Population Is in Decline

We never hear about a shortage of honey, and hence, have never had to envisage a shortage of bees, but these little critters are, in fact, at risk.

In the winter of 2006, a strange phenomenon fell upon honeybee hives across the US. Without a trace, millions of bees vanished from their hives.

A precious pollinator of fruits and vegetables, the disappearing bees left billions of dollars of crops at risk and threatened the food supply. The epidemic set researchers scrambling to discover why honeybees were dying in record numbers — and to stop the epidemic in its tracks before it spreads further.

As this was happening, something Albert Einstein reportedly said many years ago came to the minds of many. He'd said: "If the bee disappears from the surface of the earth, man would have no more than four years to live."

Not many know how valuable bees are. More than one-third of our food supply relies upon bees for pollination, which is essential for the reproduction of plants that the bees service.

Without bees, the plants would have lost an important means to spread their pollen and reproduce. These plants are necessary for the survival of not just humans, but many other animals. If they are not pollinated, they will die, and so will the entire ecosystem eventually.

Bees are also a main food source for many species of birds and mammals, as are their by-products, honey and bees wax. Scientists generally agree that bees are among the most important animals in any ecosystem.

Whether Einstein said it or not, it does highlight the importance of bees and biodiversity, the environment and our reliance on bees to pollinate and produce the much needed food, in addition to honey.

Scientists call the phenomenon "colony collapse disorder" or CCD, and it has led to the disappearance of millions of adult bees and beehives.

According to the US Department of Agriculture, in late 2006, about a quarter of participating beekeepers in the US started reporting missing colonies amounting to an average bee loss of 32%. And the number of apiaries reporting CCD climbed to 36% from 2007 to 2008. In 2009 year, winter bee losses have dropped to 29%, while in the winter of 2010, reported losses stood at 34%.

"If the average loss is 20–25%, it's sustainable to maintain a bee business," said Dr. Eric Mussen, a honeybee expert at the University of California, Davis. "If it's much higher than that, you'll have to have some other income source."

The bee population decline is not a good sign. The UK's *Guardian* reports that the abundance of four common species of bumblebee in the US has dropped by 96% in just the past few decades. Scientists say that the alarming decline, which could have devastating implications for the pollination of both wild and farmed plants, could be a result of disease and low genetic diversity in bee populations.

Research conducted in 23 US states and Canada and published in the Public Library of Science journal found 121 different pesticides in 887 samples of bees, wax, pollen and other elements of hives, lending credence to the notion of pesticides as a key problem.

Awareness of the problem and funds for research could lead to solutions, but there is no getting away from the fact that the global bee population is in decline. In the US at least, that's a major problem.

Honey has been used by humans for centuries, but has honey ever been used to bring people together and raise awareness about the plight of the bees whose industriousness transforms nectar from flowers into the "food of the gods"?

That is the aim of the Honey Club, which launched in London's King's Cross. A collaboration between international brand consultants, Wolff Ollins, and charity, Global Generation, the club draws its members from businesses in the district. The club is about taking a hands-on, more grass-roots attitude to social responsibility, with the focus on sustainability.

To date, the club has installed two beehives which house some 100,000 bees on the roof of the Wolff Olins building. Working with young people from local schools, The Honey Club organises lectures, workshops and other events, with the mission to save bees.

The Guardian's sustainability manager, Hannah Judge-Brown, says: "Bees have a lot to teach us and the life of the healthy hive is rich in metaphors for the life of any healthy, sustainable community of people working together. There needs to be good morale for it to work, everyone has to have their purpose and work together to achieve the goal of the whole, being efficient in using resources and energy, and sharing the surplus."

Putting into practice a sustainable principle is what Phillips has in mind with the Urban Beehive. Like other products already on the market, it aims to provide a home solution for the shrinking number of bees.

As part of the Microbial Home design recently unveiled by the Dutch electric light and appliance company, the Urban Beehive essentially brings the hive into the home. It comprises an outdoor base which allows a flower pot to rest outside a window, with a bee entryway leading in to a tinted glass pod that houses a honeycomb frame on which the bees can do their thing. With many city dwellers trying their hand at beekeeping to help the bee cause, the Urban Beehive offers the latest way to do just that.

Race for Sustainability

See also: "World Without Bees", By Alison Benjam and Brian McCallum. Alison Benjamin is a *Guardian* journalist. She is deputy editor of Society and editor of the Environment website. Brian McCallum is studying to become an apiarist. They previously co-wrote "Keeping Bees and Making Honey".

Postscript on BEES

BEES — Burm and Emily's Elephant Sanctuary is a home for old, retired elephants. BEES gives elephants a chance to live free before their time runs out, according to the website of Wild Volunteer.

Located a 2.5 hour drive southwest of Chiang Mai through beautiful mountains and the countryside, you could find yourself having an experience like you have never imagined.

Sources

- www.storm.sg
- www.wildvolunteer.com
- www.elephantsandbees.com
- www.design.philips.com
- www.beebiology.ucdavis.edu
- www.guardianbookshop.co.uk

28

Profile — David Fogarty: Forest Carbon, REDD and DoubleHelix

David Fogarty and I have a few things in common: We have both spent a lot of time writing about climate change in recent years. We have also been keen to network and connect with others in the clean tech and clean energy field. I was a regular attender at Clean Tech Forums that David was instrumental in organising and hosting at Thomson Reuters in Singapore. He has produced some incredibly good investigative journalism and we focus on his best special reports covering the ups and downs of the forest carbon/avoided deforestation issue in Indonesia. I can say I was instrumental in getting him to examine the intriguing world of forest DNA and the work of DoubleHelix. That story is here too...

David is an international journalist whose 24-year career spans news-papers in Australia, London and Hong Kong and includes 19 years with *Reuters* in Asia. He started writing science articles, particularly on the nascent area of climate change, back in the late 1980s while he was still studying life sciences in university.

Most recently, he was *Reuters*' Climate Change Correspondent for Asia, focusing on the policy implications of climate policies on major business sectors, such as the palm oil sector, forestry and insurance.

David has led a number of investigative re-ports into palm oil corruption in Indonesia, including a firm that illegally cleared a large area of peat swamp, as well as timber conces-sion kickbacks in Sabah involving senior offi-cials, timber barons and international banks UBS and HSBC.

His in-depth environmental reporting has been submitted by *Reuters* to regional media awards over the past several years, including for 2013.

He is a very experienced editor and regional correspondent, able to handle anything from coups to natural disasters, currency and stock market meltdowns, to complex environmental policies and their business implications.

For over a decade, he was a senior desk editor for *Reuters* in Asia, based in Singapore, hand-ling news that ranged from the 1997 Asian financial crisis, the war on terror in Afgh-anistan, to the 2004 Indian Ocean quake and tsunami and the 2005–2006 birdflu crisis.

His work has been carried by media outlets globally, including *The New York Times*, *Chicago Tribune*, and online media, including *The Huffington Post*.

He has also built up a large number of contacts across many business sectors, non-governmental organisations (NGOs), specialist lawyers, governments as well as climate science and climate negotiators.

David, an Australian citizen and Singapore permanent resident, created Singapore-based Falling Apples Consultancy in 2013. There are lots of media consultancies, but few focus on organisations whose services tackle top environment and climate issues.

Here are three typical Fogarty stories for Reuters. The first about the DNA of trees; the second his Special Report on forest carbon in Indonesia (edited), and the third about a satisfactory outcome, enabling Indonesia to embark on its first UN-led scheme called Reducing Emissions from Deforestation and Degradation (REDD):

Call it CSI: Singapore

By David Fogarty for *Reuters* (19 August 2012)

Unlike the Crime Scene Investigators from the popular TV series, these detectives are hired to look for evidence of rogue wood from stores increasingly worried about being duped by a global trade in illegal timber now worth billions.

They take wood samples into their lab and put them through DNA tests that can pinpoint the species and origin of a piece of timber. They also track timber and timber products from forest to shop to ensure clients' shipments are legal.

"This is like CSI meets save the planet," says Jonathan Geach, executive director of DoubleHelix Tracking Technologies, the Singapore company that has developed and commercialised DNA testing for wood, the only firm in the world to do so.

Every two seconds, an area of forest the size of a football field is clear-cut by illegal loggers, the World Bank said in a recent study. Annually, such illegally cleared land is equivalent to the size of Ireland.

The money earned from a trade that Interpol estimates at up to US $30 billion annually is untaxed and often run by organised gangs to fund crime and conflict. The logging increases global warming with heightened carbon emissions and landslides through loss of watersheds. It causes loss of livelihoods in forest communities and dents global timber prices.

Until now, the battle against trade in illegal timber has been waged with regulations and preventive measures, and has not met with much success. Now it is increasingly focused on using the criminal justice system and law enforcement techniques.

Gibson Guitar Corp, which makes some of the world's most prized guitars, agreed on August 6 to pay a US $300,000 penalty after it admitted to possible illegal purchases of ebony from Madagascar.

Mislabeling, lying about origin or substituting one type of wood for another, have become common practices in the timber trade.

Industry officials say rapid advances and plunging costs for DNA testing of timber now make it commercially viable for companies trying to meet new regulations in the US and Europe against such practices.

Retailers such as Kingfisher, Marks & Spencer and Australian timber wholesaler Simmonds Lumber are either already using the technology or looking to add it to their existing timber sourcing practices.

The way forward

"We see this as the way forward," said Jamie Lawrence, sustainable forest and timber adviser for Kingfisher, Europe's largest home improvement retailer. Kingfisher has been using the services of DoubleHelix, as it is known, on an ad-hoc basis to unmask cases of possible timber fraud in their supply chains, he said.

A laboratory run by Andrew Lowe, the chief scientific officer at Double-Helix and one of the world's top plant geneticists, is the frontline in the global fight against illegal logging.

It was at his laboratory at the University of Adelaide in South Australia that the method of extracting DNA taken from a log, a table or even flooring was refined — the breakthrough needed to commercialise testing for timber importers, home improvement stores and law enforcement agencies.

Trees, like people, have a unique DNA, said Lowe.

"The DNA is in every cell in a wood product and you can't falsify that DNA," he told *Reuters* in an interview.

By early 2011, Lowe was able to extract degraded DNA from decades-old wood and get accurate results. That led to an increase in business and DoubleHelix has 14 clients directly using their services, with most testing done in Adelaide.

In 2004, Lowe and colleagues extracted DNA from the oak timbers of King Henry VIII's flagship the Mary Rose, which sank in 1545 and was salvaged in 1982.

When DoubleHelix opened shop in 2008, the DNA story was a hard sell. But as new US laws started to bite over the past two years, and with tougher laws set for Europe in 2013, the number of clients is growing, says Kevin Hill, DoubleHelix's founder.

Building databases

While DNA testing per se is extremely accurate due to the unique DNA signature each species has, it has a major limitation to overcome — an incomplete global map of tree genetics.

Constructing such a map is crucial because DNA for each species changes subtly from one area to another, acting like a postcode that can be used to determine a sample's origin.

Going into a forest to take DNA samples across a species' entire range is costly and time-consuming. Building a database for teak, for instance, would cost about $1 million.

At present, databases exist for 20 tree species, mostly valuable tropical timbers, and is growing annually.

On the other hand, Kingfisher's B&Q home improvement stores carry 16,000 timber related products. For consumers, it is a bewildering choice of goods. For the illegal timber gangs, it is an opportunity for wood laundering.

Kingfisher has progressively put in place tougher checks of its timber sources to ensure all wood comes from sustainably managed forests.

Race for Sustainability

They use chain of custody certification schemes to follow the timber from forest to shop, but these are not foolproof and illegal timber occasionally slips in.

The weakest link in timber supplies is between the forest and the sawmill, where stolen timber can be added to legitimate wood. In sawmill yards, too, logs from illegally cleared forests can be mixed with legal timber. DNA testing can overcome this, say DoubleHelix and their oldest customer, Simmonds Lumber, one of Australia's largest timber importers.

Simmonds imports merbau, a much-sought-after hardwood, from Indonesia, where illegal logging accounts for nearly half the timber cut in Indonesia, according to the World Bank study.

Using DoubleHelix's system, each shipment of merbau logs is tracked from forest to sawmill by taking DNA samples to ensure no other timber has been added. These DNA samples are then matched up with pallets of finished timber decking from the sawmill to Simmonds' warehouse in Australia.

The curse of stolen timber

As a forklift loads pallets of decking into a container at a sawmill near Surabaya, Indonesia, Paul Elsmore, Simmonds' former chief executive and now a consultant to the Australian firm, explains that each container-load is worth around $45,000.

The cost of DNA testing and verification services was $250 for a container, equal to about 0.5% of the wood's value.

DoubleHelix says the ultimate goal is to make DNA testing so cheap all companies will do it.

Doing so would help tackle one of the perversities of the illegal timber trade: An abundance of stolen timber depresses prices, slashes margins and can deter investing in better due diligence of their wood supplies.

Arguably, the biggest push for DNA testing are new laws in the US, Europe and possibly Australia, which will make it easier to prosecute timber criminals.

Lawrence at Kingfisher said better wood forensics just makes sense.

"Any retailer worth their salt should not just be thinking about risk, brand protection or even legality. They should be thinking this is a damn good idea."

Special Report: How Indonesia Hurt Its Climate Change Project

By David Fogarty for *Reuters* (16 August 2011)

In July 2010, US investor Todd Lemons and Russian energy giant Gazprom believed they were just weeks from winning final approval for a landmark forest preservation project in Indonesia.

A year later, the project is close to collapse, a casualty of labyrinthine Indonesian bureaucracy, opaque laws and a secretive palm oil company.

The Rimba Raya project, on the island of Borneo, is part of a UN-backed scheme designed to reward poorer nations that protect their carbon-rich jungles.

Deep peat in some of Indonesia's rainforests stores billions of tonnes of carbon, so preserving those forests is regarded as crucial in the fight against climate change.

By putting a value on the carbon, the 90,000 ha (225,000 acre) project would help prove that investors can turn a profit from the world's jungles in ways that do not involve cutting them down.

After three years of work, more than $2 million in development costs, and what seemed like the green light from Jakarta, the project is proof that saving the world's tropical rainforests will be far more complicated than simply setting up a framework to allow market forces to function.

A *Reuters* investigation into the case also shows the forestry ministry is highly skeptical about a market for forest carbon credits, placing it at odds with President Susilo Bambang Yudhoyono, who supports pay-and-preserve investments to fight climate change.

Hong Kong-based Lemons, 47, a veteran of environmentally sustainable and profitable projects, discovered just how frustrating the ministry can be to projects such as his.

"Success was literally two months around the corner," he said. "We went through — if there are 12 steps, we went through the first 11 on time over a two-year period. We had some glitches, but by and large we went through the rather lengthy and complicated process in the time expected."

That's when the forestry ministry decided to slash the project's area in half, making it unviable, and handing a large chunk of forested deep peatland to a palm oil company for development.

The case is a stark reminder to Norway's government, the world's top donor to projects to protect tropical forests, on just how tough it will be to preserve Indonesia's rainforests under its $1 billion climate deal with Jakarta.

Unlimited corruption

The dispute has turned a spotlight on Indonesia's forestry ministry, which earns $15 billion a year in land permit fees from investors. Indonesia's Corruption Eradication Commission (KPK) said last month it will investigate the granting of forest permits and plans to crack down on corruption in the resources sector.

"It's a source of unlimited corruption," said Chandra M. Hamzah, deputy chairman at the KPK.

Indonesia Corruption Watch, a private watchdog, says illegal logging and violations in issuing forest use permits are rampant. It estimates ill-gotten gains total about 20 trillion rupiah ($2.3 billion) each year.

A forest ministry official connected with the UN-backed forest carbon offset scheme was sentenced in April to three years in prison for accepting a $10,000 bribe to ensure an Indonesian company won a procurement tender.

Wandojo Siswanto was one of the negotiators for Indonesia's delegation at the 2009 UN climate talks in Copenhagen, despite being a bribery suspect. His case has highlighted concerns about the capacity of the forestry ministry to manage forest-carbon projects.

The forestry sector has a long history of mismanagement and graft. Former trade and industry minister Bob Hasan, a timber czar during the Suharto years, was fined 50 billion rupiah ($7 million) for ordering the burning of forests in Sumatra and then imprisoned in a separate case of forestry fraud after Suharto was toppled from power in 1998.

In an interview in Jakarta, senior forestry ministry officials denied any wrongdoing in the Rimba Raya case and criticised the project's backers for a deal they made with Russia's Gazprom, the world's largest gas producer, to market the project's carbon credits.

Showcase project

The Rimba Raya project was meant to save a large area of carbon-rich peat swamp forest in Central Kalimantan province and showcase Jakarta's efforts to fight climate change.

Much of the area is dense forest that lies atop oozy black peat flooded by tea-colored water. Dozens of threatened or endangered species such as orangutans, proboscis monkeys, otter civets and Borneo bay cats live in the area, which is adjacent to a national park.

Rimba Raya was designed to be part of the UN's REDD programme. The idea is simple: Every tonne of carbon locked away in the peat and soaked up by the trees would earn a steady flow of carbon credits. Profit from the sale of those credits would go to project investors and partners, local communities and the Indonesian government. That would allow the project to pay its way and compete with palm oil farmers and loggers who might otherwise destroy it.

Rich countries and big companies can buy the credits to offset their emissions.

By preserving a large area of peat swamp forest, Rimba Raya was projected to cut carbon emissions by nearly 100 million tonnes over its 30-year life, which would translate into total saleable credits of about $500 million, Gazprom says.

It would also be a sanctuary for orphaned or rehabilitated orangutans from elsewhere in Borneo. Rimba Raya teamed up with the founder of Orangutan Foundation International (OFI), Birute Mary Galdikas, in which OFI would receive a steady income from annual carbon credit sales.

It was the sort of project President Yudhoyono and Norway have pledged to support. Yudhoyono has put forests — Indonesia is home to the world's third largest forest lands — at the centre of a pledge to reduce greenhouse gas emissions by at least 26% by 2020.

He tasked a senior adviser to press for reforms to make REDD projects easier and for greater transparency at the forestry ministry.

In June last year (2010), Forestry Minister Zulkifli Hasan asked for a map that would set the final boundary of the project, according to a copy of the instruction seen by *Reuters*. This mandatory step normally takes a few weeks. Once the map is issued, a project is eligible for a license to operate.

But by September last year it was clear something was wrong, according to Lemons. Despite repeated promises by ministry officials, the final map had not been issued. No explanations were given.

On 31 December 2010, PT Best was granted 6,500 ha of peat swamp land for palm oil development, next to a smaller parcel of deep peatland granted a year earlier — part of PT Best's broader plan to connect its palm oil plantations in the north with a port on the coast nearby. The land granted last December was part of the original area set aside for Rimba Raya.

The December allocation to PT Best came despite assurances from Forestry Minister Hasan that he would not allow deep peatlands to be converted for agriculture.

The allocation also came a day before a two-year moratorium on issuing licenses to clear primary forests and peatlands was due to start on 1 January 2011. The moratorium is a key part of the climate deal with Norway.

After months of delay, the forestry ministry finally ruled that PT Rimba Raya was only eligible for 46,000 ha, a decision that cut out much of the peatlands covering nearly half the original project area.

Ombudsman investigates

The case has now been brought before the office of the Indonesian government's Ombudsman. In an interview, senior Ombudsman Dominikus Fernandes told *Reuters* he believed the forestry ministry should issue the license to Rimba Raya.

"If Rimba Raya has already fulfilled the criteria, there should not be a delay in issuing the license," he said.

"This is a model project in Indonesia that should be prioritised. If we don't give an example on the assurance of investing in Indonesia, that's not a good thing."

Officials from the forestry ministry, in a lengthy interview with *Reuters*, said the area was given legally for palm oil development because PT Best had claims to the land dating back to 2005.

Hadi Daryanto, Secretary-General of the ministry, stressed the peatland areas originally granted to Rimba Raya were on a type of forest called convertible production forest, which can be used for agriculture but not REDD projects. Handing that nearly 40,000 ha to Rimba Raya would be against the law, he said.

Yet in 2009, the ministry was ordered to make the title switch for this same area of peatland so it could be used for a REDD project. The instruction to immediately make the switch, a bureaucratic formality, was never acted on.

In the October 2009 decree seen by *Reuters*, former Forestry Minister H.M.S. Kaban issued the order as part of a broader instruction setting aside the nearly 90,000 ha for ecosystem restoration projects. Kaban left office soon after.

Indonesian law also bans any clearing of peatlands more than 3 m deep. An assessment of the Rimba Raya area by a peat expert hired by InfiniteEARTH showed the peat is 3 to 7 m deep, so in theory it was out of bounds for PT Best to clear for agriculture.

In a letter dated June 16 to the Indonesian government, the Russian firm criticised the ministry's failure to issue the license for Rimba Raya and threatened to abandon clean-energy projects in Indonesia estimated to be worth more than $100 million in foreign investment. The government has yet to respond.

Carbon dreams?

Secretary-General Daryanto and Iman Santoso, Director-General for forestry business management, said another major problem was InfiniteEARTH's deal with Gazprom, which was made in the absence of any license.

"We didn't know about the contract with Gazprom. They had no legal right to make the contract," Daryanto told *Reuters*.

Santoso described it as the project's "fatal mistake."

Gazprom became involved, he said, because it was a project that looked to have official support. The Russian company agreed to a financing mechanism that ensured the project's viability for 30 years, regardless of the price level of carbon markets.

Those markets, centered on the European and UN carbon trading programs, were valued at $142 billion in 2010, the World Bank says. National carbon trading schemes are planned for Australia and South Korea, while California is planning a state-based scheme from 2013. NZ's carbon market started in 2008.

"If you ever want a successful REDD scheme, you are going to have to have a process that people believe in," Gazprom's Dan Barry said.

"The Ministry of Forestry ought to be doing everything it can to support a programme that benefits forestry as opposed to favouring a programme that's there to cut it down and turn it into palm oil."

"Ahead of its time"

Kuntoro Mangkusubroto, the head of the REDD task force in Indonesia who is also in charge of the president's government reforms unit, said the Rimba Raya case highlighted deep flaws in the bureaucracy and the need for sweeping reforms to underpin the 40 other REDD projects in Indonesia.

Legal action is a path Lemons and his business partner Jim Procanik may eventually take but for now they have proposed a land swap deal with PT Best in which the firm gives PT Rimba Raya 9,000 ha of peatland in return for a similar-sized piece of non-peatland held by PT Rimba Raya in the north of the project near other PT Best landholdings.

PT Best rejected an earlier offer by Rimba Raya of 9% of the credits from the project, Lemons said.

Based on recent satellite images, PT Best has yet to develop the disputed 9,000 ha area.

The delays mean it is too late for Rimba Raya to become the world's first project to issue REDD credits. That accolade has since gone to a Kenyan project.

"Our whole point here is to show host countries that REDD can pay its way," said Lemons. "And if it can't pay its way, then we haven't proven anything."

In a sign that a resolution could still be possible, Ombudsman Fernandes, Forestry Minister Hasan and PT Rimba Raya are scheduled to meet on 19 August.

Indonesia Approves Landmark Forest Protection Project

By David Fogarty for *Reuters* (5 December 2012)

Indonesia on Wednesday approved a rainforest conservation project that sets aside an area roughly the size of Singapore and rewards investors with tradable carbon credits in the first of its kind to win formal backing in the country.

Four years in the making, the Rimba Raya Biodiversity Reserve will protect nearly 80,000 ha (200,000 acres), much of it carbon-rich peat swamp forest at risk of being felled for palm oil plantations.

Russian energy giant Gazprom and German insurance firm Allianz are backers of the project, the world's first on deep peat.

A senior Indonesian official announced the approval on the sidelines of UN climate talks in Doha, Qatar. Forestry Minister Zulkifli Hasan signed a letter last week saying the project had passed all the key steps. *Reuters* has seen a copy.

"We hope projects like Rimba Raya will lead the way in proving that conservation can address the rural development needs of the communities and also preserve our forests for generations to come," Hasan said in a statement.

Indonesia has the world's third largest expanse of tropical forests but these are disappearing quickly in the rush to grow more food and exploit timber and mineral wealth. Forest clearance is a major source of greenhouse gases.

By saving the forest and locking away planet-warming carbon, investors such as Gazprom will receive carbon credits they can sell for profit or use to cut their own emissions. Money from credit sales will also fund local livelihood projects.

The project area, in Central Kalimantan province on Borneo island, is brimming with rare animal species and adjoins a national park. It is designed to be a sanctuary for endangered orangutans.

Rimba Raya is part of a UN-led scheme called REDD. The aim is to show forests can pay for themselves and compete with powerful palm oil, mining and timber interests.

"This is a small but significant step in terms of contributing to the government's efforts to reduce carbon emissions and showing that larger volumes of forest carbon credits can be sold to credible buyers," said Andrew Wardell, programme director, forests and governance, at the Center for International Forestry Research in Indonesia.

But he said REDD projects remain costly to develop and validate.

Over Rimba Raya's 30-year life, the project will generate about 104 million credits, each representing a metric ton (1.1023 tons) of carbon. In total, that equates to 300 million to 500 million euros ($390 million to $650 million) based on current market rates for REDD carbon offsets.

————◄◦►————

Sources

- www.reuters.com
- www.abccarbon.com
- www.fallingapplesconsultants.com
- www.doublehelixtracking.com

Resourceful
Management of
Waste

Section 8

29

Adding Waste to the Climate-Water-Energy Nexus

This article was written to draw attention to issues and help promote the CleanEnviro Summit Singapore, held in July 2012 — and due again in 2014 — at the Marina Bay Sands. It was in a series of articles around waste, waste management, waste to energy and recycling which appeared on the CleanEnviro Summit website and in other places, including Green Prospects Asia, Eco Business.com and **abc carbon express***, drawing on some useful "Waste to Asia" studies by Responsible Research…*

Photo by Michael Coghlan (2013) taken from WikiMedia Commons (CC BY-SA 2.0): www.commons.wikimedia.org/wiki/File:Impromptu_Rubbish_Dump_(8408779543).jpg.

N
o longer can waste be viewed as a problem on its own. It is a critical component in the climate, water, and energy nexus.

Water problems in many parts of the world are chronic and, without a crackdown on waste, will worsen as demand for food rises and climate change intensifies.

Reducing waste is a simple way to cut stress on the environment while easing pressure on farmers, who will be called on to feed an expected nine billion people around the world in 2050, versus nearly seven billion today.

Responsible waste management drives sustainability, a prerequisite for continued economic progress in Asia.

The urban areas of Asia now spend about US$25 billion on solid waste management per year and this figure will increase to at least US$50 billion by 2025.

Asian waste companies are active in developing energy recovery systems such as landfill gas capture, incineration plants and biogas extraction units.

In 2011, the world generated an estimated two billion tons of Municipal Solid Waste (MSW). Although more than 800 thermal Waste-to-Energy (WTE) plants currently operate in nearly 40 countries around the globe, these facilities treated just 11% of the waste generated worldwide compared to the 70% that was landfilled.

Drawing attention to the massive problem of waste in the world, National Environment

Agency (NEA) Chief Executive Officer Andrew Tan said the first Clean-Enviro Summit in Singapore from 1–4 July 2012 brought together people, companies and countries with waste management problems as well as solutions, including those with experience in WTE.

With the theme "Innovative Clean Enviro-Solutions for Asia's Growing Cities", CleanEnviro Summit, along with WasteMET Asia (a trade exhibition) was held together with the Singapore International Water Week and World Cities Summit.

According to recent studies undertaken by Pike Research[1], WTE encompasses thermal and biological conversion technologies that unlock the usable energy stored in MSW to generate electricity and heat.

Population growth, urbanisation, and rising standards of living are expected to drive this number higher, increasing global demand for WTE solutions. Already in the midst of scaling up capacity, growth in China is expected to shift the centre of the WTE universe away from Europe to Asia Pacific.

High upfront capital costs and attractive economics for landfilling, according to Pike Research, represent persistent barriers to widespread adoption. Although combustion technologies continue to dominate the market, advanced thermal treatment (ATT) technology deployments such as pyrolysis are expected to pick up as diminishing landfill capacity improves WTE economics.

No longer can waste be viewed as a problem on its own. It is a critical component in the climate, water and energy nexus. This is one very good reason why the CleanEnviro Summit Singapore climate made its debut with the Singapore International Water Week and World Cities Summit.

"Water problems in many parts of the world are chronic and, without a crackdown on waste, will worsen as demand for food rises and climate change intensifies." This is from the UN highlighting the linkage of waste and water in March this year (2012) on the eve of a six-day gathering on world water issues.

Focusing on world water issues, the UN said many daunting challenges lie ahead, including providing clean water and sanitation to the poor, feeding a world population set to rise from seven billion to nine billion by 2050 and coping with the impact of global warming.

"Pressures on freshwater are rising, from the expanding needs of agriculture, food production and energy consumption to pollution and the weaknesses of water management," UN Secretary General Ban Ki-moon said in the report.

From Takeaway to Throwaway Food

A report from the Reuters Global Food and Agriculture Summit in Chicago (also in March 2012) cast a spotlight on the finding that an estimated 30 to 50% of the food produced globally goes to waste.

The average American throws away about 33 lbs (that's 15 kg) of food each month which adds up to 396 lbs (or 178 kg) in lost groceries a year, according to the Natural Resources Defense Council.

In 2010 alone, 33 million tons of food that could have been eaten, ended up in landfills and incinerators across the US, according to the US Environmental Protection Agency.

But the impact of food waste stretches far beyond the kitchen.

To begin with, agriculture is the world's largest user of water, a big consumer of energy and chemicals and major emitter of greenhouse gases during production, distribution and landfill decay.

Hence, experts say reducing waste is a simple way to cut stress on the environment while easing pressure on farmers, who will be called on to feed an expected nine billion people around the world in 2050, versus nearly seven billion today.

Solid Waste Management in Asia

The urban areas of Asia now spend about US$25 billion on solid waste management per year and this figure will increase to at least US$50 billion by 2025.

Every country or region within Asia has its own background and characteristics in relation to solid waste management and material-cycle policy, even though they share the same global region, according to the International Review for Environmental Strategies (www.enviroscope.iges.or.jp).

MSW generation ranges between 0.5 kg and 1.4 kg per capita per day in all countries and regions within Asia (with the exception of China).

Organic Matter — Main Component of MSW in Asia

Landfill is the most common disposal option used in many Asian countries because it is inexpensive.

"Waste in Asia"[2], a comprehensive survey conducted by Responsible Research in 2011, examined the environmental, social and governance (ESG) issues in the waste sector in Asia.

It found that "responsible waste management drives sustainability, a prerequisite for continued economic progress in Asia".

The report also pointed out that "hazardous waste management in Asia requires urgent action to keep up with expanding industrial activity".

In some cases they noted there were "deficient environmental regulations and poor enforcement in developing Asia, resulting in the illegal dumping of waste by industrial generators, devastating the environment and also reducing business opportunities for hazardous waste treatment companies".

Responsible Research identifies a paradigm shift in Asia's waste sector:

- waste as a source of renewable energy rather than a problem to be hidden;
- evolved from simple collect and dispose models to technology-driven treatment systems that convert waste into thermal power; and
- while landfill remains the dominant method of waste disposal, energy recovery systems that can reduce the final amount of waste for landfill disposal are gaining in popularity throughout the region.

Asian waste companies are active in developing energy recovery systems, such as landfill gas capture, incineration plants and biogas extraction units.

"Waste in Asia" also drew attention to the fact that waste should be seen as a renewable energy which creates new opportunities through climate change projects and companies can seek financial assistance via the sale of carbon credits for waste projects that reduce greenhouse gas emissions.

Endnotes

1. This Pike Research report analyses the global market opportunity for WTE across three key technology segments: combustion, gasification, and anaerobic digestion. The report provides a comprehensive assessment of the demand drivers, business models, policy factors, and technology issues associated with the rapidly-growing market for WTE. (www.pikeresearch.com)
2. The executive summary of the "Waste to Asia" report by Responsible Research can be downloaded from www.responsibleresearch.com.

Sources

- www.cleanenvirosummit.sg
- www.greenprospectsasia.com
- www.abccarbon.com
- www.eco-business.com

30

Aiming for a Zero Waste Future

Zero Waste is more than a concept. It is a very active global campaign to get people to think and act differently. "Dream, the impossible dream" might well be the words on many lips even with the mention of the term "Zero Waste". That was how I referred to it in my newsletter and when this article was written at the time of the CleanEnviro Summit in Singapore (July 2012). It was also published on the Australia online newsletter Eco Voice, which reaches out to many readers who have already started to embrace Zero Waste...

Waste is one of the major threats impacting the health of the planet and all life on it, but even the various strategies which have been implemented to manage it produce adverse side effects on the environment and people.

Zero Waste has come to be touted as the solution to a more sustainable way to treating waste by taking a cradle-to-grave approach in managing resources.

This article looks into the status of Zero Waste as an approach and as a solution. At the same time, drawing attention to the CleanEnviro Summit Singapore, which began exploring issues and opportunities to deal with waste, pollution, recycling and environment problems globally.

Is Zero Waste a pipedream or is it the approach all countries and cities must take to deal with the global health and environment problems associated with mountains of waste?

Questions like this are being asked in many countries round the world and at global forums in Rio and Singapore.

"Dream, the impossible dream" might well be the words on many lips even with the mention of the term "Zero Waste".

Surely, such a concept is beyond the realms of possibility and practicality. The world is too far mired in the mess of waste to seriously consider eliminating it.

Yet many believe in it and many more are putting into practice Zero Waste programmes around the world. Zero Waste is taking hold in Europe (most notably Italy), 30 states and cities in North America as well as in Asia, with Philippines leading the way, followed by Japan and India.

Australia is an early mover for Zero Waste, but coming out ahead is NZ which became the first country in the world to adopt a national policy of Zero Waste in 2002.

The vision "Towards Zero Waste and a Sustainable NZ" resulted from an extensive, community-led campaign that has so far (mid 2012) resulted in 38 of NZ's 74 local authorities adopting Zero Waste targets. (www.zerowaste.co.nz)

So what is Zero Waste all about?

Simply put, "implementing Zero Waste will eliminate all discharges to land, water or air that may be a threat to planetary, human, animal or plant health", according to the Zero Waste International Alliance.

It is a whole-system approach to addressing the problem of society's unsustainable resource flows.

It encompasses:

- waste elimination at source through product design and producer responsibility;
- waste reduction strategies further down the supply chain;
- introduction of cleaner production methods; and
- effective product dismantling, recycling, re-use as well as composting.

Communities that implement Zero Waste strategies are aiming to switch from wasteful and damaging waste disposal methods to value-added resource recovery systems that will help build sustainable local economies.

As such, Zero Waste is in complete opposition to landfilling and incineration.

The Zero Waste International Alliance was pushing for the UN to endorse a resolution recognising a universal definition of Zero Waste during the Rio + 20 UN Conference on Sustainable Development (June 2012).

The resolution declared, among other things, that voluntary recycling goals haven't cut waste enough. It says that the placement of materials in waste disposal facilities such as landfills and waste-to-energy plants causes damage to human health, wastes natural resources and/or transfers liabilities to future generations.

The alliance was requesting the UN to adopt the definition of Zero Waste that it developed, which basically calls for "no burn or bury".

Coming hot on the heels of the Rio Conference was the Clean Environment Leaders' Summit (CELS), one of the three pillar events of the Clean-Enviro Summit Singapore (1–4 July 2012), where Zero Waste was one of the serious issues and opportunities on the agenda.

The Summit was a gathering the world's top environment leaders from the public and private sectors, international organisations and think-tanks, to discuss and help develop sustainable environmental management solutions.

The Zero Waste International Alliance has been established to promote positive alternatives to landfill and incineration and to raise community awareness of the social and economic benefits to be gained when waste is regarded as a resource base upon which both employment and business opportunities can be built.

The next CleanEnviro Summit is scheduled for 1–4 June 2014.

————◄○►————

Sources

- www.cleanenvirosummit.sg
- www.zwia.org
- www.ecovoice.com.au
- www.abccarbon.com

31

Effective Waste-to-Energy Technologies

*This article was originally written as part of the run-up to the Clean-Enviro Summit Singapore in July 2012. It was also published online and in print by Green Prospects Asia and **abc carbon express**, among others. It explores the global trend towards waste-to-energy, and highlights some of the large-scale and innovative schemes to deal with waste as a resource — not something to throw away. Like making the most of biomass and algae — even to power aircraft — British Airways decided to use municipal waste for jet fuel "in the air", hence the SOLENA aircraft image above...*

Photo Credit: Photo courtesy of Solena Fuels.

In a land-scarce urban society like Singapore, waste-to-energy (WTE) plants offer the best solution, by reducing waste volume efficiently to conserve landfill space and also contribute significantly to resource recovery. Along with waste minimisation and recycling, it is a key component of the city state's integrated solid waste management system.

Singapore has found that WTE incineration is the most cost-effective option too: It can reduce waste volume by over 90%. In 1978, the first WTE plant was opened and today the solid waste disposal infrastructure consists of 4 WTE plants (Tuas, Senoko, Tuas South and Keppel Seghers Tuas), and the Semakau Landfill.

Singapore is not alone. WTE technologies are seen globally as economical, near-term solutions for producing base-load electric power, meeting renewable energy targets and cutting greenhouse gas emissions.

WTE technologies convert chemical energy stored in residues associated with human activities into heat, steam and electricity. Primary fuel sources include municipal solid waste (MSW) and other materials diverted from disposal facilities, as well as gases rich in methane generated when organic substances decompose in the absence of oxygen.

Globally, WTE capacity has grown greatly in recent years, according to the Electric Power Research Institute, driven largely by policy considerations. In 1999, the EU directive banned the landfilling of combustible MSW fractions to control methane emissions, avoid un-productive use of land and other resources, and prevent water and soil contamination.

In Europe, Asia and elsewhere, such policies — along with climate change mitigation and renewable energy targets — have motivated the construction of hundreds of mass-burn incinerators, the early commercial application of various advanced thermal conversion technologies, and the proliferation of smaller-scale landfill gas and digester gas systems.

Frequently, these WTE plants supply heat or are combined heat and power (CHP) facilities; in fact, 18% of the district heating load in Denmark is served by MSW combustion.

Advanced biofuels that use waste feedstocks to deliver a low-carbon footprint and do not compete with food crops are entering a critical stage of development as a number of new facilities prepare to enter service.

Here's a glimpse at some current developments in WTE around the world:

Anaerobic Digestion and Biogas Facility in California

Construction has started on a commercial-scale anaerobic digestion (AD) and biogas facility in California that could fuel 80 buses a year. Clean World's organic waste recycling centre in Sacramento will convert 25 tonnes of food waste per day, collected by Atlas Disposal from food processing companies, restaurants and supermarkets, into renewable natural gas. The facility will be able to process 100 tonnes of waste daily, which will make it the largest commercial-scale, high solids AD system in the US.

Vehicle Fuel from Organic Waste in the Philippines

London-based Gazasia will develop a vehicle fuel made from organic waste products from landfills. It has signed an agreement with the Philippine power, financial services and food group, Aboitiz Equity Ventures, that secured US$150 million for creating liquid biomethane from organic waste. By refining natural gas from landfill, Gazasia will produce liquid biomethane: a carbon-neutral, sustainable and high-quality vehicle fuel.

160 Million Euro French Algae Biofuel Project from Wastes

In France, the Institut National de la Recherche Agronomique has launched Green Stars, a 160 million euro collaborative platform to develop efficient biofuels and high value-added substances from microalgae feeding on nutrients found in waste and industrial emissions of CO_2. Led by

INRA in collaboration with 45 partners, Green Stars aims to have, by 2016, industrial prototypes based on advanced technologies to build a viable economic and environmental model.

Canadian Biofuels Firm Prepares for Construction

Canadian CORE BioFuel has selected French engineering and project management firm Technip for the construction of its first wood-to-gasoline biorefinery. This will fuse proven industrial equipment and processes in a new and efficient way, to produce 67 million litres of renewable gasoline and over 20 million litres of water yearly from wood waste.

Green Diesel from Scrap Tyres Using Slow Pyrolysis

Pyrolysis creates renewable fuels by degrading waste tyres in a high-temperature, oxygen-starved environment. Diesel fuel is the primary by-product, synthetic gas (syngas) is a secondary benefit. Some syngas is then used to fuel engines or gas/steam turbines and drive generators to power the facility. Energime has verbally commited to 1,200 tonnes of tyres weekly for this facility and is negotiating further tyre feedstock agreements, including a source that will supply about 100,000 tonnes annually.

British Airways to Get Jet Fuel from London Rubbish

Solena and British Airways have partnered to build Europe's first sustainable jet fuel plant. Located in East London, close to municipal waste sources, the plant is expected to create 200 jobs when fully operational in 2014. Solena, a renewable energy technology company based in Washington DC, offers a pathway to sustainable aviation fuels by converting waste biomass into fuels, renewable energy and heat.

———◦———

Sources

- www.cleanenvirosummit.sg
- www.greenprospectsasia.com
- www.solenafuels.com
- www.waste-management-world.com

32

Profile — Douglas Woodring: How Can Oceans Cope with Plastic Waste?

This article was originally written for, and published on, the CleanEnviro Summit website as a lead up to the 2012 event. While it quotes Doug Woodring extensively — and I've added a biographical piece here — I did not have the pleasure of meeting the man until the recent Carbon War Room event in Singapore (May 2013). Here's a man who is so committed and works tirelessly to draw attention to a very serious environmental problem, through the organisation he set up, Ocean Recovery Alliance. Get plastic out of the oceans and put it to good use. It can be recycled. It is a resource...

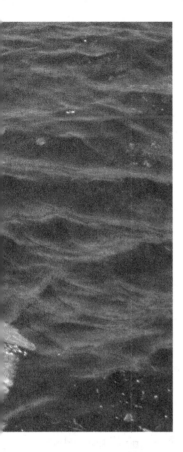

Photo of Douglas Woodring by Donald Chiu and Ocean Recovery Alliance.

Plastic has become one of the biggest waste pollution problems of our age. Even though all plastics can be recycled, there are serious environmental consequences for throwing them away. Put simply, the ever-increasing volume of plastic trash is causing major problems on land and at sea.

As Douglas Woodring, founder of the Ocean Recovery Alliance, says: "Only 27% of plastic bottles are recycled, while 73% end up in the landfill or the ocean."

Already, over 10% of fish tested in our oceans contain pollutants from plastic in their tissue. Woodring sees the growing plastic waste stream as a resource worth capturing and channelling into products that enhance life, rather than degrade it.

Ocean Recovery Alliance hosted Plasticity Rio '12 on June 21, 2012, alongside the UN Conference on Sustainable Development. Plasticity Rio '12 explored opportunities that can transform the way that plastic is designed, used and reused.

"Plastic is one of the materials that links almost all of our companies and industries to the ocean and our environment. By focusing on the newest technologies and innovations in design, packaging, materials, recovery, recycling and re-use, we will be able to showcase where leaders are going in this space and how great improvements can be made in reducing the environmental impact."

A cosmetics maker from the UK is the first business to agree to measure its "plastic footprint", using tools developed by the Plastic Disclosure Project (PDP).

"If you don't measure something, you can't manage it," explains Doug Woodring, founder of the international project launched at the 2011 Clinton Global Initiative. As a first step toward plastic reduction, PDP encourages companies to calculate their baseline footprint by tallying their use of plastics for manufacturing, packaging, and shipping.

The UN Environment Programme (UNEP) is most concerned with-marine debris — much of it plastic. This came from UNEP's Executive Director Achim Steiner:

"Marine debris — trash in our oceans — is a symptom of our throwaway society and our approach to how we use our natural resources. It affects every country and every ocean, and shows us in highly visible terms the urgency of shifting towards a low-carbon, resource-efficient green economy as nations prepare for Rio+20 in 2012."

"However, one community or one country acting in isolation will not be the answer. We need to address marine debris collectively across national boundaries and with the private sector, which has a critical role to play both in reducing the kinds of wastes that can end up in the world's oceans, and through research into new materials. It is by bringing all these players together that we can truly make a difference."

Plastic Is Not Food for Fish

There is little doubt that plastic in the oceans is responsible for the deaths of millions of sea animals. Plastic bottles floating on the surface of the oceans can look like food to larger sea life — often with fatal consequences. In addition, fish, sea birds, and other ocean creatures often get caught in plastic rings that strangle them or constrict their throats so that they cannot swallow.

Plastic is a major pollution problem everywhere, but in the US alone, people throw away 2.5 million plastic bottles an hour. Plastic is one of the most disposable materials in the US culture. Plastic makes up much of the street-side litter found in cities and throughout the countryside, and it's rapidly filling up our landfills as well.

Making new plastic requires significant amounts of fossil fuels. Studies suggest that between 7% and 8% of the world's fossil fuels are used in producing new plastics. Recycling could preserve these fuels — even reuse them in other markets.

Surprisingly, perhaps, plastic is easy to recycle. In fact, all plastic can be recycled. Some studies show that only 10% of plastic bottles created are recycled, leaving that extra 90% to take up space in landfills and in oceans, killing ocean life.

Plastic bottles take up space in landfills. Plastic bottles make up approximately 11% of the contents of landfills. And many coastal cities use the ocean as a dumping ground, resulting in depleted fish stock, polluted beaches, and other health issues for the inhabitants.

Not Designed to Burn or Bury

Incinerating plastic contributes to greenhouse gases. To save space at landfills, plastics are often burned in incinerators. When this is done, chemicals, petroleum, and fossil fuels used in the manufacturing process are released into the atmosphere, adding to greenhouse gas emissions.

Plastic takes a long time to degrade. Nobody is quite sure how long it takes for plastic to biodegrade — it hasn't been around long enough, and the first plastics made are still around today. Scientists believe, however, that plastics will take hundreds of years to degrade fully — if not longer.

Plastics contain harmful chemicals. These include cadmium, lead, PVC, and other pollutants in the form of artificial colouring, plasticisers, and stabilisers. Some of these have been discovered to be harmful and are not in currently manufactured plastics, but the older, more toxic plastics are still filling up our landfills and floating around in our oceans, releasing pollutants into the environment. These can seep into groundwater from landfill runoff and cause health risks for both wildlife and humans.

It makes sense doesn't it, when you realise that recycling plastic actually saves energy. Studies show that the energy saved by recycling a single plastic bottle — as compared to producing a new one from scratch — is enough to power a single 60 W bulb for six hours. Think of those 2.5 million bottles thrown away per hour in the US — we could practically power our homes on the energy savings we would gain by recycling every one of those plastic bottles.

Recycled plastic is useful. Recycled plastic is found in many unexpected places — including carpeting, the fuzz on tennis balls, scouring pads, paint brushes, clothes, industrial strapping, shower stalls, drainpipes, flowerpots, and lumber. It also contains oils that could be recycled and reused as fossil fuels.

Recycling and resource recovery — from plastic and other materials — was a major issue being dealt with at CleanEnviro Summit Singapore 1–4 July 2012. One event, the WasteMET Asia's ISWA Beacon Conference, focuses on globalisation, urban metabolism and waste management.

It addressed the challenges faced by urban cities, and discussed solutions and technologies available for a rapidly-urbanising Asia, from the perspective of lessons learnt and distilled into good practices, and the support provided by technological developments in waste management.

All Plastics Can Be Recycled

Addressing issues like plastic waste and reviewing best practices in recycling technologies and waste management were among the major aims of the first CleanEnviro Summit Singapore.

By tapping into the best solutions the world has to offer, attendees learnt to deal with plastic waste in a constructive fashion. Japan was one such country represented at the summit committed to recycling plastics.

Japan registered a 77% plastic recycling rate in 2010. This is twice the rate of the UK and 20% higher than the US. The rate to which Japan recycles its plastic waste is a rise from its 73% rate in 2006 and the 39% figure in 1996, according to the nation's Plastic Waste Management Institute.

Since Japan implemented its disposal and treatment of plastic waste, the list of plastic items has included other items like boxes and cases, cups and containers, wrappings, plates and trays, tube-shaped containers, lids and caps.

It was in 1997 when Japan mandated businesses and households to separate plastic waste for the first time. Many laws on waste disposal have been passed since then.

"Japan has been able to make progress in plastic recycling because waste-processing agencies have won the support of manufacturers," said institute spokesman Takushi Kamiya.

Japan recycled 72% of polyethylene terephthalate (PET) bottles in 2010, compared with 48% in Europe and 29% in the US.

The products from the recycling include textiles, industrial materials, sheeting and household items such as egg boxes. Furthermore, large quantities are being transported to countries like China, Hong Kong and other parts of Asia.

Use of new technology is also contributing to the steady improvement in the country's recycling rate. The food company Ajinomoto, for example, has recently disclosed a plastic bottle made entirely from recycled PET; and the firm says about 4,500 tonnes of recycled PET will be used in its drink bottles every year.

There were speakers and delegates from Japan participating at the Clean-Enviro Summit, including the Tokyo-based International Environmental Technology Centre of UNEP and Clean Association of TOKYO 23. A key founding sponsor of Singapore event was the leading Japanese company in the waste management and recycling fields, Dowa Eco-System.

By attending one critical summit event — the WasteMET Asia's ISWA Beacon Conference — delegates heard how cities and countries are addressing the problem of waste management. It highlighted the challenges and the difficulties that exist, but also outlined emerging solutions and best practices and, finally, provided "road maps" and strategic guidance for successful waste management.

Experts in the three main waste management solutions — landfill; waste-to-energy; and resource recovery/recycling — presented the case for each, including the adoption of each as a city's predominant solution, the constraints, as well as the advances to be expected for that solution.

Whether dealing with plastic pollution or marine debris — or for that matter any major environment issue — as UNEP's Executive Director Achim Steiner says, "one community or one country acting in isolation will not be the answer".

It requires a collective approach. That is precisely what CleanEnviro Summit is all about. Addressing issues, exploring solutions and adopting the best practices, extending across national boundaries and involving the public and private sectors. The next CleanEnviro Summit is scheduled for the first week of June 2014 in Singapore.

Doug Woodring: Founder, Ocean Recovery Alliance

Doug Woodring is the founder of the non-profit organisation, the Ocean Recovery Alliance, which is focused on bringing innovative solutions, technology, collaborations and policy together to improve the health of the ocean.

Two of the group's main projects relate to the broad scale reduction of plastic in the ocean and the environment, and were announced at the Clinton Global Initiative in 2010.

Global Alert/Floating Trash, is a web-based platform to link the world's rivers to the ocean using citizen reporting, and the PDP, which is similar to that of carbon reporting, aims at driving efficiencies in the use of plastic and reducing the environmental impact of waste.

Doug has worked in Asia for the past 18 years in a number of industries which have been at the forefront of technology, mainly related to the environment and new media platforms. Prior to working with technology startups, while at Merrill Lynch Asset Management Hong Kong in 1998, he proposed the company's first global environmental technology fund.

Doug has a dual Masters degree from The Wharton School (MBA) and Johns Hopkins University, School of Advanced International Studies (SAIS) where he studied Environmental Economics. He has an undergraduate degree from the University of California at Berkeley.

But it doesn't take a degree of any sort to see the plastic problem and deal with it. Doug gets more than his feet wet and his hands dirty! But he knows it is worth it if more people — companies, countries and cities — learn how to stop dumping plastic and instead see it as a useful resource.

———◄O►———

Sources

- www.cleanenvirosummit.sg
- www.abccarbon.com
- www.oceanrecov.org

Energy
Literacy and Creative
Education

Section **9**

33

Energy Education and a Green Campus

*Perhaps from a surprising source I gained insight into a very different form of energy education. For the second year (in 2012), CNBC television joined forces with Shell to organise a video brainstorm, called Energy Opportunities. I was invited to partake again and asked to write a review of the event. Here I also draw attention to the work of the IEC in Brisbane, Australia and the educational work of agencies in Singapore. As the objective is to impart knowledge on how energy efficiency can be achieved in an industrial setting, a Green Campus has sprung up in Singapore to help companies to systemise their energy efficiency drive. This was reported on the E2 Singapore website and through **abc carbon express**...*

The term "Energy Literacy" first came to my ears from Tim McLennan, CEO of the Australia-based organisation International Energy Centre (IEC),when he visited Singapore and I agreed to introduce him to potential partners and collaborators with a view to educating and training people for a low-carbon energy future.

We met the Energy Studies Institute (ESI), which does a wonderful job in research into all things energetic, as well as the CEO of Energy Market Authority (EMA), Chee Hong Tat, along with some of his colleagues. Education is important for EMA and one of the reasons why it goes to so much trouble with its annual Singapore International Energy Week.

We also met with the Sustainable Energy Association of Singapore (SEAS), which plays a very important role in energy training, as well as key people at National Environment Agency (NEA), with its strong focus on energy efficiency and resource management.

Around the same time, I came across the energy education startup, the Green Campus, a product of the McKinsey organisation. More on that later. But first let's look at how one section of the media, in the form of CNBC, views energy opportunities. An education in itself!

———◄◑►———

My review of the occasion, as reported on the CNBC Energy Opportunities website:

Brainstorm Call to Monetarise Efficiency, Effectively Price Energy and Carbon

Ken Hickson, Chairman and CEO of Sustain Ability Showcase Asia, participated in the 2012 Singapore brainstorm event and gives his thoughts on the topics discussed.

None of the brainstormers could contain themselves. Ideas and opinions flowed freely and flew across the table and across the room.

Cameras caught at least some of the action, while elevator pitch deliveries from chosen representatives from the ten tables contained essential highlights of the wide-ranging energy issues and opportunities aired.

Having Minister Grace Fu on hand — from the Prime Minister's office no less — did not deter anyone else from raising thorny issues or extreme clean energy options, and whether they had relevance at home or abroad didn't seem to matter.

Vocal contributions were extracted from all, even from my table which was also graced by the presence of Jose Maria Figueres, President of the Carbon War Room, brother of UN Climate Change boss Christiana, former President of Costa Rica and son of Costa Rica's game-changing former President.

He freely shared his thoughts and wisdom too, as did fellow participant Dr. Geh Min, the noted conservationist and former President of the Singapore Nature Society.

The good thing about the CNBC Shell brainstorm format is that everyone has the chance to have their say, unlike many conferences and forum where the "big-wigs" monopolise the show and the rest of us — whether media or common delegates — might be lucky enough to get an odd question in.

So what's the verdict for the future energy scenario in Asia in 2035, for which we were all asked to do some considered crystal ball gazing?

Consistently, the matter of a price on carbon — and a more realistic price for energy — was something raised repeatedly which came out

242

tops. The world must face up to and implement effective pricing — which will drive, and be driven by, energy efficiency and investment in renewables — to maintain a liveable climate, energy security and a safe environment.

Maybe there wasn't one single great idea, but there was enough energy and brain power in the room to give some hope that we are in good hands. Maybe we can plan ahead and effectively manoeuvre our way through a minefield to deal with a volatile and unpredictable future.

Energy was obviously at the heart of the matter and here are some of the brainstormed highlights:

- Governments must work with business and provide incentives to effect a move to a low-carbon economy and a clean energy future.
- There are "multiple benefits" in energy efficiency — save energy, save money — which would make carbon taxes or higher energy prices more affordable and palatable.
- The need for effective regional sourcing and distributing of renewable energy with cross-country grids, is underway in Europe and necessary in Asia.
- Accessing and utilising energy and environmental data more effectively to help to "monetarise efficiency" — the winning idea from Table 4!
- Let's create wealth from waste — it's a resource and not something to destroy, but instead turn into energy.
- The government must be an enabler to drive change through public-private partnerships and boost economic performance to manage population growth.
- Maybe it will take a global catastrophe —in the order of a Fukushima — to make us accept the inevitable: a global energy tax and a pan-Asian high voltage grid.
- To boost private sector investment in renewable energy and achieve "grid parity", regulations must be reduced.
- There will be — or needs to be — "transformational technology" to de-carbonise economies, along with a mindset change through research and education.
- Cities are where change can best take place — change the culture, and reduce energy consumption without reducing levels of comfort.

Green Campus Focuses on Energy Efficiency for Industry

A new approach to learning on the job, that's the Green Campus in Singapore. It is actually a model factory in a fully operational refinery and unlike traditional work experience or university studies.

As the objective is to impart knowledge on how energy efficiency can be achieved in an industrial setting, Green Campus is helping companies to systemise their energy efficiency drive, as the desire to be sustainable grows with the demand for energy.

McKinsey started its Green Campus on Jurong Island in March 2012 in partnership with the Economic Development Board (EDB) and NEA, and it was officially inaugurated on 25 October 2012, by Minister in the Prime Minister's Office, Mr. S Iswaran, who is also the second Minister for Trade and Industry.

EDB, NEA and McKinsey have signed a Memorandum of Understanding in the spirit of promoting energy efficiency training. NEA's role is to promote courses conducted at the Green Campus for Energy Efficiency National Partnership (EENP) members and Singapore Certified Energy Managers (SCEMs), where applicable. EDB intends to introduce potential clients to the facility for training courses.

NEA has also been working with McKinsey on energy efficiency related courses for senior management. These courses may be accredited as EENP learning events, which NEA could co-fund if EENP members are participating.

NEA has also facilitated meetings between McKinsey, senior representatives of small and medium enterprises and representatives from the Institution of Engineers, Singapore (IES), Singapore Manufacturers' Federation (SMF), Singapore Food Manufacturers' Association (SFMA), Print and Media Association, Singapore (PMAS) to seek feedback on the training courses.

As the first Green Campus in Asia, it is also McKinsey's first process model factory in the world. It is located within the Chemical Process Technology Centre operated by Petrofac.

At the facility's official opening, Mr. Andrew Tan, CEO of NEA, said that "as part of our ongoing efforts to promote energy efficient practices, NEA is pleased to work with knowledge partners like McKinsey to disseminate best practices in industry processes that lead to more efficient use of energy and cost savings. This will also support the introduction of Singapore's Energy Conservation Act (in 2013) where major energy users are required to put in place a good energy management plan."

Green Campus uses a kerosene distillation plant to train staff across a range of core operations, where McKinsey provides trainers and expertise.

Companies with manufacturing activities in Singapore and the region can benefit from the curriculum provided and it will be used to train executives and front line operations managers. This will give participants the opportunity to learn energy efficient processes across six live learning stations — from a water cooling system to an operational furnace.

Besides having on-site hardware to provide participants with experiential learning, the Green Campus courses are also designed to effect energy efficiency transformations in companies through people management training. The duration and content of the courses can be tailored to the needs of the participants.

Mr. Oliver Tonby, Managing Partner of McKinsey & Company Southeast Asia, says the establishment of the Green Campus is part of the McKinsey Innovation Campus in Singapore.

"It underscores our commitment to bring the best of our global experience to companies in Singapore and across Asia to help them address their toughest challenges. Our decision to locate these new capabilities in Singapore reflects the growing focus on innovation in this market, the commitment to energy efficiency and drive for excellence."

From working with companies in Singapore and across the region, McKinsey has come to the conclusion that there is real scope for companies to transform their operations to become more energy efficient and at the same time more competitive.

As the energy bill for the world's ten largest companies has now hit US$1.8 trillion, energy efficiency has gone to the top of the agenda for many companies.

According to McKinsey, research shows that only one in ten companies remained successful in their energy transformation efforts four year later. Studies showed that 70% of the failures were due to incorrect employee or managerial mindsets.

Dr. Mads Lauritzen, the managing partner in Southeast Asian operations practice of McKinsey, said: "Essentially, it is having one common goal, mindset, culture (on energy efficiency) across the entire company. Many companies that failed — they don't have this. They have, what I call, islands of projects all over the company and that won't lead to one single culture."

The Green Campus starts off by building capabilities, which in turn can lead to a change in mindset or habits. If enough people do the same thing, McKinsey believes, it eventually becomes a culture.

In its first nine months of operation, 500 executives and plant managers from 50 companies have received training at the Green Campus in Singapore.

Sources

- www.greencampus.mckinsey.com
- www.energyopportunities.tv
- www.internationalenergycentre.com
- www.ema.gov.sg
- www.esi.nus.edu.sg
- www.seas.org.sg
- www.nea.gov.sg
- www.e2singapore.gov.sg

SERIOUS GAMES IN

34

Games for Good: For Sustainability's Sake

In doing some work for Serious Games International over a few months of 2012 and 2013, I realised the incredible potential to use this "fun" technology for good. There is a strong affinity between gamification — games technology and platforms — with education, training, social enterprise and sustainability. Everyone plays games it seems — on computers, mobiles, consoles — and young people take the technology seriously. Collectively, we call it "games for good" compared with all the rest of the massive gaming industry. I've written about in my newsletter and also sourced what other people are doing and saying about this…

While we've been hearing a lot about the nexus between climate, water, waste and energy, we've uncovered another vital communication connection. Sustainability and technology come together to help us better understand and educate ourselves — particularly the younger generations — about our world, our behaviour and how to make things better.

As a relatively new convert to gaming — not the gambling kind —I have discovered a lot is being done around the world to use "gamification", video games, virtual reality, avatars, digital mobility, even "interactive visualisation technology", to educate and to train. It's being called Serious Games — or to coin a phrase, "Games for Good". Its applications are many and varied as I have recently discovered through my work with Serious Games International (SGI), which now goes by the name of the Game Science Group.

Now we learn that in the US a competition has been organised to challenge designers to use social gaming to combat climate change. And the UN Environment Programme (UNEP) is involved with a new programme for students using serious games.

This was introduced in Africa and Asia in 2013:

Aqua Republica is a new online strategic game that taps into social networks and the phenomenon of serious games. It helps raise awareness and educate stakeholders of the importance and challenges of managing limited natural resources in the face of multiple and often competing demands in the drive towards sustainable development. This serious water resources game is being developed by DHI and UNEP.

There is also PSFK's Future of Gaming report. It presents key trends emerging within the gaming space that brands, non-profits and communities can leverage to build engagement and motivate their target audience towards achieving a desired goal or outcome.

It is designed to inspire anyone tasked with creating compelling user experiences, whether that be on a digital screen, in the real world or somewhere in between.

There is a tremendous amount of research and study taking place around gaming, and this report reflects PSFK's contribution to that conversation.

The report provides a current snapshot into the innovative ways that games are being used within the broader marketplace, examines their expanding role in effecting change on an individual and societal level, and highlights the new technologies that are making these experiences possible.

We also came across this article from *Mashable* on Gaming for Good, which is more than a year old:

Can Gaming Change the Climate Change Conversation?

By Dory Carr-Harris (2 December 2011)

From Foursquare to Angry Birds to Farmville, there's no denying social gaming is exploding. Riding this trend, new ideas and inspiration site PSFK recently challenged designers to use social gaming to combat climate change.

At this month's Gaming for Good in New York City, ten finalists presented gaming concepts, which address challenges presented by The Climate Reality Project. Environmental activist and former US Vice President Al Gore selected five gaming concepts he believes have the potential to change conversations about climate change.

In his opening remarks, Gore said private companies — such as the PSFK gaming entrants — rather than governments, are leading the way to slow the rate of climate change. "Our democracy has been hacked," he said. "It no longer functions with the integrity of our founding fathers."

Gore is a known supporter of climate change prevention and believes the US government does not do enough to protect the environment. Despite the evidence, some people are still not convinced that climate change and its effects are real.

One innovative gaming solution Gore loved was REALiTREE, a digital representation of the local environment and our role in sustaining its well-being. Large video screens, powered by renewable energies, display images of conversation-provoking trees. Creators Stark Design compare it to a communal Tamagotchi, essentially a digital environment where you'll feel compelled to take care of the trees.

Other favorites included Zemoga's Climate Trail, based on retro favorite Oregon Trail, in which players follow a money trail tied to false information, and use that information to work toward a healthy environment in 2036. Awkward Hug's Greensquare is a geo-location game where you get points based on your check-ins' green scores.

Arnold Worldwide's Reality Drop provides you with the tools to win any climate change argument on online discussion boards — and gives you points for each time you "drop" a reality fact. Parlor's Climate Reality Patrol users tag their online comments with deeper explanations relating to climate change, earning rewards and badges.

While these games might not share the addictive appeal of World of Warcraft, their combination of a pressing topic and points and badges make them exciting educational tools and conversations starters. If these concepts come to fruition, do you think they can impact climate change?

Mashable is a leading source for news, information and resources for the connected generation. Mashable reports on the importance of digital innovation and how it empowers and inspires people around the world. Mashable's 20 million unique visitors monthly and six million social media followers have become one of the most engaged online news communities. Founded in 2005, Mashable is headquartered in New York City with an office in San Francisco.

To put gamification and sustainability in the same sentence, I turned to this article by Ashok Kamal, an authority on green social media marketing.

Green Gamification: Combining Social Media and Game Mechanics to Promote Sustainability

Games are like ketchup: widely loved and diversely applied, with an appeal rooted in childhood. In fact, a new report reveals that over 90% of US kids aged 2–17 are gaming today.

Yet the gaming generation has been on the rise for three decades, leading to not only an army of young gamers, but also an influential adult segment. It is small wonder, then, that "gamification" is the most disruptive force to impact marketing since the arrival of social media.

Typically defined, gamification refers to the use of game mechanics, such as points, badges, leaderboards and challenges in non-game settings. Traditional examples include airline frequent flyer programmes and "Buy 10, Get 1 Free" loyalty offers. But the proliferation of social media and smartphones along with the cultural adoption of gaming has increased both the scope and sophistication of gamification.

At its core, gamification is about one thing: fun. In today's competitive battle for mindshare, games are the most effective tool for leveraging technology, rising above marketing noise and engaging the socially networked consumer.

Like any marketing strategy, gamification can be applied to encourage frivolous consumption or provide superficial entertainment. But games are also uniquely suited to change the world for the better. As gaming enthusiast and renowned author, Dr. Jane McGonigal, points out: "when we are playing games, we are tapping into our best qualities, our ability to be motivated, to be optimistic, to collaborate with others, to be resilient in the face of failure."

The power of gaming is derived from the underlying behavioural psychology that motivates people to play. Successful gamification design involves understanding player personality traits that can be identified through models such as Bartle Types and Keirsey Temperaments. A key finding of gaming studies is that the vast majority of players are driven by cooperative social interaction.

Gamification guru, Gabe Zichermann, developed the "SAPS" rewards model to further outline the behavioural drivers "Status", "Access", "Power" and "Stuff". While extrinsic rewards, such as free products (Stuff), can be short-term motivators, Zichermann reveals that intrinsic rewards, such as community recognition (Status), are superior mechanisms for fostering engagement and loyalty. The most compelling rewards fulfill innate human desires for achievement, reciprocity and appreciation. Great games make us feel alive.

The Gaming Era is upon us. Gartner analysts predict: "by 2014, a gamified service for consumer goods marketing and customer retention will become as important as Facebook, eBay or Amazon, and more than 70% of Global 2000 organisations will have at least one gamified application."

As a result, gamification presents an exciting opportunity to advance sustainability initiatives. Research from OgilvyEarth suggests that games can be a vehicle to create brand equity while also promoting green behaviors.

The synergy between gamification and sustainability is based on the fact that, like gaming, greening is largely a social action that triggers an emotional response. Innovative companies recognise the opportunity to tap into consumer passions and have begun to employ 'green gamification' to create shared value for individuals, businesses, communities and the environment.

The recent union of Recyclebank and Greenopolis affirms the traction of two leading platforms that reward people for everyday green actions. Recyclebank's "Green Your" challenges use quizzes, pledges and social sharing to educate and incentivise players on interactive microsites. Greenopolis' RecyclePix mobile app encourages users to share pictures of recycling to earn rewards. The interface includes a dynamic photo stream that can be voted on for bonus points.

Solar manufacturer, SunPower, recently ran a Facebook contest to teach people about solar energy in exchange for badges and prizes. Startups such as Simple Energy and Practically Green use the social web to calculate metrics like household energy savings and reward users for their relative performance. These companies validate that people are proud to share eco-conscious habits and that a little friendly competition positively reinforces their green activities.

Traditional industries are green gaming too. The Nissan Leaf includes CARWINGS, which is a digital tracker that both measures fuel consumption and ranks drivers according to fuel efficiency. The Ford Fusion Hybrid adds graphical flair by incorporating a Tamogochi-style game, in which a small dashboard plant grows and shrinks based on green driving practices. Even social games on Facebook are experiencing a makeover; for instance, Guerillapps and upcycling pioneer, TerraCycle, partnered to introduce Trash Tycoon, which applies Zynga-like gameplay to bridge the gap between virtual and real-world sustainable living.

Gamification and game development are still in their formative years, evolving to exhibit more purpose and tangible impact. As the sustainability movement also matures, it behooves the stakeholders to embrace the potential of green gamification.

In order to propel green into the mainstream, we need to make it enjoyable, accessible and rewarding. As my fellow eco-entrepreneur, Anthony Zolezzi, proclaims, let's embrace "fun and fame, not guilt and shame". This is the new spirit of sustainability and green gamification is leading the way.

Ashok Kamal is the Co-Founder and CEO of Bennu, which is the leader in green social media marketing. To learn more about green gamification and engage with companies highlighted in this blog, Ashok draws attention to the Social Media Week on 23–27 September 2013 and 17–21 February 2014.

Sources

- www.socialmediaweek.org/newyork/blog
- www.mashable.com
- www.aquarepublica.com
- www.gamesciencegroup.com
- www.psfk.com
- www.abccarbon.com

35

Art and Nature: Creatively Connecting Sustainability

It doesn't take long for me to find an excuse to associate myself and my writing with the arts. As an art lover, supporter and collector — not only because I have a wife and a son who are artists — but because I see a strong connection between artists and the environment. Natural bedfellows. I once organised an Art and Nature exhibition, and organised concerts by the Australian String Quartet to support the University of the Sunshine Coast's art gallery. Often, the "art" word will be strongly emphasised in "articles" in my newsletter and other writing. And I have also made sure it has a family flavor too, with a contribution from my son, better known in Australia as the artist Dave Hickson...

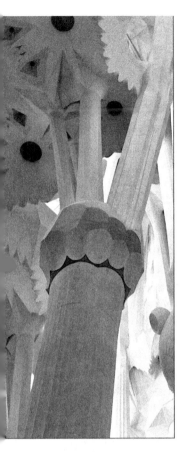

It is more than connections and connecting the dots. It is making things and people work together. Water and oil don't mix, but water-colours and oil paintings do. Water and earthly objects can cohabitate our planet and have mutual dependency. Art and the environment are convenient and creative bedfellows. Creatively managing resources and inventing eco products draws on — and inspires — the innovativeness and energy in us all. Climate change and sustainability also share a common enemy and there are co-joined solutions to deal with both.

State of the Art for the Climate

Art and nature seem to go together comfortably. Artists are often at the forefront of efforts to protect the environment and they put a high value on managing the earth's resources. They are neither wasteful nor destructive. So we have had a lot of art to take on board in Singapore of late, which also drew our attention to an article on art and activism, bringing sustainability and poverty into the purview of the artist.

Dave Hickson's mixed media sculpture "Byangum Road" (left), a model for a larger sculpture "All the World's a Stage", and his photograph (above) of the interior of Barcelona's Sagrada Familia.

Art has long been used as a medium to transmit messages or intent, from artists to audience, and they can be from a diverse range of topics. A climate-themed art exhibition, called Unfold, was staged by Cape Farewell in Beijing, looking at themes and debates provoked by climate science.

It includes the work of more than 20 artists, all of whom have travelled on and been inspired by expeditions to the Arctic and the Andes.

Climate Change Art Exhibition Opens in Beijing

By Jennifer Duggan in *The Guardian* (25 May 2013)

The exhibition, called Unfold, aims to merge culture and science to provoke climate debate in China.

With its greenhouse gas emissions continuing to soar and environmental concerns a hot topic, China is perhaps the perfect venue for a different way of looking at the issue of climate change — through art.

A climate-themed art exhibition opened in Beijing and looks at themes and debates provoked by climate science. The exhibition, Unfold, is being staged by not-for-profit climate change arts organisation Cape Farewell, which aims to prompt what it calls a cultural response to climate change. The exhibition has travelled to a number of cities, starting in Vienna, and has also been shown in New York, London and Chicago.

"All of the artists in the show have travelled on one of the three voyages (organised by Cape Farewell). So they have all had direct experience of the effects of climate change in a part of the world which is probably at the frontier of change. It's a kind of frontline where you can see quite dramatically the way the glaciers have retreated," said Chris Wainwright, co-curator of the exhibition and pro-vice chancellor of the University of the Arts London (UAL).

"What we do is we embed them [the artists] with a scientist, that's a very important part of it. The scientist informs the artists and then the artist is being inspired to try and create something," said David Buckland, Cape Farewell's founder and director.

The issue of climate change and environmental issues in general are the topic of much debate in China, both among the public and in the media. "It seemed logical that we bring it to China because the issues about climate change are often focused around China," said Wainwright. On the issue of climate change, Buckland believes China is "very engaged and very aware on a people level".

China has become the world's largest emitter of greenhouse gas emissions, burning huge amounts of coal and, for this reason, Wainwright believes it is an important venue for the exhibition. "China is seen as one of the countries that has a significant responsibility for addressing climate change, one of the countries that is one of the highest creators of CO_2 emissions and it was felt that there was a need to bring the show, not just to China, but to parts of the world where these issues could be addressed and discussed," he said.

They also hope to "empower" artists and people in China to address climate change issues, "not necessarily in a confrontational way but in an empowering way so that people can think about how they can positively change their lives and change the way they behave", said Wainwright.

One of the pieces included in the exhibition is an artificially grown diamond, made from the ash of a polar bear bone by artistic duo Ackroyd and Harvey. The pair found the bone on one of the expeditions organised by Cape Farewell. "We attach huge importance to the value of things like diamonds, they are the symbol of our wealth, the symbol of our status. I think the work asks the question: Which is the most valuable, the polar bear or the diamond?" said Wainwright.

Another piece of note in the exhibition is an LED text display by Atonement author Ian McEwan, entitled "The Hot Breath of Our Civilisation", which was written after he took part on an exhibition to the Arctic. The expedition also inspired McEwan's novel *Solar*.

The Unfold exhibition took place at the Central Academy of Fine Arts (CAFA) in Beijing from 29 May until 19 June and in AMNUA, Nanjing University, from 28 June until 20 July.

About Cape Farewell

In 2001 the artist David Buckland created the Cape Farewell project to instigate a cultural response to climate change. Cape Farewell is now an international not-for-profit programme based in the Science Museum's Dana Centre in London and with a North American foundation based at the MaRS centre in Toronto.

Cape Farewell is a charitable organisation made possible through sponsorship, partnerships and donations.

Artworks Dramatically Highlight Our Relationship to Urban Environments

Dave Hickson tells his own story of his work and its relationship to the environment. Inspired by a trip to Singapore, Spain and the US in 2012, he brought together an exhibition of works that highlights our relationship to our urban environment.

His photography, sculpture and drawings explore architecture and the interaction of objects in particular spaces, taking in the grandeur and occasional intimacy of public buildings and structures. The exhibition "New York, Barcelona, Murwillumbah" recognises the quiet drama being played out in the shapes and colours of our everyday lives:

The work explores architecture and the interaction of objects in particular spaces, taking in the grandeur and occasional intimacy of public buildings and structures. I have attempted to make works that highlight our relationship to our environment, and the relationship of shapes and colours to each other.

I started this series of work by photographing towns in my region. In 2012, I signed up for the Endless Sunrise project, where a group of photographers documented the sunrise each day for a month. Rather than taking images of the sunrise at the beach, I began photographing the towns in my area, from Billinudgel to Crabbes Creek and Mullumbimby.

I was inspired by the beauty in the buildings and trees of these areas, and when I had the opportunity to travel overseas with my partner, I wanted to continue developing this interest in architecture and urban landscape.

Travelling first to Singapore, I visited the newly built Marina Bay Sands Hotel, a 55-storey, three-tower building with a 150 m swimming pool on its roof. The complex includes a shell-shaped theatre and the Art Science Museum, which is inspired by a lotus flower.

Then on to Spain to visit Madrid's amazing art museums, Frank Gehry's Guggenheim Museum in Bilbao, where Jeff Koons' floral puppy guards the entrance to what locals call the "Dog House". This is a building that has brought millions of visitors a year to a part of Bilbao that was, for a long time, an industrial area and port. Constructed of stone, steel and concrete and clad in titanium, it is a revolution in architecture using computer-aided design to bring Gehry's organic, poetic forms to life.

Although I was amazed by the history and decorative quality of the buildings and monuments in Spain, it was in Barcelona that I had an architectural spiritual experience. Antoni Gaudi's cathedral, the Sagrada Familia, has been under construction for 130 years. Gaudi died in 1926 and the construction is expected to be completed in 2026, the centenary of Gaudi's death. The organic exterior, with sculptures growing out of the stone in every direction, is remarkable, and inside the power of the massive columns leading to an undulating ceiling of different coloured stone and marble is incredible.

Reluctantly leaving Spain, we arrived in New York and quickly made a bee-line to Frank Lloyd Wright's spiraling Guggenheim, and the Met with its buildings within buildings. From New York, we drove to Lloyd Wright's Falling Water house at Mill Run. Its cantilevered structure and natural location are a great example of architecture that interacts with its environment. The original rock formations jut into the interior of the house and the waterfall under the house acts as a natural air conditioner. We then travelled to Washington, San Francisco and Los Angeles before flying home.

My photographs of these buildings and urban landscapes were the starting point for both drawings and sculptures. I have simplified forms and played with scale and colour to produce works that sometimes only vaguely show their connection to the original image.

The series of work displayed in New York, Barcelona, Murwillumbah is simply an attempt to interpret our urban environments, to recognise the quiet drama being played out in the shapes and colours of our everyday lives.

At art school I majored in sculpture, and I find I have always had a strong affinity for architectural spaces, whether it is simply the relationship of objects in a particular space or the grandeur and drama of public buildings and structures.

I wanted to create work that looked at these relationships: us to our environment, shapes and colours to each other, and the abstraction of our everyday lives.

In this exhibition I'm showing a series of photographs that represent most of the places I have visited on this trip: Barcelona, Madrid and Bilbao in Spain; New York, Washington, San Francisco and Pennsylvania in the US; and Singapore.

I translated some of these photos into drawings, simplifying the compositions, shapes and colours, then translating them further into sculptures; using wood off cuts or reshaping recycled wood using a jigsaw, then playing with the colour, scale and composition, letting accidental associations happen, until it seems to be right. Sometimes looking nothing like the original image — but still containing the essence and memory of the starting point, whether it was standing in the Metropolitan Museum in New York or in the Sagrada Familia in Barcelona.

If the viewer feels inspired to check out one of these buildings or to look at their surroundings with a different perspective — I think that's great.

Dave Hickson's Biography

Dave was born in Auckland, but grew up in Christchurch and Singapore. After leaving school, he studied broadcasting and worked for a small music television station in Christchurch. He moved to Sydney in 1997, where he completed a Bachelor of Fine Arts, with honours in Sculpture, at the National Art School.

He won the sculpture prize in 2002 at NAS, for a series of wood and welded steel constructions, inspired by painters such as Matisse, Bruegel and Poussin.

Since art school, Dave has gained teaching qualifications; and has taught at schools and at TAFE. He continues to make artwork in a variety of media; including sculpture, photography, collage and drawing.

He has been shown in the Salon des Refuses at S.H. Irvin Gallery, Swell Sculpture Festival, and the Olive Cotton award for Photographic Portraiture.

Dave has lived and worked in the Northern Rivers region since 2008.

————

To show parental interest in the work of this "artist as a young man", I ventured to the small town in northern New South Wales, Australia, where the exhibition was being staged in March 2013 and wrote a little personal account in my newsletter of my encounter with art and the environment:

Exhibiting a Close Relation to Art

Arriving at Gold Coast Airport around 8am Australian East Coast time, was as good as anywhere to land. The weather/temperature was sunny and pleasant.

I was driven through the pleasant green countryside, across the border into New South Wales, to meet up with my artist son Dave Hickson. Inspecting his home and studio alongside the canal at South Golden Beach, it wasn't long before it was time to get ready to attend the launch of the art exhibition at Tweed River Gallery. This was, primarily, the reason for my journey.

His first one-man exhibition with drawings, small sculptures (assemblages in wood and paint) and photographs, mainly covering his observations during his travels which included Europe, US and Asia last year. Singapore figured, but predominantly his work exhibited his impressions of art and architecture, the life and soul, of Spain and the US.

Of course it was a mix of fatherly pride and appreciation of art when Richard Weinstein flew especially from Sydney to launch the show — he is a barrister and art collector — and likened David's art to that of Picasso and Matisse!

He also spoke of the art which had been commissioned and acquired by the late and great Roddy Meagher, a strong supporter of "Dave Hickson", who he described as one of Australia's leading sculptors. One of the local papers gave the show and the artist a worthy mention.

The weekend was spent in a very pleasant part of the world: Tweed Valley, South Golden Beach, Byron Bay and Murwillumbah. Windy roads, rolling countryside, where sugarcane grows on the flat and banana palms on the side of hills. Where everything is green.

And art abounds. Not only at the Tweed River Gallery where the works of Margaret Olley have a welcome home. Plans for a new wing for the gallery dedicated to the memory and art of Olley — plus an artist-in-residence retreat — will make this place one of the best regional galleries in the whole of Australia.

The towns and countryside boost many galleries and studios. A vibrant artistic community thrives in Byron Bay and beyond, competing with the surfing and fishing enthusiasts. It all made me determined to visit again, to explore the art and environment, to write about it to a larger audience. And purchase an excellent map of the artistic attractions of the place!

————◄◊►————

Another article and another place for art and the environment. This time in California. The Annual Festival of Art in Paso Robles also combined arts and sustainability, featuring a sustainable landscaping exhibit:

Fifth Annual Festival of Art in Paso Robles Combines Art and Sustainability

Local art enthusiasts were in for a special treat Saturday. It was the Fifth Annual Festival of Arts in Paso Robles. The event was held at Paso Robles City Park.

There were several new features this year, including a new bar and lounge area, featured artists, and a sustainable landscaping exhibit.

"This is like no other art festival around, since it celebrates the environment, it celebrates the artists, and it celebrates kids, and it's all free," said Barbara Partridge, the event chair.

The event was free to attend, but guests could also purchase art, souvenirs, and food.

A portion of the proceeds benefit the Festival, Studios on the Park, and the Salinas River Corridor Project.

The vision of the Paso Robles Festival of the Arts is to be the premier multi-day arts festival in Central California honoring and preserving the natural beauty and character of the region through the arts.

The Paso Robles Festival of the Arts celebrates the arts and promotes Paso Robles as an arts destination through an annual festival connecting world-class artists, the Paso Robles community, and visitors of all ages.

Beneficiaries: Salinas river corridor project update

The community has connected with a new vision of an enhanced river corridor where conservation, recreation and enhancements to the natural habitat are all possible — and the Festival's connection to the Salinas River Corridor is still going strong.

Last year's success story was in acquiring the 154 acre Salinas River Parkway Preserve with over $1.5 million in state grant funds. That purchase would not have been possible without the matching funds generated in previous years by the Festival of the Arts.

The artistic pathway to sustainability

A Leonardo influence? The promotion of environmental sustainability can take multiple pathways, besides the familiar technological and business means. Promoting the idea of the arts as a form of activism by providing visual images that raises awareness of the issue of sustainability is the goal of the student art show "Art + Activism", collaboratively organised by organisations at Dartmouth College in the US. By tapping into the striking emotional power that art has, the exhibition also hopes to spark a conversation among Dartmouth students and the community on how to better act on the challenges presented. This was how I introduced the subject and the article which appeared in my newsletter:

"Art + Activism" Links Poverty and Sustainability

By Simone D'luna (29 January 2013)

The Dartmouth, founded in 1799, is the student newspaper at Dartmouth College and the campus's only daily. *The Dartmouth* is published by The Dartmouth, Inc., an independent, nonprofit corporation chartered in the state of New Hampshire.

Featuring a perhaps unexpected combination of sustainability, poverty and art, the student art show "Art + Activism" was held in the student gallery of the Black Family Visual Arts Center.

The show, which will run until the end of the term, is the result of collaborative efforts between the Office of Sustainability, the "A Monstrous

Octopus: The Tentacles of Poverty" symposium team and "This Is Not a Group", a student organisation responsible for running, curating and installing exhibits in the gallery.

"I think that art, especially throughout history, has been used a lot to make people step back and think about society and choices and the way we treat other people," Amanda Wheelock '13 said. "I think that's also the main goal and spirit of activism in most places, so I think that they are often very intricately linked and I think that art can be used as a form of activism and vice versa."

The theme "Art + Activism" originated when the Sustainability in the Arts interns and representatives from the "A Monstrous Octopus" symposium approached student gallery co-managers Luca Molnar '13 and Sabrina Yegela '13 about combining the arts with their respective focus areas.

Both student groups were especially eager to incorporate their ideas with the arts to align with the Hopkins Center's Year of the Arts initiative, Sustainability in the Arts intern Anna Morenz '13 said.

"We really felt that the arts can be a form of activism in terms of providing powerful visual images that get people thinking about social issues or raise consciousness about issues in a different way than say, a lecture or some of the other opportunities on campus," Morenz said. "We were interested in tapping into that striking emotional power that art has."

"I think a lot about who is alienated by sustainability because it's definitely been 'consumerised' into the American diet," Meegan Daigler '14, who came to the gallery to make art from recycled materials, said. "I don't think that sustainability should be alienating because the issues of sustainability are things that are affecting people across race and gender, and art is a very different mode of communication than numbers and statistics so I'm interested in who you can reach."

Participants at the studio sessions generally expressed a belief that art and activism complement each other.

Sources

- www.thedartmouth.com
- www.davehickson.net
- www.prcity.com
- www.capefarewell.com
- www.ksby.com
- www.abccarbon.com

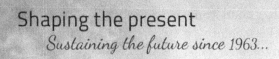

Shaping the present

Sustaining the future since 1963...

36

Profile —
Kwek Leng Joo:
Socially Responsible
Corporate Compact

I have met Kwek Leng Joo and heard him speak on important occasions, like the opening of the International Green Building Conference and the annual meeting of Singapore Compact. I admire him for his leadership and commitment not only in one of Singapore leading businesses, but his commitment to sustainability and corporate social responsibility (CSR). He is also a very talented photographer and lover of nature. I told my friend Esther An, who is herself a leading light in sustainability — and head of CSR for City Developments Limited (CDL) — about my idea to include an article on CDL's sustainability journey. She provided me with a tailor-made profile in the words of Mr. Kwek himself...

Kwek Leng Joo was appointed as Director and Managing Director of City Developments Limited (CDL) on 8 February 1980 and 1 January 1995 respectively. He is the chairman of the Corporate Social Responsibility and Corporate Governance Committee.

Mr. Kwek holds a Diploma in Financial Management and has extensive experience in property development and investment.

Mr. Kwek contributes actively to the business community through several public appointments, including Honorary President of the Singapore Chinese Chamber of Commerce and Industry. He is also the Chairman of the Board of Trustees of the National Youth Achievement Award Council and a member of the Board of Trustees of Nanyang Technological University, the National Climate Change Network and the Marina Bay Public Advisory Panel. In 2012, he was elected President of the Singapore Compact — the national CSR society and the country's focal point for the UN Global Compact.

Mr. Kwek emerged joint winners together with brother Mr. Kwek Leng Beng, as "Partners in the Office of the CEO" in the Brendan Wood International — SIAS TopGun CEO Designation Award given out at the SIAS Investors' Choice Awards in October 2012.

Its Sustainability Report was the first amongst Singapore companies to achieve Global Reporting Initiative (GRI) checked status in 2008. In the 2010 Asian Sustainability Rating, CDL was again ranked top amongst all listed developers in Asia.

A Strategic Approach to CSR — Looking at the Business and Beyond

By Kwek Leng Joo

Natural calamities. Climate change. Economic crisis. Business failures. Governance let-downs. Food shortages. Resource scarcity. Ethical lapses. Social breakdowns.

These are daily headline grabbers as one flips through the newspapers every day. Yet many companies in Singapore and around the world continue to operate in a seemingly indifferent manner, either ignoring or oblivious to the impact and risks these environmental, social and governance issues have on their business.

As a pioneering practitioner of CSR in Singapore, CDL takes a strategic and systematic approach to ensure our business sustainability by focusing on the triple bottom line. Although CSR is very much visible in all aspects of our business activities today, as we measure our success by looking at our financial, environmental and social performance, we still have much to learn and accomplish before we can achieve a complete integration of CSR within our business.

Globally, CDL is the first Singapore corporation to be listed on the three leading global sustainability benchmarks — FTSE4Good Index Series since 2002, Global 100 Most Sustainable Corporations in the World since 2010 and the Dow Jones Sustainability Indexes since 2011.

CDL's CSR journey

As one of Singapore's largest companies by market capitalisation, CDL has over 30,000 quality homes in Singapore and abroad, in addition to owning one of Singapore's largest commercial property portfolios. While building quality, innovative, comfortable and functional spaces has always been a business priority; a more formalised concept of CSR came to focus only in the late 1990s when it was integrated as part of our corporate mission and vision.

CDL's corporate vision is to maintain industry leadership in innovation, product quality, service standards, profitability and CSR. More specifically, our CDL has been proactively incorporating green features into our

270

Race for Sustainability

developments long before these guidelines were even put in place, guided by our own philosophy to environmental sustainability established in mid-1990s — simply put, to "conserve as we construct". We remain faithful to this.

For property development, we take a comprehensive life-cycle approach towards sustainability. We believe that sustainable developments should take into consideration the economic, environmental and social aspects and have adopted a three-pronged strategy to achieve a sustainable and balanced triple bottom line.

Thus, our green commitment is applied across our entire operations — from design, construction, procurement, maintenance and community engagement, involving both internal and external stakeholders at various stages of the development and maintenance. We have also set the target to achieve a minimum BCA Green Mark GoldPlus rating for all new developments.

To achieve this, we have committed to investing between 2% and 5% of the construction cost of a new development on green building design, features and innovations. Through the years of creating progressively greener properties, we have demonstrated that sustainability and financial viability do not have to be mutually exclusive.

Our committed green investment has provided the capacity to adopt and adapt a myriad of innovative technology and systems within our developments. The "adapt" aspect is especially critical as many existing green designs and features were not created with a tropical climate in mind and they had to be modified to better fit local cultural use.

CDL is also supportive of Singapore's national carbon target to reduce our greenhouse gas emissions by some 16% below Business-As-Usual (BAU) levels by 2020, contingent on a legally binding agreement, in which all countries implement their commitments in good faith. CDL has set a target to reduce the company's carbon intensity emissions by 22% from baseline year 2007 and to achieve a 25% reduction by 2030.

Applying innovative firsts across CDL's value chain

In the area of design, CDL has extensively utilised technology for effective sustainable solutions. Examples include incorporating Sunpath Analysis for effective building orientation and solar-related strategies, being a pioneering adopter of Building Information Modelling (BIM) in Singapore for optimised project development outcomes as well as having a strong focus on passive and low-energy architectural design features.

We recognise the importance and power of stakeholder influence and in 2001, we introduced the CDL 5-Star Environmental, Health and Safety (EHS) Assessment System to audit and track the EHS performance of our builders.

Over the years, the system has undergone considerable refinements with significantly improved EHS performance as more builders adopted best practices on site because of our encouragement. The CDL 5-Star EHS Award was introduced in 2005 to recognise builders who have excelled in the CDL 5-Star EHS Assessment over a one-year period.

During the maintenance stage, we have progressively installed cutting-edge green features for sustained environmental impact for users. These include the Dual-chute Pneumatic Waste Disposal System to segregate recyclable and domestic waste in condominiums, the Pontos Grey Water Recycling System, Heat Recovery System, Home Energy Management System, extensive use of solar panels in residential and commercial buildings and the Rainwater Harvesting System.

Examples of innovative developments

– 7 & 9 Tampines Grande — one of the largest use of solar panels in a commercial building which incorporated three different types of solar technologies;
– 11 Tampines Concourse — the first Carbon Neutral® development in Singapore and Asia Pacific;
– City Square Mall — Singapore's first eco-mall and first private commercial building to attain the BCA Green Mark Platinum status;
– D'Nest — national record for "Largest Solar Panels in a Condominium";
– Tree House — possibly the world's tallest and largest green wall; and
– Lush Acres — Singapore's first custom-made Agri-Cube Hydroponic Farm to promote hygienic community farming.

Promoting eco-consciousness amongst our homebuyers and tenants has also been our priority for many years now and some of our progressive and sustained green outreach initiatives include:

- Project: Eco-Office since 2002 — an initiative promoting eco-habits amongst office workers which has since expanded to the national level;
- 1°C Up programme since 2007 — encourages tenants to raise air-con temperatures in the premises by 1°C and participation has maintained at 100% since 2009; and
- Let's Live Green! — an initiative to encourage homeowners to lead an eco-friendly lifestyle and to effectively understand the green infra-structure and utilise the green features we provide in a CDL property.

Today, CDL has a portfolio of 67 BCA Green Mark certified projects of which 23 are of the highest Platinum-tier, the most for a private developer on both counts. As a testament to the success of our commitment to sustainable development and Singapore's built environment, CDL was awarded the Green Mark Platinum Champion Award in 2011, the Built Environment Leadership Platinum Award in 2009 and the Quality Excellence Award Quality Champion (Platinum) in 2013 by BCA.

Bringing business value to sustainability

For CDL, our 37 BCA Green Mark certified buildings between 2008 and 2011 have helped save an estimated S$19.7 million in electricity costs annually. This includes new buildings as well as retrofitted buildings. In 2012, our commercial flagship building Republic Plaza was awarded the BCA Green Mark Platinum, an upgrade from its previous Gold certification. We expect to save close to 4,000,000 kWh of energy, translating to an annual savings of approximately S$870,000. This is equivalent to about 17.5% reduction in energy consumption for the building. We estimate to recover the retrofitting cost for Republic Plaza from these savings in five years' time, or even earlier, should electricity tariffs continue to rise.

We have also conducted surveys on our homebuyers and the findings indicate that they are appreciative and welcome the green features placed in their homes. In the leasing market, tenant mindsets are beginning to change with a preference for greener spaces, especially amongst multi-national corporations reporting on their environmental performance.

When we were advocating the cause on our soapbox more than a decade ago, we were challenged by sceptics who were unable to look beyond

cost. As the industry and more companies come forth to share their story, the business case begins to look compelling.

A joint study by BCA and the National University of Singapore reported that retrofitting commercial buildings to achieve the standard Green Mark level resulted in significant energy savings of 17% with the potential increase in capital value of 2%. In the Jones Lang LaSalle publication "Global Sustainability Perspective", in the US, the premium for LEED-certified or ENERGY STAR label buildings is about 13% (in a 2011 study by Eichholtz, Kok and Quigley). The SmartMarket Report cites that rental rates for LEED-certified buildings are 13% more than non-LEED ones.

CSR for the community

Beyond our business operations, our CSR commitment calls for us to be active citizens where we share in the concerns of our society and take on the responsibility for its betterment. While there are many worthy causes to support, we have remain focused on four major community involvement areas — conserving and raising awareness for the environment, enhancing youth development, caring for the less fortunate and promoting the arts. We also sustain our corporate volunteering culture through City Sunshine Club, a staff volunteering platform established in 1999. The staff volunteerism participation rate stands at a commendable 89% in 2012.

To effectively engage the community, we have been a strong supporter of the Government's 3P Partnership model. In addition to CDL's own signature community initiatives such as CDL E-Generation Challenge and CDL Sculpture Award, we also collaborate with government agencies and non-governmental organisations to promote youth development by co-creating initiatives like the CDL-Singapore Compact Young CSR Leaders Award and BCA-CDL Green Sparks Competition. We also support the Corporate and School Partnership Programme by National Environment Agency, Elderly Programme by Lions Befrienders, Assisi Hospice, Arc Children's Centre, Boys' Brigade and Viriya Community Services.

As CDL continues on our mission to green our built environment, we have embarked on two special initiatives, My Tree House and the CDL Green Gallery — where we have applied our green expertise and resources to green public spaces for the community in celebration of our 50th anniversary this year.

My Tree House — the world's first green library for kids

Located at the Central Public Library, My Tree House has been purposefully conceptualised, constructed and operated with environmental sustainability in mind and is the first library in the world to be steered by green principles in all facets from design, infrastructure and use of sustainable materials, to collection and programming.

A dynamic collaboration with the National Library Board, this special green library features eco-friendly fittings and furniture, lighting, interactive learning tools and an extensive green book collection to encourage children to explore, discover and challenge their curiosity in learning and caring for the environment.

CDL green gallery at the SBG heritage museum

The CDL Green Gallery, located at the Singapore Botanic Gardens (SBG), will be Singapore's first zero-energy green gallery and the first here to use the bio-material Hempcrete when it opens in November. Designed to be a new green icon, all aspects from conceptualisation, design, construction, material selection and maintenance will support principles of sustainability and environmental protection.

To achieve zero energy, this extraordinary green gallery will be fitted with solar PV cladded roof panels that are expected to harvest all the energy required for the building's operations. A partnership with the National Parks Board, the Gallery will feature botanical- or greening-related exhibits and is open to the public.

Communicating sustainability to stakeholders through reporting

Alongside our commitment to performing credibly in all financial, social and environmental aspects to maintain a balanced triple bottom line, we also firmly believe in the importance of sustainability reporting. CDL voluntarily discloses information pertaining to sustainability through reporting as we believe in upholding the principles of corporate transparency and open communication to our stakeholders and it adds credence to the credibility and trustworthiness of a company. We also subscribe to internationally accepted guidelines and models to improve our CSR engagement and performance.

Thus, in 2008, we voluntarily published a dedicated Sustainability Report (a shorter CSR Report has been included within our Annual Report since 2004) and became the first company in Singapore to publish a report successfully checked at Level C by the GRI.

Reaching out — CSR advocacy

Our deeply embedded CSR conviction also drives us to support other CSR-related platforms and we are a founding member of the Singapore Compact for CSR (SC) and Business Council for Sustainable Development Singapore.

When I was elected to be the President of SC last year, my key priority was to bring sustainability to a higher level in the business community. Even though most businesses no longer equate CSR with philanthropy, convincing companies to understand and embrace CSR in Singapore remains an uphill task. Many companies fail to recognise the tangible benefits that good CSR practices and processes can bring to their bottom line. The eventual goal should be for CSR to become an integral component of a business's culture, as reflected in its day-to-day operations.

Another priority was for SC to expand their youth outreach, particularly of those between the age of 17 and 25, as part of an extended strategy to increase awareness.

In the last year, SC has established a new youth network with over 160 members to date. To further extend the youth outreach, SC partnered the National Youth Achievement Award Council and launched the inaugural National Youth Forum in April, where about 200 youths aged between 17 and 30 from various universities, polytechnics and ITE attended and learnt more about CSR from experienced practitioners.

What lies ahead

While it is heartening to see that the building industry in Singapore is finally turning a green corner as the island is now home to some 1,500 green building projects, it is with hope that the man on the street will be the next to jump on the eco-band wagon.

For the next leapfrog to occur in the building industry, it is critical for green consumerism to rise and take hold to generate the demand

sorely needed for green buildings. When there is increased demand for green products from consumers, businesses will be quick to respond with greater supply.

Even as CSR and Sustainability Reporting remain slow on the uptake amongst companies in Singapore, things are set to change in the wake of the revised Code of Corporate Governance issued by the Monetary Authority of Singapore in May 2012, to promote a high standard of corporate governance among listed companies in Singapore, with various revisions that relate to CSR issues. The importance of CSR and reporting is similarly echoed by the Singapore Exchange (SGX). It is with hope that these factors will provide the impetus to drive the message home to companies of the importance of CSR and for them to begin their own CSR journey.

Ultimately, one clear message must be communicated — CSR is no longer a good to have but a must have for companies to continue to operate. Increasingly, regulators are demanding it, investors are demanding it and consumers are demanding it. Companies that continue to disregard CSR are at peril of putting themselves out of business.

———◁◦▷———

Sources

- www.csrsingapore.org
- www.cdl.com.sg

Ethics,
Media and
Communication

ection 10

37

Hacking Is Not in the Sustainability Dictionary

*Not only was the world shocked by the revelations in 2011 in the UK of the prevalence of hacking by journalists, I was disappointed that News Corporation, established and managed by Rupert Murdoch, seemed to be directly implicated in phone hacking to get access to people. Freedom of information was not the issue, but a serious invasion of privacy by illegal means. It wasn't long ago when I was praising News Corp for setting an example through its commitment to go carbon neutral. I think I created something of a stir in my newsletter **abc carbon express** on 25 July 2011 with this hard-hitting headline…*

As we sit and watch Parliamentary Inquiries on live TV and see Rupert Murdoch and his son James put through the hoops by earnest MPs, and we learn day by day of further resignations and arrests, we can only wonder where this will lead to.

Such behaviour by numerous journalists from more than one newspaper, who not only invade the privacy of innocent individuals, but also use all sorts of illegal means to gain incriminating evidence or gossip, is not to be condoned in any way whatsoever.

Now, you well ask, what this has to do with **abc carbon express** or Sustain Ability Showcase Asia (SASA).

Sustainability goes beyond helping the environment and committing to charitable causes.

In a business sense, it involves CSR, governance, ethics and transparency. It impacts on labour policies and trade practices. It means running the business in a sustainable way for the benefit of all stakeholders, not just major shareholders.

We need to see the corporate world, including media owners, committing to genuine sustainability and setting some high standards in the boardrooms, offices, newsrooms, factories, as well as through their communications.

As someone who has worked in the communications industry — media, publishing and public relations — for 51 years, I cannot but be horrified at the revelations in the ongoing "hacking and denial" saga unfolding in the UK, involving Murdoch-owned News Corporation newspapers.

Of course, many will try to dismiss it as "quite normal" goings-on to be expected of the tabloids, also known as "gossip" and "gutter" press. But such behaviour by numerous journalists from more than one newspaper, who not only invade the privacy of innocent individuals, but also use all sorts of illegal means to gain incriminating evidence, is not be condoned in any way whatsoever. And to learn that police members have been bribed and private investigators paid to solicit all sort of unsavoury facts and fantasies, is beyond belief.

More press freedom or less? More resignations and arrests? The downfall of a media empire? More revelations of cosy relationships between politicians, police and media?

Media and public relations (PR) people — working for police, the government, business or media — have never enjoyed a guilt free existence or lily-white reputation. But as someone who has worked in and with the media, I have often come to the defense of the professionalism and dedication of many fine men and women, who are doing their job — often in trying and tiring circumstances — to bring news, facts, comments, features and visuals to the general public.

There is now, obviously, a very large credibility gap which seems impossible to fill. But we must not lump every journalist in the same heap of "hacks". (The uninitiated might be interested to know that journalists are often — amongst themselves — described as "hacks", but whichever meaning you take from the Oxford Dictionary, none refer to the disgusting practice of illegally "hacking" into private phones and computers.)

We need to put this in perspective. We have all heard of unsavoury and illegal behaviour coming from various professionals. There have been rogue doctors, lawyers, accountants, bankers — even politicians. But we don't put the whole profession in the "bad basket".

So let's hear it from the very professional, capable and ethical journalists and PR people. And let's expect — and even encourage — the authorities to deal very firmly and finally with those amongst them, be they from the media, government, legal profession, PR or the police, for their crimes.

There is a connection between media, communication, ethics and sustainability — a few actually:

- The News Corporation has been rated very highly for its commitment to deal with climate change. It was announced by Rupert Murdoch himself in May 2007 that the global empire would become carbon neutral by 2010. It achieved that and set some very good examples around the world.

- Sustainability, we must re-emphasise, involves CSR, governance, ethics and transparency. It means running the business sustainably for all stakeholders, not just shareholders. The Dow Jones Sustainability Index measures performance in all these areas.
- A few years back I wrote an article for the *Journal of Communication Management* on ethics, highlighting key areas for professional communicators: cultural practices, personal, professional, political, religious, racial, trade, business, legal, financial, environmental and social.
- Recently, I gave a paper to the Sustainable Energy Association of Singapore on the four E's of Sustainability — Environment, Economy, Ethics and Energy. This goes beyond the accepted triple bottom line, to give added emphasis to energy and ethics as critical factors.

We need to see the corporate world, including media owners, committing to genuine sustainability — the four E's of sustainability — and setting some high standards of ethical practice.

This has added relevance, not only as I edit and produce an online newsletter — thus I am "in the media" and consider myself a journalist (what I was trained to be many years ago) — but I also practice as a sustainability advisor and directly assist companies in the sustainability sector, which incorporates energy efficiency, carbon measurement, clean tech, clean energy, water and waste management. And not forgetting ethical behavior!

Phone Hacking: How the *Guardian* broke the story is available on Kindle, or go to its website for more information.

Sources

- www.abccarbon.com
- www.eco-business.com
- www.guardian.co.uk

Race for Sustainability

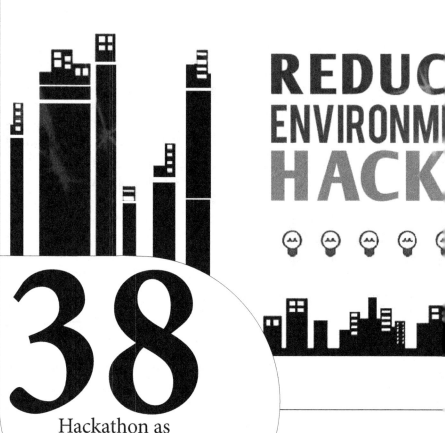

38

Hackathon as a Means to Reduce Our Environmental Impact

*I attended the final presentation of entries in the Hackathon on Reducing Our Environmental Impact in January 2013. Very enlightening! Nothing to do with hacking of the "evil" sort we are seeing, as nothing but good is coming from this form of technological communication. I greatly admire the work of Newton Circus, UP Singapore and in particular, the guiding hand of Daryl Arnold. This is based on an article contributed first to the E2 Singapore website but also used in **abc carbon express** and other places...*

H ackathons have arrived in Singapore and they are being put to good use. The "Clean and Green Hackathon" was organised by the National Environment Agency (NEA) in April 2013 in partnership with Newton Circus "to create solutions that safeguard the environment and conserve precious resources".

The previous Hackathon, also organised by Newton Circus through its UP Singapore initiative, took place in January this year, carrying the theme "Reducing Our Environmental Impact". Organised in partnership with the NUS Entrepreneurship Centre and Earth Hour, games and apps were being developed to highlight energy efficiency.

So what is a Hackathon? Also known as a hack day, hackfest or codefest, it is an event in which computer programmers and others in the field of software development, as well as graphic designers, interface designers and project managers collaborate intensively on software projects.

Moving Eco-Actions Beyond an Hour with Mobile Applications

The January Hackathon produced ideas and apps which were creative and practical, encouraging greater public participation in energy saving and events like Earth Hour.

At the launch, Andy Ridley, CEO and co-founder of Earth Hour, said the "I Will If You Will" campaign was a way to promote positive environmental action beyond an hour each year. The premise is simple: someone promises to do something if a set number of people commit to an ongoing action for the environment, beyond Earth Hour.

What came out of the Hackathon was a winning idea. Called "5 Degrees", it involved a mobile app game of environmentally friendly activities. Based on the "I Will If You Will" campaign, users send pre-defined challenges to their friends through mobile devices and social media, which are measurable in categories such as energy and water efficiency.

For example, putting at stake a population of pandas under the threat of global warming, users will alleviate their condition by completing eco-friendly challenges with friends. This visualisation of completed challenges engages users and lets them see their progress.

Leveraging on the user's social and viral dynamics, the app can reach out to those previously unaware of the Earth Hour campaign. Its accessibility and interactivity also attract new users keen to help the environment.

Upon completing a challenge, verified by photos and peer-checks, users receive points to unlock new challenges. Along with constant challenges and counter-challenges from social networks, this app stays engaging.

By completing many challenges after challenges aimed to enhance energy efficiency over an extended period, users eventually cultivate the habit of efficient energy use. The app is an effective platform to encourage the public to make significant reductions in their environmental impact.

Other ideas raised in the competitive atmosphere of the Hackathon are also aimed at increasing energy efficiency.

"Aircon+3" is an air conditioning management system that monitors energy use, monetary savings, building temperature and user feedback. Another was "eSave", an energy monitoring and user collaboration portal.

By bringing together thinkers and solvers across disciplines (sustainability experts, programmers, web designers and marketers), the Hackathon successfully generated multiple solutions for today's global warming challenges. Many ideas involved community engagement to induce behaviour change and enhance awareness.

Over 120 people attended the January Hackathon, totalling over 2,000 hours of voluntary work.

Hothouse of Ideas for a Cleaner and Greener Singapore

For the "Clean and Green Hackathon", from 26–28 April, participants examined many interesting datasets and collaborated to create solutions that safeguard the environment and conserve precious resources. Open to amateurs and professionals, students and working adults, developers, environmental activists, and creative and concerned citizens jointly built solutions for the public to safeguard and nurture Singapore's environment.

The scope of the "Data Sandbox" was also extended to include data from NEA and other agencies. Using this, participants were also challenged to test out latest technologies to help individuals and businesses optimise energy usage, and tackle environmental challenges creatively.

Participants could also try the impressive technology on offer from Samsung, Amazon Web Services (AWS), and SAP, including SAP HANA One (an in-memory computing platform, hosted on AWS's public cloud) and SAP Visual Intelligence, a powerful query and visualisation tool.

The Clean and Green Hackathon was designed to engage communities in Singapore to co-create solutions towards the challenge of resource conservation and protecting the environment.

UP Singapore is a ground-up innovation platform that creatively uses data and technology to improve urban environments. It seeks active community participation and strong collaboration across communities, governments, corporate and NGOs. It is managed by Newton Circus. An interview with Daryl Arnold also appeared on UBrain TV.

———— ❦ ————

Sources

- www.upsingapore.com
- www.cgs.sg/hackathon
- www.newton-circus.com
- www.e2singapore.gov.sg
- www.abccarbon.com
- www.ubraintv.com

39

How to Communicate Sustainability and Do It Sustainably

I agreed to write an article on sustainable communication for the Institute of Public Relations Singapore (IPRS) newsletter and it appeared in July 2011. I also organised a lunch panel on sustainability which featured Straits Times journalist Jessica Cheam, CDL Sustainability chief Esther An, and Howard Shaw, the former director of the Singapore Environment Council and now the Corporate Social Responsibility head at the Halcyon Group. Besides journalism and media, I do have a "history" in public relations and in fact served as President of the IPRS for a time. I have also been involved in public relations in Australia and NZ and lectured on the topic at the University of the Sunshine Coast, Australia…

Photo by Корзун Андрей (2009) taken from WikiMedia Commons (CC BY-SA 3.0): www.commons.wikimedia.org/wiki/File:Typewriters_01.JPG.

Sustainability means different things to different people. To some it is all about the environment and being green. Others see it as another word for corporate social responsibility (CSR).

Some sum it up as the triple bottom line — concerned with economic, environmental and social factors in business. A sustainable society is said to cover people, planet and profit.

In 1986, the Brundtland Commission defined "sustainable development" as meeting the needs of the present without compromising the ability of future generations to meet their own needs.

The much respected Dow Jones Sustainability Index talks about corporate sustainability as "a business approach that creates long-term shareholder value by embracing opportunities and managing risks deriving from economic, social and environmental developments".

Sustainability has become "a defining megatrend of the 21st century", according to business schools and noted commentators. The chairman of Ford Motor Company Bill Ford himself says sustainability is the biggest issue facing global business this century.

So with all these definitions and comments on its importance, shouldn't we as communication professionals in Singapore be sitting up and taking notice — and action!

To some extent we are. It is interesting to see that many communication and public relations professionals here and around the world are getting CSR and sustainability responsibility added to their job description.

Because when you think about it — and in my experience — communication makes up a large part of the task in delivering a sustainability practice for any business.

But let me first broaden the concept of sustainability a little. Instead of three essential pillars, I make it four.

To me there are the four E's of sustainability:

- Environment;
- Economy;
- Ethics; and
- Energy.

I have added Energy to the mix because it is essential in this day and age to manage energy more effectively, along with all the other resources a business utilises. Energy is critical as it also determines the carbon footprint for the business.

Ethics is a better word to use when it comes to business than just "social" which can mean just giving to charity. Whereas ethics covers corporate governance, transparency, and all the ways a business must operate, taking into account different legal, cultural, social, racial and religious situations.

Singapore has certainly embarked on the sustainability journey. The Singapore Business Federation (SBF) has for the second year presented deserving businesses and government agencies with Singapore Sustainability Awards. A book of case studies of 2010 winners was titled "Riding the Megatrend of Sustainability".

The Singapore Compact for CSR — bringing together the government, employers and unions — recognises the importance of sustainability with two books of cases studies of Singapore businesses. There's "CSR for Sustainability and Success", produced in 2009, and "Socially Responsible and Sustainable", produced earlier this year (2011).

The Singapore Exchange has just released a "how-to" guide so firms can prepare sustainability reports and it wants all listed firms to produce such reports. Some are already doing it. I just saw the latest report from Keppel Corporation, for example.

So where do communication and public relations professionals come in?

If you haven't already been given the job of masterminding sustainable practices in your place of employment — whether it is a government agency, PR consultancy, multi-national corporation or small and medium enterprise — make it your job to find out who is doing it. If no one is, you should step in to make sure it is happening.

But it is not just a matter of seeing what clean and green things your business is already doing. It must come from the top. Your board, your directors, CEO or MD, must be convinced that it is important and you as a key communicator must make sure that all stakeholders are aware of the commitments your business is making to become sustainable.

If you need guidance, there is plenty of good advice and practical tips from the Singapore Compact books and from the SBF.

There are a number of agencies around specialising in helping companies get to grips with sustainability. I would include Paia, Kleef Consulting, Sustainable PR, CSR Asia, GreenBizCheck, as well as my own consultancy SASA.

Then there are organisations like the Singapore Environment Council which helps business on the sustainability journey through its Eco Office and Eco Food Court programmes.

Then you can look at some of the best examples in the world — Interface, GE, Walmart and Marks & Spencers — who have progressed dramatically on this journey and set very high standards.

Winning awards and recognition locally and globally is only part of it. Gaining a reputation as a sustainable and responsible organisation is something you have to work hard at. But communication is the key.

Commit to sustainability and communicate what you are doing internally and externally.

Sources

- www.iprs.org.sg
- www.abccarbon.com

40

Profile — Ken Hickson: Harnessing the Media to Fight Climate Change

I was visiting Kuala Lumpur in Malaysia to promote the up-coming CleanEnviro Summit 2012 where I was asked to give a presentation on waste and why waste management was so important. Surprisingly, I was interviewed by Siaw Mei Li and the subsequent article appeared Green Prospects Asia (29 April 2012). There was also an interview with the New Straits Times. I say surprisingly, because it is rare for journalists to end up being interviewed. Not because they don't have anything worthwhile to say. So, in place of me writing about myself in profile, I pass that task to Mei Li. Also, because I cannot complain that she misrepresented me in anyway...

Over the course of his long career, veteran sustainability communicator Ken Hickson has witnessed many significant developments in environmental issues as well as in the media. He talks to Siaw Mei Li about how harnessing modern communications can help save the planet.

"I started out as a journalist 50 years ago this year," Ken Hickson reveals cheerfully, noting with a quick look around that he must be the oldest in the room. "Now I've made the transition from being a print or newspaper journalist to an online journalist, I've become reasonably modern!"

And so he has. In addition to providing sustainability communications services to corporations and government agencies, the founder and chief executive officer of Singapore-based consultancy Sustain Ability Showcase Asia (SASA) tweets periodically and helms SASA's twice-monthly email news digest on climate change issues.

Photograph by Bryan Loke Design of Ken Hickson, the journalist (with microphone), at the Sir Richard Branson/Carbon War Room media conference at Marina Bay Sands, Singapore, May 2013.

Lately, he was also involved in promoting the Singapore National Environment Agency's (NEA) inaugural CleanEnviro Summit and the WasteMET Asia exhibition and conference, the latter of which is co-organised by the Waste Management and Recycling Association of Singapore (WMRAS). Both events took place in the first week of July (2012) in conjunction with Singapore International Water Week and the World Cities Summit.

Wanted: Integrated Solutions

Hickson sees a much-needed synergy in this upcoming events cluster. "We've got to accept that there's a nexus between climate change and energy, water and the environment. We can no longer say, 'I'm just dealing with water here' or 'I'm just dealing with food here.'"

"Climate change has an impact on all of that, and waste is a component we have to deal with much better in terms of using it for energy and also reducing the amount of waste we create. It's not something we should be dumping or filling up holes in the ground or our water resources with; we should be converting it to energy — using it as a resource."

While some of the information that Hickson receives in his work may sound worrying, the business and social potential in turning such problematic situations around are also tremendous. As an example, he relates how experts at the recent Reuters Food and Agriculture Summit in Chicago reported that an estimated 30 to 50% of the food produced in the world goes uneaten and ends up in landfills.

"We've got to better manage our production, distribution, buying and consumption habits, and also how we manage waste," says Hickson, citing waste minimisation and reutilisation projects such as converting used cooking oil into biofuel, running community and commercial composting initiatives, and salvaging discarded supermarket food items not yet past their due date, to be channeled to the needy via charitable organisations.

In other words, resolving the food waste problem creatively means not only feeding more people, but also diverting waste from landfills and supplementing the society's need for fuel and agricultural resources.

Nothing Wasted

These principles of maximising resources, avoiding waste, recycling and prolonging the useful life of a product apply equally well to the realm of climate change communications, particularly in the era of multi-platform communications.

"Some journalists may be writing for newspapers but their material is also being used online, and they're also blogging and working with social media," Hickson points out, giving as an example, veteran journalist Michael Richardson, whose work on climate change and alternative fuels enriches regional think tanks while also reaching wider audiences in the form of the Singapore *Straits Times*' print and online readership.

Meanwhile, *Reuters* climate change correspondent David Fogarty's journalism is disseminated not only by the agency's newswire, but also reaches the public via the @reutersclimate Twitter profile. With each additional re-post, news and research gains longevity along with new audiences.

"You need to be working in all media that's available," says Hickson. "You might use social media to refer to an article that appears online or on a web portal that, in turn, comes from a newspaper. So nothing goes to waste — not even the work of journalists."

Biodata of Ken Hickson

- Native of NZ, currently lives in Singapore;
- Governor of WWF Australia; and
- Author of *Flight 901 to Erebus*, a non-fiction account of a 1979 major airline disaster in the Antarctic.

Sources

- www.greenprospectsasia.com
- www.abccarbon.com
- www.sustain-ability-showcase.com

Epilogue

Actions Speak Louder than Words

Why does a book of 40 chapters and close to 80,000 words need an epilogue? What more is there to say?

Good questions — I will attempt to answer that by providing some additional information which supplements what has gone before and gives the reader some additional value. I will also attempt to "bring things up to date" where required. This I will do by way of short items which connect with the earlier text and with upcoming events:

Green Purchasing Network

More than passing mention has been made to the importance of introducing sustainability to the supply chain (Walmart, Chapter 2) and the adoption of sustainable manufacturing of products using less energy, water and thereby reducing waste and incorporating recycled materials. The best example is carpet tile maker Interface (Chapter 2) and automobile companies (Chapter 11). The construction industry increasingly draws on sustainable materials for green buildings (Chapters 9–14). Energy efficient lights have been widely adopted and we are seeing portable solar chargers for mobile people with digital equipment needing power off-grids. And to make events more sustainable (Chapters 21–23), the selection of environmentally friendly paper and eco-products is important.

So all this leads to the fact that I have been asked to provide some leadership for the Green Purchasing Network in Singapore, to promote the international activities of the movement operating in dozens of countries and to speak at the 4th international Conference of Green Purchasing in Kuala Lumpur, Malaysia (18–20 September 2013).

Make Shopping Green

We have also been working with Servé Sondeijker to "Make Shopping Green" with his Directgreen framework for assessing companies' sustainability initiatives and giving customers reassurance that their purchases are making a genuine difference. He has built a system that allows sellers to choose from three different pledge plans and for shoppers to earn loyalty points when they purchase from Directgreen sellers. More than that, shoppers can use points to support global projects through the Directgreen Foundation. To complete the sustainability circle, Servé has also made sure Directgreen has a strict code of practice in the partners and projects chosen for the programme. Watch this space!

The Blue Economy

For some time now Martin Blake has been telling me and others that we should not be equating everything green with everything sustainable. We should be turning blue. The blue economy is a progressive metamorphosis from the green economy. Based on the notion of thinking ahead so as to create more good, instead of less bad, it uses a strategic, opportunity-driven rationale to connect the environmental, social and financial puzzle. It is a business response to a changing economic landscape in which resource depletion and social costs are unsustainable.

Martin, who we have worked closely with in recent years, set up the consulting firm called **be sustainable,** which practices principles from *The Blue Economy* as coined by author Gunter Pauli. It aims to develop business solutions that are at once environmentally, financially and socially beneficial.

Integrative Design

We have made passing reference to integrative design — see Chapter 6 — and it keeps cropping in association with green buildings, retrofitting and energy efficiency which is covered fully in Chapters 9–12. But concentrating attention on integrative design — as part of **be sustainable** and the blue economy — is Nigel Grier, now based in Singapore. As the CEO of BE Integrative Design, Nigel says the goal is to transform the design industry, by bringing together entrepreneurs and investors, and enabling them to develop solutions that address our fundamental human needs: namely, water, energy, food, waste, shelter, health, education and employment. "Our solutions are inspired by nature and can be practically as well as commercially deployed."

Nigel, who has formerly ran the Australian ecological design consultancy Zingspace, is actively engaged on a number of projects in Singapore now. And he is also instrumental in linking up with international expertise to stage the first Blue Cities Forum in Singapore in April 2014.

Sustainable Buildings

Someone who understands integrative design and applies it to real life situations is David Strong — who has also worked with Martin and Nigel as well as energy engineering guru Lee Eng Lock (Chapter 12). David is an internationally recognised expert in energy efficient sustainable building design and refurbishment. He has a wealth of knowledge associated with the low- or zero-carbon buildings and is a specialist in whole system thinking, building physics and integrative design. He has a particular interest in eco-minimalism and bio-mimicry — exploiting and optimising the use of natural systems for heating, cooling, ventilating and illuminating buildings.

While he is often called on to consult and advise in Singapore and other parts of Asia, he is based in the UK, where he is Chairman of the Energy Efficiency Partnership for Buildings and chair of the Green Deal Installer Accreditation and Qualification Ministerial Forum. He has a history as well. He was presented with the 2007 Building Sustainability Leadership award for establishing the UK Green Building Council, with the judges describing him as "one of the most influential figures in the drive to make the industry sustainable".

Connecting Energy and Sustainability

Singapore and Asia are fortunate to have on tap these experts who can apply sustainability and not just talk about it. Collectively — along with our own SASA consultancy and the people at Energenz— we can join up the dots. We can find the strong connections between energy efficiency and sustainability. Maximising the resources that are available and minimising or eliminating waste.

It all goes to confirm that sustainability must involve the four E's — Energy, Economy, Environment and Ethics.

Sustainability is more than green and it's more than blue. People are inclined to latch on to the term sustainability and apply it to only a part of their business or industry. So many times recently have I heard knowledgeable business people talk about sustainability only in economic terms. They are talking about survivability, not sustainability. I also attended an arts industry "sustainability" event only to discover that the focus was on how arts and artists could survive...economically.

So we have a long way to go to achieve a full understanding of sustainability in all senses. The book is hopefully a step in the right direction.

Sustainable Events

In the same way, we can bring the sustainability approach to events as we can to property or business. Events — we have said in Chapters 21–24 — might be inherently unsustainable, but if you adopt a systematic approach or go as far as working toward the international gold standard ISO 20121 like the London Olympics did, you can achieve remarkable savings in energy, water and waste, as well as make the event enjoyable and accessible with a positive legacy.

SASA is doing its best to introduce sustainable practices, starting with sustainable assessments, of some major events in Singapore in coming weeks and months. Hopefully this will include the International Green Building Conference, World Engineers Summit, the BEX Expo as well as — against all odds — the F1 motor sport event (Chapter 1).

We have a track record for events with the 2012 i Light Marina Bay as a case in point (Chapter 22). SASA has now been appointed to work with URA and Pico for the next event, billed as Asia's first and only sustainable light art festival (7–30 March 2014) with the theme "Light+HeART", making us the most experienced event sustainability team in Singapore.

Energy Literacy

Educating people, companies and communities on energy issues and opportunities is a full-time job and it has been satisfying to work with NEA on both the E2 Singapore website content as well as promote and be involved in the National Energy Efficiency Conferences (Chapter 6).

Energy literacy goes a step further and now SASA has been appointed to work with the International Energy Centre to promote educational programmes to advance a low-carbon future. There will be more work to do, as well as opportunities to link up with other active agencies and organisations like Energy Market Authority, Energy Studies Institute and Sustainable Energy Association Singapore.

Big events, like those scheduled for the Singapore International Energy Week (28 October to 1 November 2013) and in Bangkok with its Clean Energy Expo and Energy Efficiency Asia (25–27 September 2013) are in the diary, as is the next CNBC/Shell Energy Opportunities brainstorm (in Bangkok this time).

Energy 2020 Asia

We have to admit to a failed attempt in the current year. We have tried to get a campaign underway in Asia called Energy 2020 Asia, a campaign for a cleaner energy environment, a private sector initiative to encourage companies, cities and countries in Asia to set the 2020 target to commit to:

- reduce greenhouse gas emissions by 20%;
- increase the share of renewable energy to 20%; and
- make a 20% improvement in energy efficiency.

This is based on what the European Council decided on in 2007. It adopted ambitious energy and climate change objectives for 2020 — to reduce greenhouse gas emissions by 20%, rising to 30% if the conditions are right, to increase the share of renewable energy to 20%, and to make a 20% improvement in energy efficiency. This is not unlike what the ADB's Energy for All campaign aims to do or the UN's Sustainable Energy for All efforts, but they have failed, in my opinion, because they have not set achievable targets or made any serious effort to get the private sector — and the public — on board.

Maybe 2014 will see Asia moving more positively in a sustainable energy direction and Energy 2020 Asia — including the excellent identifiable logo Bryan Loke designed for me — will see the green light of day.

Funding Energy Opportunities

It is always a challenge to get people and companies to put money into sustainability, clean energy and energy efficiency. But there are some positive signs. Last year we started promoting the work of Armstrong Asset Management with its Clean Energy Fund for Southeast Asia (Chapter 15) and it expects to have a final close this September with $150 million to allocate. It has already committed to two major solar projects in Thailand.

Then we've just met the people who have set up a $200 million fund for energy efficiency in Singapore — Sustainable Development Capital (Asia) Limited (SDCL) —with the encouragement and support of the Economic Development Board. With no upfront investment, companies can cover up to 100% of the capital cost of energy efficient technologies, systems and equipment. It is paid for out of the energy cost savings achieved through performance guaranteed agreements with suppliers.

Sustainable Forests

Making sure this book is printed on a suitable sustainable paper has been a little harder than it should be in Singapore. Not only do you have to source for the certified paper — FSC or PEFC — and expect to pay more for it than "normal" paper, but you have to use a printer who has gone through the certifying process. Through my dogged enquiring, I came into contact with the Programme for the Endorsement of Forest Certification (PEFC), the world's largest forest management certification system — Genevieve Chua in Singapore and Thorsten Arndt in Geneva. Of course, I had heard of PEFC before, in fact, I shared the platform a few years ago in Sydney with the chairman of PEFC, William Street. I have been invited to promote and participate in the Forest Certification Week in Kuala Lumpur (11–15 November 2013).

As I told Genevieve, it really should not be the case where you should have to pay more for sustainable paper, which comes from legal, certified forests and mills, against much more freely available cheaper paper from "unsustainable" sources. Does that mean most of the paper we use comes from illegal logging companies, the same as those responsible for rampant destruction of our rainforests, contributing to excessive emissions of greenhouse gases and the indiscriminate burning of trees and peatlands (in Indonesia)? Issues I will keep raising and questions I will keep asking until countries like Singapore insist on banning paper and other goods which are unsustainably (unethically and illegally) produced and sold.

Last Words?

There will always be more to say, write and do in my world, but as with my previous book "The ABC of Carbon" (2009), I was able to continue the story — and continue to feed appropriate, necessary and urgent messages — to willing ears and eyes around the world through my fortnightly newsletter **abc carbon express**. Now in its sixth year, it will continue and maybe even produce a few offsprings with imaginative titles, like Green Purchasing Network News, Energy 2020 Asia Express, Energy Literacy Digest or — how about? — Race for Sustainability Reporter.

Ken Hickson

August 2013

Bibliography

Here are the books and major reports read and/or referenced in the researching and writing of *Race for Sustainability*. The reader will note that at the end of every chapter we show one or more sources, usually websites or links, either for further information or indicating the place to go for verification or elaboration on topics or issues raised in the text. These are unlikely to be repeated here, except where major reports or documents have been cited:

American Council for an Energy-Efficient Economy (ACEEE). 2013. "Overcoming Market Barriers and Using Market Forces to Advance Energy Efficiency", March, www.aceee.org.

Anderson, Ray and Robin White. 2009. "Business Lessons from a Radical Industrialist", New York: St. Martin's Press, www.interfaceglobal.com.

Anderson, Ray and Robin White. 2011. "Confessions of a Radical Industrialist", New York: St. Martin's Press, www.interfaceglobal.com.

Armstrong Asset Management. 2013. "Entering a New Phase of Growth; Renewable Energy in SE Asia", April, www.armstrongaam.com.

Asian Development Bank (ADB). 2013. "Same Energy, More Power: Accelerating Energy Efficiency in Asia", June, www.adb.org.

Branson, Richard. 2011. "Screw Business as Usual", UK: Virgin Books, www.randomhouse.co.uk

City Developments Limited. 2013. "Changing the Landscape", Sustainability Report, www.cdl.com.sg.

Commission for a Sustainable London. 2013. "Beyond 2012 — Outcomes, Commission for a Sustainable London 2012", March, www.cslondon.org.

Energy, Energy Efficiency and Renewable Energy (EERE) US Department of. 2012. "Energy Literacy: Essential Principles and Fundamental Concepts for Energy Education", www.eere.energy.gov.

Faulks, Sebastion. 2011. "Faulks on Fiction", UK: BBC Books, www.sebastianfaulks.com.

Federation Internationale de l'Automobile (FIA). 2013. "A World in Motion", www.fia.com.

FIA Institute for Motor Sport Safety and Sustainability. 2012. "Environmental Certification Framework, Accreditation Guidelines Checklist", July, www.fiainstitute.com.

Freeman, Damien. 2012. "Roddy's Folly: R.P. Meagher QC", www.connorcourt.com.

Heald, Henrietta. 2010. "William Armstrong: Magician of the North", Newcastle: Northumbria Press, www.mcnidderandgrace.co.uk.

Hickson, Ken. 2009. "The ABC of Carbon: Issues and Opportunities in the Global Climate Change Environment", Australia: ABC Carbon, www.abccarbon.com.

Hickson, Ken. 2013. "Forty: Building a Future in Singapore", Singapore: Lend Lease Asia, www.leadlease.com.

Jones, Megan. 2009. "Sustainable Event Management: A Practical Guide", UK and USA: Earthscan, www.greenshootpacific.com.

Jones, Megan and Fullerton-Smith, Jane. 2012. "ISO 20121 Events Sustainability Management Systems Guide to Understanding the International Standard", www.greenshootpacific.com.

Lovins, Amory and Rocky Mountain Institute. 2011. "Reinventing Fire: Bold Business Solutions for the New Energy Era", USA: Chelsea Green Publishing Company, www.rmi.org.

Ocean Recovery Alliance and Flynn Consulting. 2012. "Water Margin: Hong Kong's Link to the Sea", www.oceanrecov.org.

Singapore Compact for CSR. 2011. "Sustainability Reporting in Singapore: Non-Financial Reporting Among Mainboard Listed Companies in Singapore", www.csrsingapore.org.

Singapore Institute of International Affairs. 2012. "Clean City Air & the Haze: A Three-fold Approach Towards Breathing Easy", www.siiaonline.org.

The Guardian. 2011. "Phone Hacking: How the Guardian Broke the Story", www.guardian.co.uk.

Index

Race for Sustainability

Race for Sustainability

Race for Sustainability

Acknowledgements

First and foremost, thanks to Max Phua and World Scientific Publishing for taking me on with this collection, even though it did not fit into the normal mould of academic paper or scientific treatise. They took me at my word — or around 80,000 words — that this would make a useful contribution to the "business of sustainability" and they were prepared to put their good name to it.

Much of the substance of what is produced in this book has appeared in some form, in print or online, over the past year or so. Each section and chapter identifies not only sources — and where to go for more information — but also indicates websites or publications where it made its first appearance.

Special appreciation therefore to the National Environment Agency (NEA) of Singapore for allowing me to reuse and recycle quite a number of articles which were expressly written for www.e2singapore.gov.sg. Promoting energy efficiency comes naturally to me and as I've been a vocal advocate of it for some time, NEA wisely hired me and my team to provide content for the website and also used my services at their annual National Energy Efficiency Conferences.

Some content — on waste and recycling — was also first provided to promote another NEA event — the first CleanEnviro Summit in Singapore in July 2012.

I would also like to thank the following organisations and publications for commissioning me to write something for them, willingly publishing a piece of my writing, or for providing me with access to editorial material which I have made good use of. They are:

- Lien Centre for Social Innovation's Social Space (2012) — "Sense and Sensibility" and "12 Steps Towards Sustainability in Business";

- Asian Development Bank's RTF Mirror (2012) — "Is Solar the Renewable Energy of Choice in Asia?";

- Halcyon Agri — for access to and use of material in their Sustainability Report and newsletter *Halcyon Days*;

- Lend Lease — for extracts from "Forty: Building a Future in Singapore" (2013), which resulted in the profile on Mann Young and CLT;

- International Energy Agency (IEA) — for providing content and images for chapter "Multiple Outcome Benefits of Energy Efficiency" and access to Fatih Birol;

- CEI — Conventions, Events, Incentives — Magazine (January 2013) — for the article "Taking Sustainability Seriously in Asia" (Chapter 21);

- Marina Bay Sands Singapore — for providing content for Chapter 23 — "Can a Luxury Hotel and Convention Centre be Sustainable";

- UBrain TV — for access to videos and materials which originally appeared on the web-based channel and provided content for the book;

- Storm Magazine — which first used my article, entitled "What's the Buzz? Bee Populations in Decline and Elephants Feel the Sting";

- Thomson Reuters — for use of reports by David Fogarty providing the excellent content in the profile: "Forest Carbon, REDD and DoubleHelix"

- Eco-business.com — partners in "crime", for the use of writings by Jessica Cheam and Jenny Marusiak, which pop up in a number of chapters;

- CDL — Esther An, for willingly lining up the content for the profile on Kwek Leng Joo;

- CNBC — for re-use of the review I wrote on the Energy Opportunities event, appearing in "Energy Education and a Green Campus";

- Green Prospects Asia — in particular Siaw Mei Li — for the very acceptable profile article on me which I have made into Chapter 40; and

- Eco Voice and Eco TV Australia — for access to editorial material online and on video.

Thanks also to Andrew Affleck of Armstrong Asset Management for encouraging me to publish the article "The Price is Right! Renewable Energy Is Cheaper than Fossil Fuels", originally by Edward Douglas and based on an excellent report, which first appeared in **abc carbon express** and eco-business.com. Andrew also introduced me to William Armstrong, which resulted in Chapter 16 of this book.

There are many more people involved in the production of a book, both providing moral and physical support to the author — my dear wife M is number one! — as well as work colleagues, friends and business partners, namely Adam Lyle, Adrian Bukmanis, Atiqah Ali, Yang Yi Yong and Yap Beng-Ai.

Special thanks to the team at World Scientific, especially Lee Xin Ying, for her patience and professionalism in turning a "mixed bag" of articles into a very acceptable collection in book form.

Ken Hickson
August 2013

About the Author

Ken Hickson is a sustainability consultant, public affairs specialist, lecturer and writer, who has edited a fortnightly newsletter **abc carbon express** for the past five years. He has produced hundreds of talks, lectures and articles for media — in print and online — the world over. He is the author of four non-fiction works: *Flight 901 to Erebus*, *The Future South*, *Forty: Building a Future in Singapore* and *The ABC of Carbon: Issues and Opportunities in the Global Climate Change Environment*.

A journalist and communications specialist in NZ for 20 years, he came to Asia in 1983 as a consultant for Singapore Airlines. He set up his own communications consultancy with clients like DHL, BMW, Intel, Hitachi, Canon and Lend Lease. In 1996, Hickson PR was acquired by Fleishman Hillard. Ken lived in Australia from end 2000 for ten years. He was in demand as a consultant, writer and lecturer (as an adjunct associate professor at the University of the Sunshine Coast).

He returned to Singapore in September 2010 to establish Sustain Ability Showcase Asia (SASA), while managing a publishing business **ABC Carbon** and soon after, acquired a communications consultancy, which he re-branded as H2PC Asia. He and his team worked for clients in the private sector, including Armstrong Asset Management, Singapore Road Safety Council, Third Wave Power, Serious Games International and the International Energy Centre — and with the Singapore Government agencies, including the National Environment Agency (NEA) and the Urban Redevelopment Authority (URA).

Ken has been associated with the World Wide Fund for Nature over the years, acting as its honorary representative in Singapore in the 1990s and he remains a Governor of WWF Australia. He has recently taken on the role of Chairman of the Green Purchasing Network Singapore.